American Protestant Ethics
and the Legacy of
H. Richard Niebuhr

MORAL TRADITIONS SERIES
Edited by James F. Keenan, S.J.

Aquinas and Empowerment:
  Classical Ethics for Ordinary Lives
  G. Simon Harak, S.J., Editor

The Banality of Good and Evil:
  Moral Lessons from the Shoah
  and Jewish Tradition
  David R. Blumenthal

Bridging the Sacred and the Secular:
  Selected Writings of
  John Courtney Murray
  John Courtney Murray, S.J.
  J. Leon Hooper, S.J., Editor

The Catholic Moral Tradition Today:
  A Synthesis
  Charles E. Curran

Catholic Social Teaching,
  1891–Present
  Charles E. Curran

The Christian Case for Virtue Ethics
  Joseph J. Kotva, Jr.

The Context of Casuistry
  James F. Keenan, S.J., and
  Thomas A. Shannon, Editors

Democracy on Purpose:
  Justice and the Reality of God
  Franklin I. Gamwell

Ethics and Economics of
  Assisted Reproduction
  Maura A. Ryan

The Ethics of Aquinas
  Stephen J. Pope, Editor

The Evolution of Altruism and the
  Ordering of Love
  Stephen J. Pope

The Fellowship of Life:
  Virtue Ethics and Orthodox
  Christianity
  Joseph Woodill

Feminist Ethics and Natural Law:
  The End of Anathemas
  Cristina L. H. Traina

Jewish and Catholic Bioethics:
  An Ecumenical Dialogue
  Edmund D. Pellegrino and
  Alan I. Faden, Editors

John Paul II and the Legacy of
  Dignitatis Humanae
  Hermínio Rico, S.J.

Love, Human and Divine:
  The Heart of Christian Ethics
  Edward Collins Vacek, S.J.

Medicine and the Ethics of Care
  Diana Fritz Cates and
  Paul Lauritzen, Editors

The Origins of Moral Theology
  in the United States:
  Three Different Approaches
  Charles E. Curran

Shaping the Moral Life:
  An Approach to Moral Theology
  Klaus Demmer, M.S.C.
  Translated by Roberto Dell'Oro
  James F. Keenan, S.J., Editor

Who Count as Persons? Human
  Identity and the Ethics of Killing
  John F. Kavanaugh, S.J.

American Protestant Ethics and the Legacy of H. Richard Niebuhr

William Werpehowski

GEORGETOWN UNIVERSITY PRESS
Washington, D.C.

Georgetown University Press, Washington, D.C.
© 2002 by Georgetown University Press. All rights reserved.
Printed in the United States of America
10 9 8 7 6 5 4 3 2 1   2002

This volume is printed on acid-free offset book paper.

Portions of William Werpehowski's essay "Christian Love and Covenant Faith-fulness," first published by the *Journal of Religious Ethics*, vol. 19, no. 2 (fall 1991), pp. 103–32, have been used in chapters 3 and 4. They are reprinted by permission of Religious Ethics, Inc., © 1991.

Library of Congress Cataloging-in-Publication Data

Werpehowski, William.
   American Protestant ethics and the legacy of H. Richard Niebuhr /
William Werpehowski.
      p.   cm. (Moral traditions series)
   Includes bibliographical references and index.
   ISBN 0-87840-383-3 (pbk. : alk. paper)
      1. Christian ethics—United States.   2. Protestant churches—United States—Doctrines.   3. Niebuhr, H. Richard (Helmut Richard), 1894–1962—Ethics.
I. Title.   II. Series.

BJ1251 . W46•2002
241′.092′273 — DC21   2002023629

To my mother, Margaret Margetich Werpehowski,
and my father, William John Werpehowski

Contents

Preface   ix

ONE   Questions in Christian Ethics   1

TWO   A Theology of Permanent Revolution   15

THREE   Love, Justice, and the Whole Idea of God   33

FOUR   Political and Medical Ethics   51

FIVE   Keeping Faith in Good Company   72

SIX   Politics, Creation, and Conversion   95

SEVEN   God Will Be God   119

EIGHT   Questions for Theocentric Ethics   143

NINE   Transcendence, Culture, and Ethics   164

TEN   Realism, Identity, and Self-Defense   183

ELEVEN   Eight Theses for Theological Ethics   203

Index   225

Preface

This book is an attempt to contribute to the practice of Christian ethics through an examination of the legacy of H. Richard Niebuhr. The approach I take is to present a critical conversation among four theologians whose work reflects that legacy. Hence, this exchange encompasses and develops into another conversation with Niebuhr's theological ethics itself. My working in and working out of these conversations exemplify, I hope, commitments that are central to the content and conclusions of my arguments and to these theologians' conclusions: close and respectful attention to what is going on in these thinkers in their response to God, given their places in church, world, tradition, and history; a response on my part that relies on discriminating argument and the need for mutual correction; and a rejection of defensiveness in the course of my inquiry.

I have learned and come to love these commitments in great measure not just through the study of H. Richard Niebuhr, but also through personal and professional engagement with the other modern moralists. I studied with Paul Ramsey as an undergraduate. He and Stanley Hauerwas were unfailingly honest and supportive critics of my ventures into Christian ethics during my graduate studies. Ramsey continued in this vein until his death, and Hauerwas continues to this day. Beyond learning so much about the discipline of Christian ethics from the work of James Gustafson, I am also indebted to him for a number of meetings, talks, and letters that have challenged and inspired me. Kathryn Tanner and I have been colleagues since graduate school. My gratitude to these good people makes me especially intent on doing right by them in this book.

I started writing in 1994–95, thanks to a sabbatical leave from Villanova University and a grant from the Center of Theological Inquiry in Princeton, New Jersey. I had a fine year as a member of the center thanks to the fine company I kept, including especially Daniel Hardy, then the center's director; George Hunsinger; James Keenan; William Placher; and Todd Whitmore. With characteristic insight and wit, Placher read all I had to say at that time, and, with characteristic generosity, did it all again in 1999 when he criticized a completed draft along with the rest of the Washington-Yale Theology Group during our annual meeting in Washington, D.C. I thank this company of friends for their two decades of spirited comments and ongoing regard.

Before the Washington-Yale meeting, Gilbert Meilaender read a full draft and offered helpful comments that I needed to hear. For years, he has been my good friend and acute critic, and this time—as always—he made good on both counts. I know I have not addressed a number of his concerns, but that is nothing new. Facing up to our disagreements about Christian ethics (and our many agreements), I hold out, here, too, for the chance of mutual correction. Darlene Fozard Weaver carefully read a later version of this book and helped make it significantly better regarding both structure and content. I also greatly appreciate the valuable suggestions I received from two anonymous reviewers for Georgetown University Press.

I am fortunate to have the kind of friends and fellow workers who deserve my thanks for their encouragement and support whether they have read (or will read) a word of this book or not. At Villanova University, my comrades at the Center for Peace and Justice Education—Carol Anthony, Bob DeFina, Rick Eckstein, Dorothy Lairdieson, and Joyce Zavarich—have made my life and work richer. Villanova students Brian Behrend, Christian DiBella, and Matthew Siblo worked hard to get the final text in shape. My friends Jack Doody, Kevin Hughes, Hank Nichols, Harry Perretta, Dan Regan, and Tom Smith have looked after me in various ways with wisdom and good humor. And then there are the pals who have nothing, and may want nothing, to do with Villanova, including Bob Brophy, Bill Collins, Bill Grant, Tom Hickey, and Fran O'Brien.

Ed Santurri has been a great friend for a quarter-century. If my arguments are clear and precise in any way, they are mostly because of his example. They won't be clear and precise enough for him, but I'm working on it.

Stephen John Werpehowski and James William Werpehowski do not realize how many fruitful theological conversations I end up having with them. Or maybe they do. I surely hope they would know that their father treasures and respects them, and that their quiet questions and enthusiasm about this book have not gone unnoticed.

Anne McGuire has been involved in this project from beginning to end. We have discussed its original conception and revisions to that. She has thoughtfully read the final chapters and walked me through final steps. In between, and with keen intelligence, she has aided me in carving out a history of writing that well fits and reflects the life we have made together not only as colleagues, but also as spouses, parents, and friends. I am very much in her debt and lovingly thank her.

I dedicate this book to Margaret Margetich Werpehowski and William John Werpehowski. My mother taught me to love the life of the mind for its own sake, and my father never let me forget that there is great honor in hard work. Perhaps above all, at their best they gave me these lessons with a light touch, with an amusement and joy that said something, I bet, about their love for me. That love sustains.

CHAPTER ONE

Questions in Christian Ethics

When Christians talk with one another about what their faith in God has to do with their moral lives, questions arise. Some of them have to do with the relation of the "church" to the wider "world," which is not explicitly Christian but which includes neighbors whom Christians are commanded to love, and "secular" institutions within which many Christians work. A related concern is about what nontheological disciplines such as history and science can tell us of our place in the world, and how this connects with what we learn from the Bible and Christian tradition about where we stand before God. Other questions begin from the sharp and painful sense that there are horrible injustices in the world, and that Christians have been responsible for a lot of them. What should be the Christian community's approach to the domination, exploitation, and cruel indifference shown toward fellow human creatures of God?

In this book, I will respond to these questions in the course of considering a selected set of recent discussions in American theological ethics. The positions I assess come out of the Protestant tradition, and a primary instrument for my analysis is the retrieval of the work of H. Richard Niebuhr. In this chapter, I give a blueprint for the space we will inhabit by presenting summaries of four contrasting contemporary approaches to the Christian moral life. In chapter 2, I will offer an interpretation of salient themes in Niebuhr's theology and ethics that pertain to the disagreements we will find in these approaches. His legacy is reflected in different ways in all four approaches, and in this richness and diversity it can foster, I think, honest and creative reflection about the character and direction of Christian ethics.

To anticipate: Niebuhr's legacy takes Christian ethics to be a critical reflection on humanity's moral response to the sovereign God who acts in the world as Creator, Sustainer, and Redeemer. This response ought to attend both to our social nature and to our irreducibly individual character and action. It should honor God's universality and transcendence at the same time as it locates both undefensively in a particular language and practice of faith loyal to God's cause, discerned in Jesus Christ.

Four Approaches to the Christian Moral Life

Covenant Love

When trying to describe the moral life of people who claim ultimate allegiance to God as known in Jesus Christ, one might refer to those biblical passages that proclaim the priority of the love of God and neighbor. In the Gospel of Luke, the parable of the Good Samaritan is framed by an exchange between Jesus and a lawyer regarding the way "to inherit eternal life": "You shall love the Lord your God with all your heart, and with all your soul, and with all your strength, and with all your mind; and your neighbor as yourself" (Lk 10:27; cf. Mk 12:29; Dt 6:4–5; Lv 19:18).

Besides the parable's depiction of the meaning of the love of neighbor, other texts that present the command to love the enemy, and that point to God's universal regard and mercy, indicate a certain shape to such love as lived before the God who is Love (Mt 47–48; Lk 6:27–28, 32–36; 1 Jn 4:8). It is universal in scope. It is directed to all of God's human creatures, including the enemy and the unjust. It does not depend on being loved first or loved in return. It is not based on rigid conditions determining who counts as my neighbor; I love the neighbor by being a neighbor to the one standing before me in his or her need (Lk 10:36–37). This kind of love is based on the vulnerable and costly love of God in Jesus Christ: "I give you a new commandment, that you love one another. Just as I have loved you, you also should love one another" (Jn 13:34).

The ethics of Paul Ramsey is an account of the Christian moral life grounded in the norm to love the neighbor in these ways. Agape defines what is right for the Christian, and what defines agape is a biblically depicted pattern of God's love for humanity disclosed in the history of Israel and Jesus Christ. In that history, God keeps faith with those with whom a divine covenant has been established. God reaches out in concern for the alien, cares for the vulnerable, loves sinners, and attends to human needs apart from considerations of comparative merit or social status. In short, the pattern of divine love displays fidelity to the well-being of human creatures, cherished for their own sake. Christians are bound to be faithful to the neighbor along the same lines and by this measure, by having their activities correspond and witness to the redeeming divine actions that preeminently identify God. For Ramsey, moral duties to oneself, though essential to the Christian life, are still secondary, being derived from and ordered to the requirement to love the neighbor.[1]

Building up from this ground floor, Ramsey's work was distinguished by his vigorous involvement in public discussions of moral controversies and by his longstanding defense of moral rules, and even exceptionless moral rules, as expressing the law of love. He decisively shaped the political ethical reflection of his day through a reconstruction and refinement of the Christian theory of "just war." Ramsey was also a leader in developing moral responses to medical dilemmas concerning human experimentation, genetic intervention, reproductive technology, and care for the sick and dying. He stressed the importance of protecting persons from violations of their well-being pursued for reasons of greater social utility or lesser quality of life. The neighbor's worth in the eyes of God is not so ordered.

The significance of rules and principles in Christian ethics seemed to make sense from two background theological convictions. The first, ironically, had to do with Christian love's liberation from "legalism." Agape, Ramsey reasoned, is free from "law" so that the neighbor may be served; when the law, whatever it demands, fails to do that, it is to be set aside, for the good of the beloved. But to rule out the moral relevance of rules governing conduct that do really serve the well-being of human creatures would be to succumb, in the name of "freedom from law," to a new legalism of freedom.[2] Christian freedom makes legitimate rules and principles of general applicability possible. More important, the demands of faithfulness or the promises of "covenant fidelity" might make some such general moral rules necessary. Being bound to the neighbor who is also one's spouse or one's patient or one's current student through adherence to rules about keeping promises or acquiring informed consent or grading on performance and effort rather than sexual attractiveness may be the most fitting way to express loyalty to him or her.

In speaking out to the secular world as a Christian ethicist, Ramsey hoped that Christian discernments can properly be presented as public ethics; particularly Christian moral insight may resonate with and be relevant to the moral aspirations and ideals of culture. Here also, two background beliefs were crucial for warranting and expressing this hope. One of them was that the entire world of creation belongs to God and is illumined by the Incarnation of the Word. Structures of "natural law" or "natural justice" in human communities, forged and seemingly sustained at a distance from explicitly Christian deliverances, may yet serve the neighbor well and deserve Christian assent. The same structures, however, are liable to ceaseless challenge and transformation in the direction of agape. Ramsey never tired of reminding his readers of this theme of "love transforming natural justice."

Second, and as the foregoing suggests, Ramsey's public ethics called, typically but not exclusively, for the protection of persons he took to be especially liable to exploitation and abuse in the name of this or that social cause or for the benefit of this or that preferred person or group. He would emphasize the intractable character of human sinfulness and the dangerous implications of sentimentally expecting too much from the good will and moral ideals of fallen human creatures. It is not surprising or inaccurate to characterize him as a sort of Christian realist after the fashion of Reinhold Niebuhr, bent on seeking a more tolerable common life in society and the world through checking with just power the abusive impulses of the prideful human spirit.[3]

A Community of Character

Stanley Hauerwas questions whether Christian ethics really can or should be made public with the aim of shaping or transforming the moral ethos of American society. He worries about the abstractness of doing Christian ethics by simply working out the implications of Christian beliefs for the purposes of moral argument. Hauerwas is more comfortable speaking of "virtues" rather than "principles" like agape. He defends Christian pacifism rather than the just war tradition, and he believes that sustaining the life of the church might be a more important way to protect the vulnerable in medical contexts than defending "informed consent" and criticizing "quality of life judgments." Ramsey calls for faithfulness to the neighbor; without denying this, Hauerwas insists that Christians be faithful as a gathered people called church.

The first responsibility of the church, Hauerwas has often said, is to be itself.[4] This is a challenge because the dominant moral ethos in contemporary American society is liberalism, which holds that the best or only moral community we can have is based on guaranteeing the freedom of each individual citizen to do as he or she pleases, as long as he or she does not thereby violate the legitimate equal freedom of others. Liberalism celebrates toleration, pluralism, and respect for personal autonomy. But the church is devoted to a particular God and a particular way of life that follows Jesus Christ. Its members know themselves not in the first instance as autonomous but as bound to God. They know themselves as they are known by the merciful and faithful God, and hence they live in trust, patience, gratitude, and forgiveness, seeking not to control history but to witness to God's rule within it as established by Jesus. At least they should know themselves this way.

The problem has been that "in our attempt to control our society Christians in America have too readily accepted liberalism as a social strategy appropriate to the Christian story."[5] Thus they have gone some way in losing the moral skills or virtues that enable a proper description of reality as the Christian story presents it. Their moral experience becomes impoverished when what they see is filtered through the dominant value of individual freedom. For example, they might be tempted to view the family as a contractual society rather than as a community whose members learn what it means to live historically in responsibility to persons one may not choose to be with. Thus the church needs to recover its distinctiveness and stand as a contrast to liberal society.

From this standpoint, Ramsey's work contains "the tension inherent in the development of Christian ethics—namely, a concern to provide a theological account of the moral life while at the same time underplaying the significance of theology for purposes of public discussion."[6] Important Christian convictions and activities either lose their proper context, or worse, are eroded by liberal ideas and practices. Agape as universal love, ceaselessly forgiving, showing hospitality to the stranger, may turn out in public ethics to look very much like mere "respect for personal autonomy." The exclusive focus on arguing to moral conclusions from basic Christian beliefs makes Christianity look more like just another philosophical theory than like a social community called to live a certain life. Yet those beliefs might become intelligible just when they are apprehended in the sight of that way of life.

By reading the Gospel narratives in a way that highlights Jesus' political act of refusing recourse to violence, Hauerwas is able to believe that pacifism is the normative mode of witness to God's reign in history. Appeals in the name of love to just war need to respond to this biblical reading as well as to pay more attention to the social location of just war discourse. This discourse is liable to being co-opted by nations to rationalize their killing exploits. The issue of social location, and hence of the relationships and virtues that give intelligibility to the moral life, also plays a role in medical ethics. The practice of medicine is about the faithful refusal to abandon those who are in pain, and health care professionals "are the bridge between the world of the ill and the healthy."[7] But in American society persons are tempted to adopt strategies that isolate the suffering and insulate the caregiver either in the name of the former's freedom (call this "respecting patient autonomy") or in the name of the power of their caregivers (call this "medical paternalism"). In this social context, medicine needs the church to offer examples of fidelity and hospitality.

Theocentric Ethics

Hauerwas's focus on the Christian tradition and the church leads James Gustafson to question whether God is thereby made to take a back seat:

> It is God with whom humankind has to reckon: God who is the source of all life, whose powers have brought it into being, sustain it, bear down upon it, create conditions of possibility within it and will determine its ultimate destiny. Theology has to be open to all the sources that help us to construe God's relations to the world: ethics has to do with the interdependence of *all* things in relation to God. This . . . nec-

essarily relativizes the significance of the Christian tradition, though it is the tradition in which our theologies develop. God is the God of Christians, but God is not a Christian God for Christians only.[8]

Gustafson sees Hauerwas's standpoint to be based on its "fidelity [to] the biblical narratives, and particularly the gospel narratives," rather than "on a concern to be responsible participants in the ambiguities of public choices."[9] The doctrine of God's creation, which affirms that God orders life through nature, is effectively omitted; so is the commitment "to interact with other ways of viewing the world with any openness to what these other ways might require as alterations" of the church's narrative-based construal of reality.[10] The Christian tradition seems isolated, valued for its own sake, and immune to critical scrutiny. "But if God is the source of how things really and ultimately are, if God is the sustainer and even destroyer of aspects of life in the world, if God is the determiner of the destiny of things, then whatever one says about how God is related to the world demands theological attention to ways in which nature, history and culture are interpreted and understood by investigations proper to them."[11]

Theocentric ethics may be summarized under four points. First, "it is *God* with whom humankind has to reckon." Gustafson thinks that too often theology has reversed this order by placing God in the service of human beings. The attack on anthropocentrism most clearly marks his thought. Theocentric piety must be ready to consent to the power and powers that sustain and bear down upon us, for our good or ill. From this starting point, and in line with the doctrine of creation, Gustafson relies "more heavily on scientific and other sources of our knowledge of the world . . . than traditional Christian ethics has."[12] In fact, his reliance can be tied rather closely to his critique of anthropocentrism, as when scientific investigation raises questions about the possibly instrumental character of beliefs in resurrection and personal salvation.

Second, theocentric ethics cannot be understood apart from "piety," the religious expression of certain general or universal human experiences of the world. Faithful consent to God's governance goes along with various human affections, or senses of dependence, gratitude, obligation, remorse and repentance, possibility, and directedness. Within the Christian tradition, Jesus decisively incarnates such piety, and the Gospel narratives show what human life "can and ought to be—a life of courage and love grounded in an object of piety and fidelity that transcends the immediate objects of experience."[13]

Third, "since ethics has to do with the interdependence of all things in relation to God," the moral life is founded on God's ordering of the "patterns of interdependence and development within which human activity and life occur."[14] The ways of nature may indicate something about this ordering. The good for human persons may be grasped through their relations with one another in families and in other so-cial and natural units defined socially, economically, politically, na-tionally, internationally, biologically, and ecologically. There is in piety "a proper incentive to expand the arenas of relationships and inter-dependencies within which particular entities are explained and understood."[15]

Fourth, human moral agency is a matter of construing God's rela-tions to the world as beings who always already interact with and par-ticipate in it in many ways. Neither spectators nor the lords of cre-ation, human beings are temporary yet responsible stewards of the patterns and processes of interdependence in which they too partici-pate. The basic moral question is "What is God enabling and requir-ing us, as such participants, to be and to do?" The answer is "We are to relate ourselves and all things in a manner appropriate to our and their relations to God."[16] Particular moral judgments are made by a keen discrimination or discernment of the "necessary conditions for life to be sustained and developed."[17]

Gustafson distinguishes his work not only from Hauerwas but also from Ramsey. Ramsey is "more confessionally Christian" and "Chris-tocentric." Gustafson also thinks that Ramsey's "love monism" re-stricts attention to the good of human individuals at the expense of not considering the wholes in which they participate and the common good to which they may contribute. For example, in medical experi-mentation exceptions to the principle of informed consent may some-times be justified, even in the case of children, for important reasons of potential benefits to others. Because a theocentric ethic calls for a more inclusive description of morally relevant circumstances than Ramsey's strict attention to covenant fidelity requires, it may lead to moral conclusions relying more on good consequences than Ramsey could countenance.

The (Progressive) Politics of God

Kathryn Tanner also thinks that Christian theology and ethics are about God. The implications for human life are all-encompassing:

> In every affair of life—in public or private, in word or deed, when active or in retirement, in matters of state or worries about economic justice, when contemplating the course of either the natural world or human history, when assessing the character of one's desire or deciding one's responsibilities to one's neighbors, when helping others or caring for oneself—one can try to witness self-consciously, in one's feelings, thoughts, and deeds, to the relationship that creatures enjoy with God. In short, one tries self-consciously to inscribe the relationship one has with God everywhere.[18]

Her account stresses, with Ramsey, "God's special concern for every individual *as such*," and, in a sense, with Gustafson, how "one's own life is given meaning *only* insofar as it is brought under the umbrella of a relationship with God enjoyed by the whole world as the creation of God and the object of God's continuing concern."[19] But she also directs us to a program of progressive politics and social transformation that perhaps distinguishes her from these others.

The key is understanding the implications of belief in a transcendent God who, as the source of all being and value, actively works immediately and universally in the world. To recognize God's transcendence is also to recognize the limited and fallible nature of human proposals and norms. In this way, at least, belief in transcendence has a critical potential for challenging social norms taken to be inevitable or otherwise absolute. Add a robust doctrine of human sinfulness, as well as a Christology that builds on divine transcendence and stresses God's utter graciousness toward human and all other creatures for their good,[20] and the critical potential before God is enhanced.

The payoff is that traditional Christian beliefs about transcendence, providence, sin, and the shape of a human life assumed by Jesus Christ can lead to a progressive and even radical program of social change. Conceding that Christian traditions historically have legitimated and

masked unjust practices through appeals to this or that divinely ordained hierarchy or role relation, Tanner intends to uncouple Christian beliefs about God and the world from these practices. For example, fixed hierarchies of superiors and subordinates cannot be
included in a theological ethic that rules out limiting the will of the
Lord by human social arrangements. The domination and exploitation
of human beings cannot stand in face of the fact that, before God,
human creatures are owed an independent and unalterable respect that
is never a matter of proof and never earned. All human creatures have
rights to life, self-development, and self-determination.

A further consequence of Tanner's analysis is that oppressed and privileged alike are enabled and required to struggle for justice, though in
different ways. "The dignity before God that psychologically empowers the oppressed to *claim* their rights psychologically empowers the
privileged to [*sic*] *forego* what they possess at another's expense. . . .
Just as identifying one's value with one's value before God corrects the
self-denigrating tendency of the oppressed to take their social standing to heart, it corrects the self-congratulatory inclination of the privileged to identify their value with their social prestige."[21] Here is a
"preferential option for the poor" based on equal status before God.

There is more to Tanner's thought that relates to our inquiry. Holding that religious beliefs generally and Christian beliefs in particular
"are prone to supply an overarching interpretive framework for the
whole of life," she argues that the Christian faith is a kind of "lived culture" with a distinct set of practices that works to forge for adherents
a particular identity or style. But one might wonder whether Hauerwas would take little comfort from this case; for Tanner's postmodern
notion of culture opposes ideas of identity based on particularly stable
boundaries between, say, Christian and liberal, church and world, and
so forth. The story that unites, calls, and directs the community of disciples must not be chained to human presumptions or predictions
about these oppositions, but must find its home in the free grace of
God. God transcends all of the human maneuvers to contain God
within static understandings of "tradition" or "rules of discourse."[22]

In a fashion that again seems to ally her with Gustafson, Tanner en-
thusiastically endorses theological dependence on nontheological disciplines and habits of inquiry. Theologians are in the business of "tak-

ing up the best thought about the cosmos and its inhabitants and subjecting it to their particular angle of vision, by investigating how all
this appears when one understands the world in its relation to the God
of all." They are "perpetual renters," "parasites," "poachers," "in-
terjecting their own distinctive viewpoint within the spaces of other
disciplines."[23] Still, theology for her remains irreducible to and crucially independent of the conclusions of other disciplines. Characteristic Christian "formalities" or "patterns of use" emerge through a
procedure of theological commentary that itself is not independent of
these disciplines.

Thus we have a theologian whose ethic of the irreducible worth of
human creatures challenges establishment Christian ethics for not caring enough about social injustice and the plight of the poor and oppressed. Tanner is also a particularist who cautions her would-be comrades not to succumb to defensiveness or idolatry, and she also is a
somewhat theocentric theologian who maintains a number of traditional commitments that Gustafson's perspective excludes.

More Questions

The approaches point to differing accounts of Christian ethics. For
Ramsey it is both church ethics and public ethics;[24] fidelity to the
neighbor and the permeability of human culture to Christ's transforming work establish a theological basis and bridge for movement
from the one to the other. Hauerwas focuses on the development of
critical skills, virtues, and relationships that articulate the church's witness as a contrast model to a world of unbelief. Challenging anthropocentric narrowing, Gustafson practices theocentric ethics by being
attuned to scientific inquiry and public canons of reasonableness. Tanner would do Christian ethics in solidarity with the victims of injustice, and with a keen eye to the value of theological diversity and critical reflection in faithfulness to God.

In the following chapters, I will consider a number of related questions that come up in the four approaches (I will return to them explicitly in chapter 11):

What is the relation between the "church" and the "world"? How
does a general answer to this question apply to the specific relation be-

tween a distinctive Christian community and American liberalism? Between the church, as it aspires, say, to a life of nonviolent discipleship, and the violent character of the nation-state? How does Christian ethics fittingly bear on broader public discussions of moral and political matters?

Why and how should Christian ethical reflection deal with "the ways in which nature, history and culture are interpreted and understood by investigations proper to them?" How does the particularity of Christian tradition relate to these and other more general or even universal understandings?

How should we gauge the emancipatory potential of traditional Christian belief? What is the full meaning of our dignity as creatures of God, or as sisters and brothers for whom Christ died?

I hope to contribute to these inquiries by analyzing and evaluating the four accounts against the background of the thought of H. Richard Niebuhr. For reasons of influence alone, this strategy makes sense. Gustafson and Ramsey were students of Niebuhr at Yale, and both have developed their thought in conversation with their mentor's work. Tanner's conception of divine transcendence resonates considerably with Niebuhr's, and Hauerwas's writings indicate toward his theology a complex relation of sympathy and criticism. Tracing these positions and their attendant controversies back to a common conversation partner will help to illumine both common themes and competing emphases.

A better reason for the strategy rests on the power and richness of Niebuhr's legacy itself. I think it contains dimensions of the four approaches in a way that sets a direction for critique, synthesis, and reconstruction. Like Hauerwas, he resisted Christian accommodation to what he saw to be American idols of nationalism and capitalism. But a good portion of his work contends with theologies that rely on "Christocentrism" to set the church apart from other human communities. He characteristically called for a conversion or transformation of the whole of life before God in Christ that seemingly is aligned with Ramsey's idea of "love transforming natural justice." But Niebuhr's "permanent revolution of the mind and of the heart" may also have a more critical edge than Ramsey's position includes. Niebuhr's later writings on "radical monotheism" have resonances in Gustafson's theocentric ethics, but there are also substantial differences between the two regarding the nature of God and the meaning of Christian theology. Niebuhr's stress on divine sovereignty, I have said, fits much of what Tanner says; but he also may focus so much on consenting to the "insurmountable givens" of human life that he loses sight of active human responsibility for social transformation. Or so Tanner contends. We find in this legacy the makings of a case for theological independence without theological isolation; for individual and social conversion corresponding to what God, and not merely some religious community or moral norm, is doing in the world; and yet for a knowledge of God that is crucially available in the church's language and practice, and that demands both the acceptance of creaturely limits and the removal of sinful impediments to creaturely well-being.

It is not the point of this study to cast Christian ethics once and for all in the mold of H. Richard Niebuhr's theology. The point is that his work can aid in exposing better ways of conceiving the practice of Christian ethics as it reflects on and responds to the Christian moral life, ways that preserve and enhance the strengths of the current proposals while reducing reliance on their weaknesses. I would like to come up with a position that, while perhaps faithful to the best in Niebuhr, is—more important—something of a more truthful Christian ethic of faithfulness. It would bring together trust in and loyalty to the entire reality of God, the accompanying call to Christians to a common life that confesses and embraces, confidently and undefensively, a particular identity before God in Jesus Christ, and the church's responsibility to God and God's cause for the world.

Notes

1. Paul Ramsey, *Basic Christian Ethics* (New York: Scribner's, 1950), 1–23; see also Paul Ramsey, *The Essential Paul Ramsey*, ed. William Werpehowski and Stephen D. Crocco (New Haven, Conn.: Yale University Press, 1994), 15–18.
2. Ibid., 1–24.
3. See the introduction to Ramsey, *Essential Paul Ramsey*, xx–xxii.
4. Stanley Hauerwas, *A Community of Character* (Notre Dame, Ind.: University of Notre Dame Press, 1981), 10.
5. Ibid., 11.
6. Stanley Hauerwas, *Against the Nations* (Minneapolis: Winston Press, 1985), 35.

7. Stanley Hauerwas, *Suffering Presence* (Notre Dame, Ind.: University of Notre Dame Press, 1986), 78.

8. James M. Gustafson, "The Sectarian Temptation," *Proceedings of the Catholic Theological Society* 40 (1985): 94.

9. Ibid., 88.

10. Ibid., 86.

11. Ibid., 92.

12. James M. Gustafson, *Ethics from a Theocentric Perspective*, vol. 2, *Ethics and Theology* (Chicago: University of Chicago Press, 1984), 144.

13. James M. Gustafson, *Ethics from a Theocentric Perspective*, vol. 1, *Theology and Ethics* (Chicago: University of Chicago Press, 1981), 276, 277.

14. Gustafson, *Ethics from a Theocentric Perspective*, vol. 2, 7.

15. Ibid., 15.

16. Ibid., 146.

17. Gustafson, *Ethics from a Theocentric Perspective*, vol. 1, 339–40.

18. Kathryn Tanner, "Why Are We Here?" in Ronald F. Thiemann and William C. Placher, eds., *Why Are We Here? Everyday Questions and the Christian Life* (Harrisburg, Pa.: Trinity Press International, 1998), 11.

19. Ibid.

20. Kathryn Tanner, *Jesus, Humanity, and the Trinity: A Brief Systematic Theology* (Minneapolis: Fortress Press, 2001).

21. Kathryn Tanner, *The Politics of God: Christian Theologies and Social Justice* (Minneapolis: Fortress Press, 1992), 232.

22. Kathryn Tanner, *Theories of Culture: A New Agenda for Theology* (Minneapolis: Fortress Press, 1997).

23. Kathryn Tanner, "The Difference Theological Anthropology Makes," *Theology Today* 50, no. 4 (January 1994): 567–79.

24. Paul Ramsey, "Tradition and Reflection in Christian Life," *Perkins Journal* 35, no. 2 (winter–spring 1982): 47 n. 3.

CHAPTER TWO

A Theology of Permanent Revolution

H. Richard Niebuhr's older brother Reinhold was, with the exception of Martin Luther King, Jr., the most influential American theologian and preacher of the twentieth century. A "public theologian" who brought a prophetic biblical vision to bear on the political and social challenges of his day, Reinhold Niebuhr's project, according to Richard, had more to do with the reform of culture, while his own addressed the reformation of the church. Yet from that point of departure the latter's influence was remarkable. During his thirty-one years of teaching and writing at Yale Divinity School until his death in 1962, H. Richard Niebuhr developed a deep and multifaceted body of thought, and established himself as an educator of the highest order.[1]

In this chapter, I consider themes basic to Niebuhr's theology and ethics. By chapter's end, the reader should have a rudimentary grasp of Niebuhr's thought and a feel for its relevance to the questions and quarrels we need to ponder. I will propose that he establishes and then positions himself within various "polarities" that orient and direct theological movement toward the end of faithfulness to God. This devotion requires humble and assured attention to a Lord sovereign over yet present in our history, to the One Beyond the Many revealed to us in the man Jesus Christ, who founds a distinctive community that confesses in His particular name a universal truth. It makes for a life in which judgments about our specific actions drive to interpretive responses to context, to what God is doing in the world. It demands in light of these responses a Christian stance toward the world that neither rejects it as God's good work nor accepts it as if it were God. Finally, faithfulness to God in the church enlists a variety of voices, self-critical and critical of one another, as this community seeks a mean or balance in its movement between these poles.[2]

The Reality of God and Our Point of View

The Sovereignty of God

In an essay published near the end of his career, H. Richard Niebuhr tells of a decisive shift in his thinking that took place in the 1930s:

> The fundamental certainty given to me then . . . was that of God's sovereignty. My fundamental break with the so-called liberal or empirical theology was not due to the fact that it emphasized human sovereignty; to interpret it in that way is to falsify it in unjustifiable fashion. It was rather due to the fact that it defined God primarily in value-terms, as the good, believing that good could be defined apart from God. And now I came to understand that unless being itself, the constitution of things, the One beyond all the many, the ground of my being and all being, the ground of its "that-ness" and its "so-ness," was trustworthy—could be counted on by what had proceeded from it—I had no God at all.[3]

Niebuhr came to believe that the method of the Social Gospel theology championed by Walter Rauschenbusch and others was not "theocentric" because its idea of the Kingdom of God was teleologically conceived as "humanity organized according to the will of God" and "as an association in love of intrinsically valuable persons." This meant that the end of Christian life was not God but a goal defined by a social ideal negating the laissez-faire social philosophy of the United States in the early twentieth century. God's action was limited, on the one hand, to being the author of nature (and, as such, the guarantor of the success of human striving), and, on the other, to its immanence within human historical action directed toward the Kingdom of God. The priority of God's approach to the human creature was compromised by this conception and the identification of divine action with a form of human love.[4]

In contrast to the Social Gospel's teleology, Christian eschatology affirmed that God sets a limit on all human activity. The mind of Jesus is directed toward revolution, "an event which has an end character, not as the 'telos' toward which men strive, but as the 'eschaton' which terminates striving, not by fulfillment but by complete denial."[5] The Kingdom that God establishes must be grasped in terms of the transcendent God's purposes, not our own, and human action, accordingly, must be seen to be a "response to the divine action which precedes, accompanies, and awaits human action in history."[6]

Hence, for Niebuhr the divine sovereignty is conceived in terms of the priority of God's majesty, graciousness, and transcendent historical activity. Divine majesty refers to God's reality as the judge and destroyer of all the idolatrous causes and loves that occupy human history, the reality of the One that "crowns with destruction the life which proceeds from it."[7] Yet for the Christian community, this God is revealed in Jesus Christ to be a reality in whom it may trust; we accept Christ "as God's word to us that God is faithful and true, that he does not desire the death of the sinner, that he is leading his kingdom to victory over all evil."[8] The revelation and the trust it makes possible are "miraculous gifts"; God's prevenient grace is apprehended in the gifts we receive in repentance and faith. Finally, Christian existence is always a matter of response to God's actions in history, who governs all things immediately, and who is, though hidden, "still the reality behind and in all realities."[9]

Relationism

Niebuhr was also convinced of the radically historical character of human existence. "I am certain that I can only see, understand, think, believe, as a self that is in time."[10] The historically particular shaping of human reflection and conception place an inescapable limit on human ambitions to speak universally, for all times and places. But historical relativity does not imply skepticism or subjectivism. Although there is no universal view escaping the limits of finite existence, there are views of the universal that are justifiable and true; "what we see from the democratic point of view," for example, "is really there, even though all men do not see it and even though our way of expressing it is not a universal way."[11] Yet again, what is underscored is the fact that we are always in time, indeed, that "time is in us," in our reasoning and apprehending and acting and undergoing; therefore, human thought and action about God are also always thought and action from some particular, temporal point of view.

Niebuhr's historical relationism is complemented by a religious or theocentric relativism. This means, first, that Christians may speak about God only from their particular standpoint of faith in God, who is the Absolute and of absolute value for us. For Christians, grasping this historical and religious point of view of faith inevitably involves attending to the distinctive, traditioned story of our life as lived before God in Christian community.

Second, "just because faith knows of an absolute standpoint it can therefore accept the relativity of the believer's situation and knowledge" by refusing to assume for oneself the absolute authority of the former and seeking instead the divine correction and completion of all one's beliefs and actions in history. Also, "to deal as we must with the relative values of persons, things, and movements does not involve us in relativism, when we remember that all these realities which have many values in relation to each other also have a relation to God that must never be lost to view." Thus a person's relative worth "for his state or his class or his biological race" can never be accepted as one's final value before God.[12] In Niebuhr's understanding, epistemological humility may combine with positive and objective discernments of the multiple relations between the finite and the infinite.[13]

The themes of the sovereign reality of God and the relativism of our point of view are given together in Niebuhr; "there is here . . . a metaphysical vision for the fullness of the divine initiative in relation to the created order, but its descriptive force is rendered solely by the given, specific 'life story' of any creature or traditional group."[14] The theologies we surveyed in chapter 1 include differing emphases with regard to these themes. Stanley Hauerwas will pay close attention to the historical narrative of the Christian community, whereas James Gustafson stresses the universal priority of a God who will not be ignored, denied, or manipulated—and certainly not manipulated by an overweening concern to defend the Christian tradition.

On another front, Kathryn Tanner holds a position approaching the theocentric or religious relativism described above. Any adequate theological movement on these matters, I propose, cannot fail to affirm what these three affirm. However one may wish to qualify the affirmations, and however sensitivity to historical context calls for a situated focus in this direction or that, none of these claims may be excluded, even if they are held in tension.

Particular Confession and Faith in the Absolute One

Confessional Theology

The first two themes help make sense of a third. Christian theology, "that response of man's nascent love toward God and neighbor which seeks to *know* the beloved,"[15] is primarily confessional, not apologetic. Starting from the standpoint of the historic faith of the Christian community, it must avoid the defensiveness by which Christians try to recommend themselves in displaying the superiority of their faith. It is enough that "we . . . proceed by stating in simple, confessional terms what has happened to us in our community, how we came to believe, how we reason about things, and what we see from our point of view."[16] This confessional dimension is an aspect of an ethic of faithfulness that I sketched at the end of chapter 1.

The aversion to apologetic theology also has roots in Niebuhr's conception of God. He thought that theological efforts to defend one's faith to others holding another point of view often reflected the intention to substitute the sovereignty of the Christian religion for the sovereignty of the God of Christian faith. This intention contradicts the fundamental Christian claim that all persons, and especially Christians in their religious strivings, are judged as sinners "wholly unworthy of sovereignty."[17] Apologetic claims to the superior knowledge and insight that Christian faith brings also tend to identify revelation with a static possession under Christian control, rather than as a revelation in action by a living God, in which the church is called anew to repentance and rejoicing.[18]

In a few paragraphs in his book *The Meaning of Revelation*, Niebuhr succinctly presents the positive work that Christian theology needs to do. First, it may identify the central patterns that give a particular historical tradition its intelligibility, seeking the "reason within that history" and distinguishing from it moments of secondary significance. In *The Kingdom of God in America*, Niebuhr sought to do this with American Protestantism from the Puritans through the religious revivals of the eighteenth century up to the period of the Social Gospel. He showed how three interrelated theological convictions about the sovereignty of God, the kingdom of Christ, and the coming Kingdom made intelligible a religious history that at different times weighted these differently. In the book, Niebuhr "gave testimony to the compelling force of the bedrock, to the unavoidable and linguistically unsubstitutable language of tradition," and showed how within it the idea of the Kingdom of God "bridged the gap between the reality of divine agency in history, as course of human events, and the symbolic part played by our own faith's constructive act. The priority belonged to the radical realism of divine action."[19]

Second, theology may undertake to present "the grammar, not of a universal religious language, but of a particular language" during a particular period in time, "in order that those who use it may be kept in true communication with each other and with the realities to which the language refers."[20] Niebuhr's analysis in *Christ and Culture* bears the clear marks of this sort of presentation. We find it especially in his remarks "toward a definition of Christ," and in his critical redescription of the doctrines of creation, the fall, and redemption in their ethical implications.[21]

Third, confessional theology may attempt to develop a method applicable to its particular faith. One could say that *The Meaning of Revelation* itself was one such attempt. Fourth and finally, theology can test and affirm the truth of its assertions about God by subjecting them to the experience of the church. "A theology which undertakes the limited work of understanding and criticizing within Christian history the thought and action of the church is also dependent on the church for the constant test of its critical work."[22]

Nearly two decades after he published *The Meaning of Revelation*, Niebuhr summarized the work of theology as developing "reasoning in faith" and "the criticism of faith."[23] By that time as well, he was writing about another mode of theological activity that could appear to compromise the more or less sharp distinction between confessional and apologetic reflection. It will figure in my discussion of the next theme.

Radical Monotheism

Niebuhr relentlessly applied his basic conviction regarding the sovereignty of God to his critique of the church and the world; more, he sought to show how a "radically monotheistic" faith played a constructive, reforming role in cultural life.

Understanding faith as trusting dependence on a center of value with corresponding loyalty to that center's cause, Niebuhr distinguished radical monotheism from two other faiths in conflict with it: "a pluralism that has many objects of devotion and a social faith that has one object, which is, however, only one among many."[24] The first, "polytheism," divides the self's valuations and commitments across a number of gods that confer worth and claim loyalty. The polytheist disperses oneself in roles and functions with no unifying center, aside from the self-defeating, arbitrary freedom to negotiate between them. "Henotheism," in contrast, holds to a single social center of value, be it family, church, nation, class, or any other grouping. This faith divides the in group from what goes on outside of it, and affirms value and worth only as it serves the closed society's cause.

Though never free of these two forms of faith, radical monotheism dethrones "all absolutes short of the principle of being itself. At the same time, it reverences every relative existent. Its two great mottoes are: 'I am the Lord thy God; thou shalt have no other gods before me' and 'Whatever is, is good.'"[25] No finite existent may be divinized or demonized by being separated from the realm of value established by the One. The self's loves are unified by its expansive affirmation of the goodness of everything that is in its relations with God.

Radical faith opposes both Christ-centered and church-centered henotheisms. The latter makes the Christian community itself the center of value; the former, which typically becomes such an ecclesiasticism, substitutes the Lordship of Christ for the Lordship of God. The special principle of the Christian community is placed in opposition to the principle of being. "To be a Christian now means not so much that through the mediation and the pioneering faith of Jesus Christ a man has become wholly human, has been called into membership in the society of universal being, and has accepted the fact that amidst the totality of existence he is not exempt from the human lot; it means rather that he has become a member of a special group, with a special god, a special destiny, and a separate existence."[26]

The life of radical faith "involves us in a permanent revolution of the mind and of the heart, a continuous life which opens out infinitely into ever new possibilities." It is a life of turning away in repentance from our narrower gods and self-defensive self-loves, and toward the apprehension of all beings "with reverence, for all are friends in the friendship of the one to whom we are reconciled in faith."[27] It is also occupied with the challenging dual project of making radical faith intensively incarnate in the particularities of embodied existence and extending its reach as universally as possible without the loss of concreteness.[28] One carries on from one's limited, relative standpoint, but with "universal intent," "as one who seeks a truth that is true of universal relations and true for all subjects in the universe."[29]

The complexity of Niebuhr's theological call to speak both confessionally and with universal intent can be gleaned from an examination of the contrasting views of Ramsey, Hauerwas, Gustafson, and Tanner. All four hold to some version of a confessional position, and none of the four would deny concern with the more universal reach of that position. But we have already noted some real disagreements. The plot thickens as we try to work out what is at stake in varying approaches to the dual commitment; but here as before, the trick, I believe, is to follow Niebuhr in seeking the mean, to affirm both in balance and, hence, without compromise.

Ethical Themes

Christ the Transformer of Culture

For Christian faith, the miraculous gift of trust in God and loyalty to God's cause of reconciling the many to the One is accomplished among us by and through Jesus Christ. Theologically, this means that Christ may be the converter or transformer of human cultural life as of all being. Two points are particularly important for comprehending Niebuhr's position. The first refers to the underlying theological perspective, and the second indicates one typical way Niebuhr discerned and described this transformation in history.

The conversionist makes a sharp distinction between God's work in Christ and humanity's work of building a social environment that materially advances and conserves values supportive of human good. "Distinction" is not opposition; human culture may be judged by God in Christ, but as a reality that is always already under God's sovereign rule. Divine creation is honored in its goodness but is never immune to proper judgment. Human corruption is thoroughgoing but crucially the corruption of human creatures. Indeed, these and all created natures may be seen to be created in the Word of God. "Hence man the creature, working in a created world lives, as the conversionist sees it, under the rule of Christ and by the creative power and ordering of the divine Word, even though in his unredeemed mind he may believe that he lives among vain things under divine wrath. . . . The Word that became flesh and dwelt among us . . . has entered into a human culture that has never been without his ordering action." Culture is converted, not replaced, though so radically that one may speak of rebirth into eternal life, a quality of existence in the here and now.[30] In brief, creation is fallen, but finite creation and the fall are not identified. The work of redemption renews creation without obliterating it in the ever present possibilities of God's historical action.

Soberly and hopefully, Niebuhr often described this process of conversion as the palpable but still mysterious working out of repentance and faith in the midst of judgment and the suffering innocent. In one famous case, he interpreted World War II as a time Christians might experience the judgment of God:

> Wars are crucifixions. It is not the mighty, the guides and leaders of nations and churches, who suffer most in them, but the humble, little people who have had little to do with the framing of great policies. . . . Christians know that the justice of God is not only a redemptive justice in which suffering is used in the service of remaking but it is also vicarious in its method, so that the suffering of innocence is used for the remaking of the guilty.[31]

Construing war in this way may lead to a defense of the innocent that is not so tainted by national self-centeredness, and to a continuing active concern for imperiled neighbors both during and after a war less conditioned by the final end of promoting "our" values. One is also freed to act with repentance. "Repentance is called for not because we shall suffer or because civilization will perish if we do not repent, but because others are now perishing for us and because we are attacking the very son of God in our endeavor to maintain our civilization at any cost. Repentance is called for not because we have chosen false means to the achievement of our ends but because our ends themselves are idolatrous."[32]

This approach is not exclusive. One can find other examples in Niebuhr's work where the theme of the cross does not loom so large. Usually, however, what is highlighted are events of reconciliation: the transitions from self-centeredness to disinterestedness, and from defensiveness to hope in God's ongoing governance in cultural life. The conversionist theme is at the center of Ramsey's theological ethics. Hauerwas sees it as a dangerous mistake. Gustafson adopts the theme in a less Christological and more radically monotheistic fashion, whereas Tanner's more Christological ethic is critical of Niebuhr yet not discontinuous with his thought.

Responsibility

Niebuhr's beliefs about divine sovereignty and human historicity affect his understanding of human moral agency. In contrast to images that focus on human fashioning for the sake of an end, or on human consent and obedience to law, he devised a third symbol or synecdoche that fixed on human responses to actions and events. Agency takes place in interaction with and response to the forces acting upon us in the natural, historical, cultural, and interpersonal worlds. Responses are fitting or not according to the adequacy of our interpretation of "what is going on" in and with these impinging, limiting, and enabling events. Responding as we interpret the meaning of actions upon us, we also respond in anticipation of answers given to our answers within an ongoing community of fellow agents.[33]

This image of the human as responder reflected in a striking way the social character of human selfhood. Niebuhr relied on but also transformed George Herbert Mead's analysis of the social self to make the point. The self possesses an ability to become an object to itself; but this reflexivity is only possible through dialogue with others. From such interaction one may take toward oneself the attitude of other selves, seeing and hearing oneself as seen and heard. "To say the self is social is not to say that it finds itself in need of fellow men in order to achieve its purposes, but that it is born in the womb of society as a sentient, thinking, needful being with certain definitions of its needs and with the possibility of experience of a common world." So the social self exists in responses to others who are members of a group or common history "in whose interactions constancies are present in such a way that the self can interpret present and anticipate future action upon it."[34]

Niebuhr also thought that the responsibility model offered a good way to understand the ethos of Christian Scripture:

> When an Isaiah counsels his people, he does not remind them of the law they are required to obey nor yet of the goal toward which they are directed but calls to their attention the intentions of God present in hiddenness in the actions of Israel's enemies. The question he and his peers raise in every critical moment is about the interpretation of what is going on, whether what is happening be, immediately considered, a drought or the invasion of a foreign army, or the fall of a great empire. Israel is the people that is to see and understand the action of God in everything that happens and to make a fitting reply. So it is in the New Testament also. The God to whom Jesus points is not the commander who gives laws but the doer of small and of mighty deeds, the creator of sparrows and clother of lilies, the ultimate giver of blindness and of sight, the ruler whose rule is hidden in the manifold activities of plural agencies but is yet in a way visible to those who know how to interpret the signs of the times.[35]

The Christian is called to discern God's action in all actions upon him or her, and to respond to all such actions in a manner fitting to this divine action.

The symbol of responsibility helps Niebuhr to interrelate radical monotheism with his confessional affirmation of Jesus Christ the reconciler. In sin, human beings respond to the One beyond the many as to the law of our destruction by which all our labors and causes and very being come to nothing. Anxiety, the law of self-preservation, and defensiveness enter into all that we do as suspicion of God the Enemy leads us to seek our own glory and the glory of our closed societies. To be saved from this body of death is to be freed from this distrust and to gain "the liberty to interpret in trust all that happens as contained within an intention and a total activity that includes death within the domain of life, that destroys only to re-establish and renew."[36]

The Christian receives this empowerment in Jesus' unceasingly trustful response to the One, and in the manifestation of his Resurrection that the One is his Father. Again, his response and its aftermath in God's mighty act offer the basis for this interpretive liberty. Disciples of Jesus may in the church respond to God as those called to a universal community, and proclaim in the Resurrection the caring goodness of the Lord who rules it.

Niebuhr's later work on responsibility is explicitly set forth as "an essay in Christian moral philosophy," or as an attempt to present, from a Christian point of view, an account of human moral life in general. Hence he will maintain both that "all human life has the character of responsiveness" and that this "universal claim" comes out of a Christian interpretation of the world. Here we have an effort to speak confessionally but with universal intent, and certainly not to do any systematic Christian apologetics. We find in Gustafson and Tanner distinctive efforts along the same path.

Church and World in Tension

In the 1930s, Niebuhr was convinced that the sovereignty of God was being usurped by the spirit of capitalism and nationalism, and he called for "the rejection of 'Culture Protestantism' and for the return of the church to the confession of its own peculiar faith and ethos."[37] Changes in the intervening quarter-century led him in 1960 (and before) to make a different but not inconsistent move. "If my Protestantism led me in the past to protest against the spirit of capitalism and of nationalism, of communism and technological civilization, it now leads me to protest against the deification of Scriptures and the church." He looked for the church's reformation "not now by separation from the world but by a new entrance into it without conformity to it."[38]

These passages display both Niebuhr's refusal of the exclusive options of the church's accommodation to the world or its isolation from it, and his promotion of a rhythm of identification and withdrawal attuned to the signs of the times.[39] Indeed, the very independence of the Christian community from all other powers for the service of God requires the capacity to respond appropriately to what is going on, and that may require conflict with the world, alliance with it, or both in proper measure.

Before God, the world is a companion of the church, "a community something like itself." It is sometimes the church's enemy and sometimes its partner, "often antagonist, always one to be befriended; now it is the co-knower, now the one that does not know what the church knows, now the knower of what the Church does not know."[40] Niebuhr's view of the church's responsibility to God for human societies is similarly diverse. It preaches the Gospel of repentance and faith to the point of prophetic critique of moral evil and injustice. It ministers to the needs of fellow human creatures. It is in its highest form a "social pioneer," assuming "representational responsibility" for the world in its own internal life by showing in the manner of Christ what is possible by the grace of God for all.

So, in a world where the evils of nationalism, racism, and economic imperialism have become so evident, "the Church meets its social responsibility when in its own thinking, organization, and action it functions as a world society, undivided by race, class and national interests."[41] As I will argue below, we may be able to address some of the disagreements between Ramsey and Hauerwas in terms of this vision of church and world.

Conclusion

Niebuhr believed that the best method available to him for delivering a definition of the Christian church was polar analysis. The analyst "must try to do justice to the dynamic character of that social reality, the Church, by defining certain poles between which it moves or which it represents."[42] The analyst of Niebuhr's thought does well to do the same, because its dynamic character, fueled by the dual commitments to human historicity and the present reality of God's initiating activity in the world, is otherwise lost or diminished.

The discussion of the last section suggests that at least five interrelated polarities define Niebuhr's thought. First, he affirms both the transcendent, sovereign reality of God and the relative, historical character of the Christian standpoint regarding God. Hans Frei noted how this creates a tension between Christian claims about the living God's reality as discovered from this standpoint and the critical idealist's recognition that the lived narrative or internal history of the Christian community is inevitably a matter of religious construction.[43]

Second, Niebuhr's radical monotheism exhibits a faith and confidence toward the "One beyond the Many" or the "principle of being," and this faith may be expressed throughout human cultures and not just in the church. But Niebuhr's thought is also strongly committed to Jesus Christ as the norm of the church, and in any case "revelation means less the disclosure of the essence of objective being to minds than the demonstration to selves of faithful, truthful being."[44] Thus Niebuhr seems to bring together metaphysical and "storied" Christian claims without reducing either to the other.[45]

Third, theology for Niebuhr is confessional through and through. Yet it should seek the truth with a "universal intent" that is loyal "to a more universal, more ecumenical truth than the immediate point of view" of particular confessional communities. We find Niebuhr moving between these poles when he works out a Christian moral philosophy of the responsible self, when he devises a confessionally informed structure of faith that supports the very process of human knowing, and when he commends theologians for employing critical historical methods in their inquiries.[46]

Fourth, ideas about responsibility and conversion, coupled with the belief in God's sovereignty, seem to generate a pressure toward moral focus on specific human actions as embodying the present possibility of human renewal, cultural transformation, and loyalty to the divine cause.[47] Different responses to what God is doing in the world are in fact more or less fitting, and more or less faithful. Yet as Niebuhr's war writings suggest, these same notions also direct the moral agent behind and ahead of the specific action, to an assessment of the preceding and anticipated succeeding acts by the agent and others. The acts come together to form a wider context for reflection on the moral life. Thus Niebuhr was able to say that the specific content of action matters less than the total "context in which each specific action is to be carried out."[48]

Fifth, his preference for a model of "Christ transforming culture" and his aversion to exclusive Christian policies of accommodation or isolation did not keep Niebuhr from recommending, and exhibiting during his career, a historically sensitive rhythm of the church's identification with and withdrawal from the world.

In sum, in Niebuhr we have a theologian who would be neither a pre-Kantian theological realist nor a post-Kantian critical idealist; neither a natural theologian (or metaphysician) nor a fideist; neither a Christian apologist nor a Christian henotheist; neither a moral situationist nor a moral rigorist or legalist; neither a cultural Protestant nor a sectarian.

These negations, however, really do not reach to the essence. Stephen Crocco has written that Niebuhr's description of Ernst Troeltsch "as one in whom antithetical interests were combined in the unity of his personality without being fused" strikingly applies to Niebuhr himself.[49] Niebuhr would have preferred "polar" to "antithetical" here, but the point still stands. Niebuhr's thought moves between these poles, resisting a static one-sidedness but moving forward, probing in love and loyalty to God what it means to find "faithfulness at the heart of things."[50] Even his well-known critique of defensiveness was double-edged, ruling out both a self-justifying apologetics and a self-justifying confessionalism that tends too much "to magnify our distinctiveness from others, and to undervalue our similarities and agreements."[51] The example of this view of theological movement well serves the current project, which places controverted positions in a critical context established by the polarities canvassed above, among others.

For example, how does Tanner's emphasis on the transcendent and sovereign reality of God make way for a necessary concentration on the incarnate reality of Jesus Christ? Does Gustafson's radical monotheism strip away too much of the storied character of Christian faith and tradition? Does Hauerwas's narrative ethic maintain a viable conception of God and God's activity vis-à-vis the whole of being or creation?

The questions multiply. What are the responsibilities of Christian theology to engage other scientific inquiries as these may embody universal intent or reflect natural law? How may we both critically redescribe Christian moral language and critically engage the natural and social sciences? How are Christian guides for character and action, specified in terms of various rules, roles, relations, or virtues, to be contextualized socially and theologically? Under what conditions can Christian ethics become public ethics, and when not?

These questions repeat and sharpen those asked at the end of chapter 1. They represent a little of what Ramsey, Hauerwas, Gustafson, and Tanner might say to one another against the background of a point of view to which all four are indebted, and which may focus and direct our more detailed analysis. More than that, the questions reflect the kind of theological conversation that is itself an implication of the devotion to God's cause that Niebuhr espoused. Truth does not belong exclusively to any individual or group. It must be sought by way of the "whole dynamic and complementary work of the company of knowers and believers."[52] And if there be a finding, this is not merely for the purpose of human comfort or security, but to inspire further through ceaseless dialogue a permanent, continuous revolution, faithful to the Lord of all active in our midst.

Notes

1. Liston Pope, "H. Richard Niebuhr: A Personal Appreciation," in Paul Ramsey, ed., *Faith and Ethics: The Theology of H. Richard Niebuhr* (New York: Harper & Brothers, 1957), 8. On Reinhold Niebuhr's impact, see editor Larry Rasmussen's introduction to the collection of Niebuhr's writings, titled *Reinhold Niebuhr: Theologian of Public Life* (Minneapolis: Fortress Press, 1991), 1–4. Niebuhr's comparative description is found in his "Reformation: Continuing Imperative," *Christian Century* 77 (March 1960): 249. Jon Diefenthaler persuasively shows how Niebuhr's characteristic concerns emerged well before the 1930s and his arrival at Yale. See his *H. Richard Niebuhr: A Lifetime of Reflections of the Church and the World* (Macon, Ga.: Mercer University Press, 1986).

2. H. Richard Niebuhr, *Theology, History, and Culture*, ed. William Stacy Johnson (New Haven, Conn.: Yale University Press, 1996), 18.

3. H. Richard Niebuhr, "Reformation: Continuing Imperative," *Christian Century* 77 (March 1960): 248.

4. Niebuhr, *Theology, History, and Culture*, 117–20.

5. H. Richard Niebuhr, "The Social Gospel and the Mind of Jesus," *Journal of Religious Ethics* 16 (spring 1988): 122.

6. Niebuhr, *Theology, History, and Culture*, 121. Here Niebuhr is interpreting and endorsing the position of Karl Barth, whom Niebuhr described as "the legitimate heir of the social gospel. . . . He has saved it from perishing with utopianism and offers a more consistent alternative to that redefinition of the social gospel which splits its intra-worldly ends from its supernatural faith and continues to think in terms of human action directed toward temporal, though not unsatisfactory, goals." Ibid., 122.

7. H. Richard Niebuhr, *The Kingdom of God in America* (New York: Harper & Brothers, 1937), 51.

8. H. Richard Niebuhr, *Faith on Earth* (New Haven, Conn.: Yale University Press, 1989), 97.

9. Niebuhr, *Kingdom of God in America*, 88.

10. Niebuhr, "Reformation: Continuing Imperative," 249.

11. H. Richard Niebuhr, *The Meaning of Revelation* (New York: Macmillan, 1941), 14.

12. H. Richard Niebuhr, *Christ and Culture* (New York: Harper & Brothers, 1951), 239–40.

13. Ibid., xii.

14. Hans W. Frei, *Theology and Narrative*, ed. George Hunsinger and William C. Placher (New York: Oxford University Press, 1994), 219.

15. H. Richard Niebuhr, *The Purpose of the Church and Its Ministry* (New York: Harper & Brothers, 1956), 112.

16. Niebuhr, *Meaning of Revelation*, 28–29.

17. Ibid., 29.

18. Niebuhr, "Social Gospel and the Mind of Jesus," 121.

19. Frei, *Theology and Narrative*, 218, 229.

20. Niebuhr, *Meaning of Revelation*, 13. Cf. Niebuhr's intentions in "The Doctrine of the Trinity and the Unity of the Church," *Theology Today* 3 (1946): 371–84.

21. Niebuhr, *Christ and Culture*, 11–29, 190–96, and passim.

22. Niebuhr, *Meaning of Revelation*, 15.

23. H. Richard Niebuhr, *Radical Monotheism and Western Culture* (New York: Harper & Row, 1960), 14–15.

24. Ibid., 24.

25. Ibid., 37.

26. Ibid., 60

27. Ibid., 126.

28. Ibid., 61–62.

29. Ibid., 88.

30. Niebuhr, *Christ and Culture*, 192–95.

31. H. Richard Niebuhr, "War as the Judgment of God," *Christian Century* 59 (1942): 631.

32. H. Richard Niebuhr, "Utilitarian Christianity," *Christianity and Crisis* 6 (1946): 5.

33. H. Richard Niebuhr, *The Responsible Self* (New York: Harper & Row, 1963), 47–65.

34. Ibid., 73, 78.

35. Ibid., 67.

36. Ibid., 141–42.

37. Niebuhr, "Reformation: Continuing Imperative," 249.

38. Ibid., 250.

39. Diefenthaler, *H. Richard Niebuhr*, 19.

40. Niebuhr, *Purpose of the Church and Its Ministry*, 26.

41. H. Richard Niebuhr, "The Responsibility of the Church for Society," in K. S. Latourette, ed., *The Gospel, the Church, and the World* (New York: Harper & Brothers, 1946), 126–33.

42. Niebuhr, *Purpose of the Church and Its Ministry*, 19.

43. Frei, *Theology and Narrative*, 223ff.

44. Niebuhr, *Radical Monotheism and Western Culture*, 46.

45. Cf. Frei, *Theology and Narrative*, 219.

46. See Niebuhr, *Faith on Earth*, pp. 43–62; and ibid., "The Seminary in an Ecumenical Age," *Theology Today* 17 (July 1960): 300–310.

47. See Frei on Niebuhr's "short range historical action" and its implications for a "carefully circumscribed progressive politics" in *Theology and Narrative*, 230–33.

48. H. Richard Niebuhr, "The Christian Church and the World's Crisis," *Christianity and Society* 6 (1941): 11.

49. Stephen Crocco, "The Place of Christ and Culture in the Niebuhr Corpus" (unpublished manuscript, Princeton Theological Seminary, Princeton, N.J., 1993).

50. Niebuhr, *Purpose of the Church and Its Ministry*, 37.

51. Niebuhr, *Responsible Self*, 150.

52. Niebuhr, *Theology, History, and Culture*, 62.

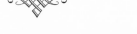

CHAPTER THREE

Love, Justice, and the Whole Idea of God

Even more than H. Richard Niebuhr, with whom he studied in the late 1930s and early 1940s, Paul Ramsey spent most of his career in one place. For forty-four years, he worked in Princeton, New Jersey, first in the Department of Religion at Princeton University, and then, following his retirement, at the Center of Theological Inquiry until his death in 1988. His younger colleague James Gustafson accurately described him as a "a towering and forceful figure" who "had a deep impact on a younger generation of authors." He was "a persistent critic of moral fads, a steadfast proponent of the Christian ethics of love, and a vigorous participant in debates about public policy and ethics."[1]

Underline "vigorous participant." Ramsey was a prolific author and avid conversationalist. Whether engaging in debate at conferences or holding court in the Religion Department's faculty-student lounge at Princeton, he possessed an almost overwhelming intellectual energy. In exchange he was, at his best, challenging but never dismissive, assured but never closed to correction. His abiding focus was to advance an activity that he described in modest terms. "As a theologian attends to the discourse in which we exhibit and help one another in our beliefs, so the ethicist attends to the moral discourse in which we manifest and help one another in fashioning Christian moral attitudes and practice. It has ever been my belief that we should watch our language if we mean to watch our morals and mean to attain and maintain a proper rectitude of behavior and any exactitude in the assessments we make. The vocation of the Christian ethicist is the care and feeding of Christian moral discourse."[2]

This passage gives us helpful clues to Ramsey's work and style. There is the focus on Christian moral discourse itself, which he tirelessly studied, displayed, worked, and reworked, and usually fought about with colleagues in controversies involving political, medical, and sexual ethics. There is also the conviction about the practical importance of this focus. Mistakes in language make for mistakes in thought, which in turn may establish bad precedents and wicked policies. When Ramsey wrote that "war first became total in the minds of men,"[3] he was pointing out (as we shall see) how "theoretical" matters about moral talk possess chilling implications for human life. Tied to these points is the positive promise of the study: the good fashioning of the attitudes and practices of Christian life, maintaining rectitude in conduct, and "exactitude"—so crucial for Ramsey—in moral argument.

In light of this understanding of Christian ethics, Ramsey set out, as I shall argue in this chapter, to develop and sharpen a proposal set before him:

> Niebuhr's lectures on ethics, in which the Christian life is viewed as simultaneously responding to "creation," "judgment" or "governance," and "redemption," have always suggested to his students the indivisibility of these approaches, since God is he with whom we are always already engaged, and he is all these eventful acts toward us, wherever we are culturally and historically in our being in the world. In this there is promise of a dynamic ethic of redemption which does not simply build upon yet does not jettison the ethics of creation.[4]

Accordingly, for Ramsey, creative and critical engagement with Christian moral discourse needs to include an exposition of the meanings of creation, judgment, and redemption for the moral life in a way permitting of a "dynamic ethics of redemption." "Love transforming natural justice" is the result, and Ramsey's career in writing on specific moral topics was an effort to mediate dynamism, transformation, or conversion via the abiding standard of covenant fidelity to the neighbor beloved of God. The mediation and the standard help make for an ethic of faithfulness, I argue, that would honor the unity and wholeness of God's activity as Creator, Preserver, and Redeemer, that theologically construes appeals to natural law as both informing and tested by Christian love, and that provides a telling alternative to various forms of utilitarianism.

A Free and Binding Love

Ramsey used the Christian Scriptures in a limited[5] and yet decisive way in the formulation of his ethics. As was mentioned in chapter 1, he drew the measure of the love to be shown the neighbor from the character of God's love for human creatures. Biblically depicted, God's love is universal, not conditioned by merit but ordered to need, and redemptive, "with special bias in favor of the helpless who can contribute nothing at all [to this or that community] and are in fact 'due' nothing."[6] The norm of human righteousness is drawn from a reading of central biblical descriptions of God's righteousness, and the appropriation of these descriptions is central to the Christian's "internal history";[7] as such the norm

> does not make man the measure. . . . If you want to know how to treat the stranger or the sojourner or alien in the land, according to the Old Testament, you would proceed to reason as follows: You know the heart of a stranger, since you too were strangers and sojourners in the land of Egypt; and the Lord your God acted rightly when He brought you up out of the predicament and so right-wised the dealings you may ever have with the littlest and unlikeliest people on this earth (Ex 22:26, 23:9). . . . The model is the same for the New Testament. . . . Jesus' words "Love one another *as I have loved you!*" are the commandment, the model, the organizing principle of all New Testament ethics. So if you want to know what to do or how to treat someone in need of help—the ungodly sinner, or an enemy of yours—the way to begin is to ask, How did God treat me when He sent his only Son to the rescue (Rom 5:6–8, 10)?[8]

Hence Jesus Christ realizes the divine righteousness, and Christians order themselves to it through an analogous pattern of regard for human creatures for their own sake.

Bound in origin, content, and authority to the righteousness of God in Jesus Christ, agape binds itself to the neighbor. In this way it is free, by God's grace, from distrusting self-partiality, and hence free from legalism and the codes of social convention. Accordingly, love is made free for the neighbor in his or her need. "While love itself never submits to external rule and does not proportion its benefaction according to some rule, it never becomes unruly, since the needs of other persons are the rule of love and quickly teach such love what to do."[9]

Given love's focus upon the neighbor, no claims of self may impede active attention to his or her need, and no conditions are set as qualifications for moral regard. Attention to the neighbor's particularity requires that he or she not be but a predicate of the self's partial desires for itself; as Ramsey argues in *Basic Christian Ethics*, his first book, the Christian is to discover the neighbor beneath friendliness or hostility, apart from enlightened self-interest, and beyond the mixed motives associated with some "common good" that the self and the other may reciprocally share.[10] Even the appeal to certain general and universally applicable standards of worth, such as "the infinite, inherent value of human personality," is rejected. Because the self would meet the requirements of the standard, "such a doctrine would logically lead to subtracting from obligation as much as the just claims of self require." Another type of condition of love, that one's own claims be included in moral deliberation, would enter thereby.

Basic Christian Ethics carries forward the notion of agape as free and binding by way of a doctrine of vocation. Love binds itself to the neighbor and is as such free from any legalism impeding the service of need; yet freedom for service in the world, where there is always more than one neighbor, implies being bound in responsibility to one's moral station within it. Responsibility within the lasting or permanent relationships that one has established or in which one is otherwise implicated, such as with families, friendship, and work, will call for preferences among the many neighbors who cross one's path. Preference for the victim over the perpetrator of injustice may also be justified in terms of worldly calling. Self-regarding actions, as they may be necessary to serve others, may be warranted vocationally; for the neighbor's sake, one needs to cultivate one's talents, care for one's health, and so forth.

Ramsey goes so far as to suggest that one's duty to others may require defending oneself coercively against attack, standing up for one's rights, and seeking to cultivate personal virtues that dispose one to the love of neighbor. He concedes that this conception of "enlightened unselfishness" is liable to selfish abuse, but he maintains it nonetheless insofar as it is rightly subordinated to the full meaning of self-giving love.[11]

Although Ramsey does not dwell on the theological bases for this account, it appears that for him Christian vocation, and the possibilities for preference that it implies, appropriately reflects the Christian's status as a creature whose contingency and limitation cannot but qualify the concrete expression of love within a particular life.[12] In addition, his defense of resistance against the unjust presupposes that in a fallen world social arrangements are morally required for the protection of persons against unjust assault.

We can see, then, that already in his first book Ramsey was trying to coordinate the divine activities of creation, judgment and governance, and redemption for the purposes of Christian ethics. He continued to ponder this issue until, by the early to middle 1960s, he arrived at a stance that characterized much of his thought thereafter. He called that view "love transforming natural justice." Also, by that time he hit upon what he found to be a more complete understanding of agape as a free and binding love.

Love Transforming Natural Justice

The weakest discussions in *Basic Christian Ethics* treat the relationship between Christian love and natural morality or natural law. Ramsey wanted to establish how the norm of agape must finally be dominant over and free from the yield of natural law, human reason, and moral conscience. No "coalition ethics" that jeopardizes this sovereignty is acceptable; nevertheless, he also affirmed that Christian love is assisted by the rational quest to discover the genuine needs of human beings, and that love inevitably makes alliance (if never concordat) with available natural norms "which happen to be convincing" in the search for general social policies. The alliances permit and require constant criticism and redirection of these norms in the interests of neighbors.[13]

But here we have to ask: What makes the case for certain alliances over others? What establishes the theological grounds for proceeding with certain accounts of human well-being over others, to which Christian love will be seriously yet sovereignly committed? We are not told. No criterion for discrimination, in terms, say, of the basic needs of human creatures, is forthcoming. Without some third term establishing their relation, Christian love and natural morality appear to remain entirely separate sources of morality, and any particular alliance between them appears to be either merely circumstantial (this is the natural moral ethos we find at this place and time) or arbitrary. Ramsey's constant stress in *Basic Christian Ethics* concerns the refusal of any necessary and permanent partnership between agape and natural moral wisdom, rather than on agape's presumptive affirmation of a sort of creaturely need to which it properly and redemptively answers. Just this sort of affirmation is needed, however, if any particular alliance between agape and natural morality is to be made theologically intelligible.

Conversion and Covenant

How, then, was Ramsey to describe the relationship between the morality of reason, conscience, or natural law on the one hand and agape on the other, such that the latter is sovereign yet fit for a theologically proper alliance with the former? He came to an answer through two logically distinct discoveries. In the first place, he conceived more exactly the problem of the relationship along the lines of Niebuhr's book *Christ and Culture*, which was published one year after the appearance of *Basic Christian Ethics*.

Second, he appropriated for his own purposes Karl Barth's view that creation is the external basis of covenant, and covenant the internal basis of creation. The two developments eventually were matched with a deeper focus on faithfulness as "the single univocal biblical concept in terms of which the meaning of 'love' in Jesus' twofold commandment has to be understood,"[14] and on moral rules as a legitimate and necessary feature of the ethics of agape.

In *Nine Modern Moralists*, a collection of essays mostly composed in the 1950s, Ramsey credited his "greater clarity" concerning love and natural morality to Niebuhr's observation that he had adopted a stance of "Christ transforming natural law" in *Basic Christian Ethics*. So it is not surprising that Ramsey argues for the centrality of this conversionist theme for Christian social ethics by contrasting it with other approaches derived from Niebuhr's *Christ and Culture*. This book presented a typology of five responses to the "double wrestle of the Church with its Lord and with the cultural society with which it lives in symbiosis."[15] These "typical partial answers," are embodied in Christian history but are not strictly historical, because they "recur so often in different eras and societies that they seem to be less the product of historical conditioning than of the nature of the problem itself and the meaning of its terms."[16]

In turn, these partial answers stress (1) a "sectarian" opposition of Christ to human culture; (2) an "assimilationist" agreement between the two, in which Jesus is seen to be the great hero of cultural achievement; (3) a "synthetic" ordering of Christ above culture, where the two are harmoniously and hierarchically related; (4) a "dualism" of affirmation and opposition, in which duties to Christ and the civil community are conceded but also distinguished to the point of rupture; and (5) a "conversionist" solution discussed in the last chapter. Niebuhr preferred this last approach while insisting that his preference was in no way a prescription for the universally applicable Christian answer.

Falling in line, Ramsey seeks in *Nine Modern Moralists* to guard his position from the *synthesist* tendency to set up a more or less independent account of natural law upon which agape builds, and the *dualist* tendency to locate the work of redemption more in subjective disposition than in actions and structures in the world.[17] The first stance risks loss of the dynamic work of redemption by insulating this or that historical moral system from critique and conversion. The second loses critical force by its tendency just to locate the redemptive work intrapersonally. He also offers interpretations of the "Egypt" and "Exodus" of natural law, which seem to rely on the logic of Niebuhr's presentation of assimilationist, or "cultural Christian," and sectarian approaches:

> The chief problem for Christian social ethics is how we are to understand the relation between the law of nature and the righteousness of the covenant. There are two ways, and only two ways of avoiding this problem. Ethics may, on the one hand, remain wholly within the "Egypt" of the natural law, deriving the standard for man solely from man and from the structures immanent in human society. This is the

path taken by every humanistic ethic. Christian ethical theory may, on the other hand, pass wholly into "Exodus," taking note only of the demands upon men who live in the immediate presence of God and ignoring the fact that they still live within the ordered forms of *some* natural community which is based, in part at least, upon agreement as to inherent principles based on creation. This is the path sometimes taken by the ethics of Protestantism with its radical doctrines of sin and grace.[18]

In Ramsey's hands, conversionist social ethics and the law of love must be free alternatively to confirm some norms of justice, to extend and reinvigorate others in their own right, and to transform and refashion others beyond these.[19] He also interprets natural law or natural injustice inductively, appealing primarily to a "sense of injustice" that reveals negatively and circumstantially conditions of human well-being.

> In . . . spontaneous reaction to whatever is inhumane, the human essence first discloses itself to our minds. Essential human nature manifests itself through innate tendencies toward its ends, and that is known to us in the context of whatever proves basically congenial to that nature.[20]

The yield of discernment is tested and refined through "ceaseless dialogue" rather than authoritative pronouncement.

Thus Ramsey sought to do Christian ethics attentive to "the whole idea of God,"[21] an ethics that indivisibly responds to God's action in creating, preserving, and redeeming humanity. For example, when he discusses orders of politics and economics that protect us from one another by the restraint of sin, he says that "there is a teleologically dynamic connection—running backward, so to speak, between redemption, preservation, and creation," and that in virtue of this connection in God's activity redemptive love may "manifest a dynamic, redirecting, and transforming influence upon the apparently given necessities of the orders of society and upon any of the standards of natural justice which may commend themselves to the minds of men."[22]

By presenting a cogent theological rubric and defending a dynamic process of moral discernment, Ramsey deepened the viewpoint of *Basic Christian Ethics* concerning love and native moral insight. The basic difficulties noted in the first book, however, remain in *Nine Modern Moralists*. Little material attention is given to a view of creaturely well-being; ceaseless dialogue risks ceaselessly proceeding, in need of a theological signpost. Without some guide demarcating the terms of relation between love and natural ethics, we are left with at least the appearance of separate moral schemes; moreover, commendation of Richard Niebuhr's stress on the Incarnation of the Word who has entered into "a human culture that has never been without his ordering action" is not paired with a proposal concerning what that ordering action amounts to as a reflection of the Word. Ramsey is left with having to think "in one direction only"; only love is available to animate a natural morality that still looks like a neutral datum standing apart.[23]

A study of Sartre on sexuality and a brief invocation of Barth are indirect indications in *Nine Modern Moralists*[24] of the interest in covenant central to *Christian Ethics and the Sit-In*. The following statement from *Sit-In* is crucial:

> Karl Barth has written that, in the Christian view, creation is the external basis of covenant, creation is the promise and makes possible the history of God's covenant dealings with mankind; while His covenant is the internal basis, the meaning or purpose of creation. An illustration of this can immediately be given: human sexuality, in its created nature, is to be understood properly as no individual matter, and certainly not as a mere biological fact, but as the external basis, the promise and possibility of the marriage covenant and the capability of nature for fellow humanity between man and woman, and as such this is an effective token and *image*, in fact *the* image, of God's covenant and fellow humanity with man; viewed in the other direction, the ordinance, law, or covenant of marriage is the internal basis and meaning or purpose of created human sexuality.[25]

Four points following from this statement are elaborated by Ramsey later in the book. First, to say that creation is the external basis of covenant is to distinguish a formal condition of relationship from its realization; but the example of sexuality shows both that these conditions ought to be honored, and that, in the realm of creation, human life flourishes in covenant. We have here a positive claim about creaturely well-being in its own sphere. "In covenant was every man made from his birth, and without fellow humanity was not anything made that was made—no man, no rights of his, no justice, no proper law."[26]

Second, the appeal to "external basis" obviously includes, but is not limited to, natural conditions such as sexual differentiation and a person's integral embodiment. Ramsey holds that "natural justice, human and legal rights, and social institutions generally, so far as these have a positive purpose under the creative, governing, and preserving purposes of God—all are the external basis making possible the actualization of the promise of covenant; while covenant or fellow humanity is the internal basis and meaning of every right, true justice, or law."[27]

Third, a normative notion of creaturely covenant in marriage and other human relationships is validated as a fitting witness to God's covenantal dealings with humanity in Jesus Christ. God in Christ's being for others is the basis of the possibility that human beings may be with and for one another across the range of their relationships. The ordering activity of the Word, active in all creation, makes way for a covenant of reconciliation that promises, among other goods, that human beings may be restored to their proper reality as creatures in and for covenant. Ramsey's celebration of Niebuhr's conversionist theology of the Incarnation is thus completed with a concrete employment of the position.

Fourth, the fellow humanity of creatures is constituted by a relationship in differentiation that is paradigmatically realized in God's covenant with fallen human persons:

> God does not unite or blend his nature with man's; He covenants with him, holding him in a life-in-community in which God remains irreducibly other than man and man a creature not himself in any way divine. I can say Thou to God only if I am maintained in difference from him as an independent creature; yet I could never say Thou to God unless this expressed the fact that in my being, however independent, I am always with and for Him, based on no will or deed of my own but on the fact that He is *my* God, i.e., because, as Christians affirm, from all eternity He is Christ for us and has bound himself not ever to be God without us.[28]

As a reflection of this pattern, life in fellow humanity recoils from both the tyranny by which selves are reduced to mere instruments, and the servility of self-denying absorption into others. It is also at odds with the idea that human beings are by nature hostile or neutral toward the other. These errors all attest to an isolation that corresponds to the overcoming of differentiation or proper relation. The covenant of fellow humanity "is not a relationship with disappearing terms. It is not pure internal relation with no irreducibly different beings to be related to each other. There is distance in the relation, and relatedness in the distance."

The relatedness, moreover, is proper to creaturely differentiation, in which essentially dependent beings meet. The self cannot be for the other as God is, nor may the other expect one to be God for it. We can say only that human creatures as such may be with one another in relations of justice; to that extent there is room for their being for one another in response to the mutual need for help and rescue; this "being for" may issue from charity in its permeation of justice. "Charity (for fellow man) is the internal basis and meaning of natural justice (with fellow man), as justice in turn is the promise and possibility of closer meeting and steadfast covenant."[29] A love-transformed justice is still justice, though always bearing promise of closer meeting.

Ramsey makes use of this normative understanding of fellow humanity in a discussion of the right to property. Generally, *man has rights because fellow humanity is precarious in him.*" The precariousness has two sources. Because it is finite, the human creature depends upon certain social conditions that enable the realization of fellow humanity; moreover, these conditions must include forms of mutual protection, given that fellow humans are also fellow sinners. Specifically, property "is a man's capability for life for and with his fellow man, that is, it is the external basis of covenant." Persons need property because it is a condition and expression of the differentiation of otherness. "I need some things to call my own in order to be with or for fellow man. Otherwise, I would be without a place on which to stand with him. . . . I would sink into relations with the state or institutions above me which would absorb us both. There would be no distancing by which I would bring more and more of a self to the bond of covenant between us."

Yet there must be relatedness in the distance; "property is mine expressly for the sake of the life of man with man. In owning I belong generically to the race of mortal and needy men. The definition of such property right should itself contain an indissoluble and *unavoidable* connection between my ownership and the good of all men who in time come to that spot with needs I have so used my property to be able to provide for."[30] The traditional "inn keeper's law," by which owners of establishments that serve travelers with bed and food are bound not to "discriminate among those who apply for these services he is in business to sell," correctly expresses the link between property right and fellow humanity. All other rights share this dimension of setting the conditions or the external basis for bonds between those who bear the human countenance.

Ramsey's use of Barth improves the account of "love transforming natural justice." It provides a theological vision of human well-being in the realm of creation that is at the same time applicable to contemporary secular moral insight regarding the value of human goods and rights. It sets a general criterion to authorize, interpret, reconfigure, and criticize varying and competing accounts of human flourishing derived from natural reason. It establishes a connection, a comparative term, between the ethics of creation and an ethics of love that is to be distinguished, not separated, from it.

Finally, the ethics of creation is given its own concrete status in light of the work of God; it may set terms to which the order of Christian love, reaching down to it, must respond. Love does good work for the good of the neighbor when it sustains the external conditions of covenant, affirming justice and fundamental rights; but love may go on "elevating, transforming, definitely shaping, and fashioning what justice may mean, if possible, more in the direction of the requirements of charity."

New possibilities for fellow humanity are always considered beyond a minimal ascription of rights, and toward the realization of the fullness of human need in fellow humanity that agape discerns. All of this is accounted for along with love's critical freedom; "the order of justice reaches up to the order of charity, submitting to its final review every judgment and proposed action based only on what 'nature itself teaches' or what society and its present laws require."[31]

Canons of Loyalty

In chapter 1, I said that Ramsey's ethics gave a prominent place for moral rules generally, and exceptionless moral rules in particular. We can trace the rudiments of his position to two developments in his thought, and to the subsequent attempt to interrelate them. First, a 1957 essay on Niebuhr questioned his teacher's tendency to describe as "relativism" a view that could less misleadingly be named "relational" or "perspectival" "objectivism." Ramsey argues that Niebuhr's best insights affirm that there are "relationally objective norms," and that, in any case, his theological commitments do not require a commitment to moral relativism. Niebuhr holds out for the idea that, though there is no one universal view of morality, there are objective, situated "views of the universal."

One cannot rule out that the conversionist's apprehension of "certain universally valid principles" may be part and parcel of an ordered response to the creative and ordering work of God. To clinch the point, Ramsey refers to the moral crimes of rape and the coercion of women for the purpose of producing more genetically or racially "pure" children. These surely are always and everywhere wrong, "relative to the structure of man's or to his mode of being in the world."[32]

Second, *Nine Modern Moralists* appeals to faithfulness as capturing the essence of the love commandments:

> Hence we may summarize biblical religion as faith in the *faithfulness* of God; and we may summarize biblical ethics as the molding of human action into the action of God's righteousness. Thus, the love commandments really mean, you shall be faithful to the Lord your God with all your soul, mind, and strength, and you shall be faithful to your neighbor's well-being as to your own—or, rather, as God has proved himself faithful to you in these events of deliverance upon which your faith rests.[33]

Ramsey connected these two features, faithfulness and permanently valid moral norms, through an account of the "covenants of life with life" that owes much to his analysis of creation and covenant. His discussion of "canons of loyalty" bears this out.

I have stressed again and again how Ramsey's ethics normatively refer the life of love to the biblical pattern of God's righteousness. With his embrace of the unifying category of faithfulness, he was able to speak of witnessing to the divine faithfulness by displaying fidelity in the "elected and nonelected covenants of life with life." These human covenants include the many roles and relations in which fellow humanity may be expressed. In Ramsey's work they extend from familial relations of husband and wife, or parents and children, to moral bonds between medical professionals and patients or experimental subjects, to fellow citizens of national and international orders.

The basic idea of these covenants involves the exploration of the specific purpose or meaning of such bonds in a world created, preserved, and redeemed by God, and of the possibilities for the communication of faithfulness or covenant fidelity within them. "In the Christian life we are driven deeper and deeper into the meaning of the faithfulness to other men required by the particular covenants or causes between us. The relevant moral features which this understanding of the moral law uncovers in every action, moral relation or situation are primarily the claims and occasions of faithfulness."[34]

The discernment and prescription of how fidelity to the neighbor may be embodied in human relations and institutions includes seeing to the external conditions of creaturely covenant, the conditions of distance and relatedness, "otherness" and "common good." Agape is faithful to human creatures in honoring the terms by which they may be faithful to one another. It may also seek to transform thought and action within moral bonds so as to realize more nearly that fellowship which is creation's inner meaning.

An ethics of covenant fidelity needs to include rules expressive of and enabling covenant fidelity. There are "rules of practice" that are justified by the good social consequences of adherence to them. The general requirement that experimental subjects give a reasonably free and adequately informed consent may help to establish conditions of trust and mutual understanding, and cut against the temptation to exploit individuals for the sake of great social benefit. One may even conclude that this rule be closed to future exceptions on similar grounds, given the presence of considerable social pressures to advance medicine or a researcher's career at the expense of exploiting subjects. It may be too easy under such pressures to rationalize activities that waive consent—better, then, to institutionalize its exceptionlessness.

But Ramsey offered a deeper theological reason for rules such as the consent requirement that relativized the appeal to "rule utilitarian" warrants. It was that they properly dictate the embodied performance of fidelity to those who would claim it as creatures of God. Informed consent, the prohibition of cruel and unusual punishment, and the immunity of noncombatants from direct attack in wartime are examples of canons of loyalty whose consequentialist justification is subordinated to the quest for what constitutes fidelity to the neighbor.

From this standpoint, Ramsey thought, departures from these rules in the name of some "greater social benefit" represent the abandonment of human creatures at risk who claim our faithfulness. With this move, Ramsey was able to use the effects of policies and practices on social values to help "build a floor under the individual fellow man by minimum faithfulness rules or canons of loyalty to him that are unexceptionable."[35] The neighbor's good—not the social good over all or the good of practices in general—remains paramount.

Summary and Conclusion

Ramsey practiced his vocation, "the care and feeding of moral discourse," with special attention to the "whole idea of God." For him the Christian moral life could not be understood apart from the divine activities of creation, preservation, and redemption. Christian moral discourse must reflect them in its accounts of the ends of human creatures, the facts of human fallenness, the need for social arrangements that preserve us in the midst of moral evil, the moral implications of divine redemption, and the way these all interrelate.

Ramsey's appropriation of Barth on creation and covenant enabled him to set a concrete direction in his theological anthropology and to reflect on human fallenness as endangering persons by endangering, in one way or another, the conditions of creaturely covenant in the roles, relations, and institutions of social life. The work of redemption is conceived to be the transforming work of Christian love, which honors creation while remaining dynamically sovereign.

Ramsey's defense of canons of loyalty displays more fully the shape his conversionism takes within the practice of Christian ethics. Love remains free to serve the neighbor, and exceptionless rules governing social life and prescribing the performance of faithfulness may do just that. Only a new legalism of "freedom from rules" could stand in the way of a free and binding love's commendation of binding rules. Creaturely covenants of life with life are to be investigated for both the particular fellow humanity they may express and the divinely authorized faithfulness they may embody. And so Christian ethics may be public to the extent that it addresses the world so that these covenants are preserved and humanized in the light of Christ. The idea is to shape a social ethos or moral culture within which these relations may flourish as witnesses to God's righteousness.

Ramsey thought that the shaping activity should generally be pursued by setting a framework of directions for public deliberation rather than by making specific directives or policy proposals. When performed by churches and their ethicists, the second practice has the danger of wrongfully faulting Christian consciences where legitimate disagreement is possible, and hence of introducing improper divisions within Christian communities. Also, conforming one's Christian voice to a culturally specified menu of "feasible policy alternatives" may sacrifice whatever would be distinctively creative and critical in that voice. Finally, proposing directives may usurp the legitimate responsibilities of moral agents who are placed within their specific vocations to make competent assessments of fact and value on the issue at hand. If there are clear violations of moral principle in public life apart from seriously controverted findings of fact, that is another matter. Ramsey did not hesitate to condemn the "policies" of the American use of the atomic bomb at Hiroshima and Nagasaki, or the Willowbrook experiments on mentally disabled children.

The Christian ethicist may also distance himself or herself from that specific vocation to speak in the public forum from his or her specific competence as a citizen, would-be patient in the health care system, and so forth. But the Christian ethicist as such should be primarily concerned to illustrate pedagogically (for the church and world) the sorts of routes that moral arguments might take, given alternative orderings of value and determinations of factual situations.[36] By showing how moral arguments move from principle to application via the discernment of an order of value in the projected specific case, practical wisdom might be taught short of advocacy of specific policies.

Notes

1. James Gustafson, *Ethics from a Theocentric Perspective*, vol. 2, *Ethics and Theology* (Chicago: University of Chicago Press, 1984), 84.
2. Paul Ramsey, "Does the Church Have Any Political Wisdom for the 1970s?" (unpublished manuscript, Princeton University, Princeton, N.J., 1972), 3–4. This long text apparently includes Ramsey's 1972 lectures at the Perkins School of Theology. Cf. the published excerpt in *Perkins Journal* 26, no. 1 (fall 1972): 29–40.
3. Paul Ramsey, *The Essential Paul Ramsey* (New Haven, Conn.: Yale University Press, 1994), 81.
4. Paul Ramsey, *Nine Modern Moralists* (Englewood Cliffs, N.J.: Prentice-Hall, 1962), 218–19.
5. Note his concession, made after the publication of Hans Frei's *The Eclipse of Biblical Narrative* (New Haven, Conn.: Yale University Press, 1974), that his work shared in the mistakes of "biblical theology" in the tendency to find the unity of the biblical canon in the development of moral and religious ideas contained in it. Paul Ramsey, "A Question (or Two) for Stanley Hauerwas" (unpublished manuscript, Princeton University, Princeton, N.J., 1982), 1–2. In this essay, Ramsey also appears to be sympathetic to Hans Frei's case for a "recovery of Biblical narrative."
6. Paul Ramsey, *Basic Christian Ethics* (New York: Scribner's, 1950), 14.
7. Cf. H. Richard Niebuhr, *The Meaning of Revelation* (New York: Macmillan, 1941), 44ff.
8. Ramsey, *Essential Paul Ramsey*, 16–18; italics in original.
9. Ramsey, *Basic Christian Ethics*, 78–79.
10. Ramsey, *Basic Christian Ethics*, 94–95, 102. Here and throughout this chapter, I use and try to advance on my discussion of Ramsey in "Christian Love and Covenant Faithfulness," *Journal of Religious Ethics* 19, no. 2 (fall 1991): 103–32.
11. Ramsey, *Basic Christian Ethics*, 157–66.
12. Cf. Ramsey, *Basic Christian Ethics*, 157–58.
13. Ibid., 344.
14. Ramsey, *Nine Modern Moralists*, 290n.
15. H. Richard Niebuhr, *Christ and Culture* (New York: Harper & Brothers, 1951), xi.

16. Ibid., 40.
17. Ramsey, *Nine Modern Moralists*, 219–20, 236.
18. Ibid., 224–25.
19. Ibid., 235–36, 254–58.
20. Ibid., 276.
21. Ibid., 258. Ramsey takes the phrase from Emil Brunner.
22. Ibid., 254.
23. Paul Ramsey, "A Letter to James Gustafson," *Journal of Religious Ethics* 13, no. 1 (spring 1985): 74.
24. Ramsey, *Nine Modern Moralists*, 94–140, esp. 135–37; cf. 302.
25. Paul Ramsey, *Christian Ethics and the Sit-In* (New York: Association Press, 1961), 22; italics in original.
26. Ibid., 30.
27. Ibid., 26.
28. Ibid., 36.
29. Ibid., 27.
30. Ibid., 32, 38–39; italics in original.
31. Ibid., 125.
32. Ibid., 222, 215.
33. Ibid., 290; italics in original.
34. Ibid., 125.
35. Ibid., 133.
36. "More than *principles* of moral and political decision-making seem to be needed in church education, and also in succinctly addressing our fellow citizens on public questions. . . . Indeed, one *must* get into specifics in order to *teach* political principles. How to impart skill in moral reasoning—skill in Christian casuistry—without partiality for outcomes [is] the issue" (italics in original); Paul Ramsey, *Speak Up for Just War or Pacifism* (University Park: Pennsylvania State University Press, 1988), 136.

    However coherent Ramsey's view was, it was difficult to realize and communicate in practice. For example, he was usually counted among the supporters of the war in Vietnam, even though he insisted at the time that he was only evaluating the kinds of arguments that "doves" were making against the war; the fact that he found those arguments wanting hardly warranted, he thought, the claim that he was as a Christian ethicist a "hawk." Yet, later in his career, he conceded that his war writings were not clear or careful enough to guard against this reading of him, and that in any event he was too slow in realizing how morally disproportionate the war had become. For a persuasive defense of Ramsey, see Philip Turner, "Social Advocacy as a Moral Issue in Itself," *Journal of Religious Ethics* 19, no. 2 (1991): 257–81.

CHAPTER FOUR

Political and Medical Ethics

In this chapter, I want to mark the theological basis of Paul Ramsey's political and medical ethics in terms of his understanding of fellow humanity. My interpretation both supports Ramsey's conversionism and leads to some critical questions about it.

Politics, War, and Fellow Humanity

The two categories central to Ramsey's ethics of Christian love—"love transforming natural justice" and the relation between creation and covenant—appear most prominently in *Christian Ethics and the Sit-In*. Even though his medical ethics seem to rely on an account of these categories, as I shall claim below, Ramsey tended merely to refer to his earlier theoretical reckonings and proceed without much comment. The virtual absence of talk of creation, covenant, and fellow humanity in Ramsey's political ethics is especially striking.[1]

Perhaps this last fact should not be surprising. Ramsey's greatest contribution in political ethics was to retrieve, reinterpret, and use with precision the theory of just war. Now at least as far as competing enemies are concerned, war is not about fellow humanity conceived as communal solidarity. "Justice" in war evidently would be entirely compatible with the absence of that. Nevertheless, I shall argue that Ramsey's just war ethics intimated and required appeal to fellow humanity. The intimations may be found in the way he argued for the limited meaning of political existence. Fellow humanity in relation to the barely human activity of war is considered not in any robust communal realization but rather in terms of the external condition of otherness, distance, or differentiation.

Ramsey applied this condition to "enemy" noncombatants and combatants alike. My claims about the requirement of fellow humanity, a creaturely norm liable to figure in love's transforming work within a sinful world, are based on the observation that without it, as qualified above, Ramsey's ethics lose their dynamic conversionist character; that, in fact, they drift in the direction of a static synthesis and cultural Christianity. I will argue, moreover, that the Christian norm and discourse of fellow humanity must inspire and be expressed in skills and practices that, in turn, protect both from corruption.

Three Themes

Nonresisting love resisting. Ramsey held (1) that Jesus' "strenuous teachings" about not resisting one who is evil must be understood in the context of what he took to be his apocalyptic expectation of the Kingdom of God. Anticipating the Kingdom's imminent arrival, Jesus directs the Christian to unqualified and exclusive regard of the single neighbor whom one may encounter "because all neighbors except the one actually present were apocalyptically removed from view and taken care of by God."[2] Nevertheless, (2) the norm of nonresisting love remains pertinent and effective outside this original context, where in fact "there is always more than one neighbor" and where Christian engagement with continuing social arrangements to maintain human life becomes a possibility.

Nonresisting love in a nonapocalyptic world intensifies the bar against the intrusion of self-love in moral activities involving many neighbors. Just at the point where we find ourselves with multiple responsibilities, we are most tempted to prefer some over others for our own sakes. Agape, in contrast, enjoins that we look exclusively to the needs of the neighbor. The language of nonresistance intensifies the call to an unclaiming love for the neighbor's sake. But (3) the notion of nonresistance also authorizes service for others of the sort excluded in utterly one-to-one, self and other relations. That is to say, precisely as the sort of love that claims nothing for the self and would serve the single neighbor by not resisting evil but overcoming it with good, agape may serve innocent victims of injustice by resisting on their behalf. We find the beginnings of a neighbor-centered preferential ethics of protection in the biblical Jesus himself, even with the impact of his apocalypticism expelling concern for the permanent organization of justice in political institutions. While refusing to resist evildoers in his own case, still "he showed indignation, even wrath, over injustice, using vitriolic words as weapons against the devourers of widows' houses."[3]

Thus (4) the justification of resistance represents a change of tactics within the general strategy of Christian ethics once "Christians . . . came to see that the service of the real needs of all the men for whom Christ died required more than personal, witnessing action. It also required them to be involved in maintaining the organized social and political life in which all men live. Non-resisting love had sometimes to resist evil."[4]

Finally, Ramsey believed (5) "that for an ethics based on reconciling, suffering, non-resisting, self-giving, Christ-like love, the passage or step or leap to resistance has most of all to be articulated; clearly the gaps between this and non-violent pressures . . . and between it and armed force are equally wide."[5] Decisions to resist nonviolently or violently are matters for prudential judgment. This view, which seems to coincide with that of Reinhold Niebuhr,[6] leads Ramsey to question Christian efforts to strike a decisive break between licit nonviolent resistance and illicit violent resistance, including killing. He asks whether these attempts compromise the ethic of Jesus both in the direction of diluting the demand for unclaiming love in utterly one-to-one relations (because the self would be permitted to resist nonviolently aside or apart from service of neighbor), and in the direction of restricting "what love may find needs to be done when weighing the claims of more neighbors than one and the actual ways they may be served."[7] He also wonders if the separation, common to some Christian pacifists, reflects a legalism of non-killing or "a superficial objection to bloodshed and physical violence and suffering."[8]

Christian realism. Ramsey's thought overlapped with Reinhold Niebuhr's in other ways. With Niebuhr, he criticized forms of Christian idealism that esteemed sinful human nature and its possibilities too highly. He believed in the inevitability of sinful self-assertion and "ideological taint" among collectives, and saw the need to balance power with power in pursuit of historical ideals of justice. Yet he also believed that the human spirit was capable of attaining some realization of these ideals. In a manner reminiscent of Niebuhr's account of the "two political instruments of brotherhood—the organization of power and the balance of power,"[9] Ramsey spoke of the dialectical relationship between order (organization), justice (balance), and the realities of power that embrace them both. As far as these instruments of fellow humanity are concerned, order and justice serve one another and are always to be seen as in some way conditional to the other. But at a particular time and place the demands of one may exact a cost from the other that cannot be ignored. "Power, which is of the *esse* of political agency, may be a conditional value only; but order and justice, which are ever in tension yet in interrelation, both are values that comprise the well-being, the *bene esse* of political affairs and the common good which is the goal of political action."[10]

Generally, then, Christian realism is justified by the acknowledgment of "God's restraining grace in every impersonal and coercive institution and in the legal order, by which he intends our good always to preserve a tolerable fellow humanity against the ravagements of sin."[11] The Christian should live before the whole reality of God, knowing that "in his response to God the Redeemer and God the Creator of our fellow creatureliness, he does not omit to respond obediently also to God's judgment, by being content to live within orders that limit and often obscure while they still make possible man's life in community and hold this back from death and destruction."[12]

With the covenant of Noah in mind, we can connect the establishment of government and its monopoly of power to the remedy God gives for the preservation of the world: "Whoever sheds man's blood, by man shall his blood be shed, for in the image of God made he man." Against the sinful human heart, evil is made legitimate for the purpose of restraining greater evil, so that a common good may be preserved. And in national and international affairs alike, any form of imposed coercion is just part of a continuum "on which the shedding of blood is simply an extreme in the use of evil to prevent greater evil. From this perspective, a local community's interest in the education of its youth is good, while the fact that this cannot be accomplished simply by an orchestration of various voluntary participants, the fact that coercion is required, is a necessary evil."[13] To deny that real good may be done under these conditions, or to assert that the good may be done apart from an expectation of the possible need for restraint, is to make the same mistake of misapprehending political reality, though from opposite sides.

Just war. Ramsey's realism and the case for resisting (nonresisting) love converge in an interpretation of the theory of the "just war." The act of politics requires considering the necessities of both power and human purpose; the political act of waging war is no different. Preferential love for oppressed neighbors may call for violent resistance; war may and must be understood along these lines. We now discuss the five rudiments of the interpretation.

First, recourse to war may be justified by appeal to agape, which serves the neighbor's real needs in a fallen world yet ruled by Christ. Love "allowed even the enemy to be killed only because military personnel and targets stood objectively there at the point where intersect the needs and claims of many more of our fellow men. For their sakes the bearer of hostile force may and should be repressed." In a sequence of thought experiments, Ramsey suggested that the Good Samaritan's proper service might well extend to defending the man who fell among thieves had he caught them in the act of thievery, or to serve on a police patrol on the Jericho Road to prevent such crimes, or even "to resist by force of arms external aggression against the social order maintaining that patrol."[14] From this perspective, appeals to self-defense are not adequate. They narrow moral regard to some circle with the self and its attachments at the center, they tend to demonize the "aggressor" enemy (but see below), and they leave ambiguous what moral limits apply to self-preservation.

Second, love may justify recourse to war, but it also limits conduct within it. Because a Christian is justified in resisting an enemy only for the sake of "the innocent and helpless of earth," he or she "could never proceed to kill equally innocent people as a means of getting at the enemy's forces."[15] Noncombatants in wartime are immune from direct attack. This "principle of discrimination" is coupled with the secondary requirement that conduct against legitimate military targets be justified through a claim of proportion between good and evil consequences.

Third, competing commonwealths, constituted by their respective agreements about the objects of their love and regarding the things which are helpful to this life, cannot be presumed to have, on either side, a universal view of standards of justice. They only have their situated views of the universal, and this fact, when allied with a realistic expectation that collectives will assert themselves inordinately, leads to the possibility that in war a measure of justice may be on both sides. Under conditions of uncertainty as to this "relative justice," it is all the more important to grasp the objective and unexceptionable limits to the conduct of war. Also, since there can be no pretension that absolute justice rests with one side, it may follow that war's destructiveness would have to be carefully limited relative to each relatively just cause itself.[16]

Fourth, the principle of discrimination condemns actions, the direct killing of noncombatants, that would utterly reduce enemy citizens to a mere means in service of war aims. Protecting citizens in this way implies a rejection of the claim that a person's value is utterly and merely reducible to his or her contribution to political life. A key for Ramsey was Saint Augustine's doctrine that followers of Christ lived in two cities in this temporal life, the *civitas terrena* and the *civitas dei*. "By relating men to an eternal end and not only to the earthly end of the common good, Christianity broke open the one world view of classical politics with its incipient totalitarianism that viewed individual men as belonging to only one city and that embraced their whole lives in one commonwealth."[17]

When Ramsey refers to war governed by just war tenets as a barely human activity,[18] I interpret him to mean "fellow human." What makes war barely human, at least, is the guarantee that one's fellow creature who is a noncombatant citizen of an enemy commonwealth would not be absorbed to the whole of his or her being into political ends. The rejection of immunity does that; treated as merely an organ of the enemy, he or she would be cut away merely to serve one's own political cause of justice. Let there rather be the honoring of distance or otherness or differentiation even in this relation of nonrelation or anti-relation between warring parties.[19]

Fifth, this last point should also apply to the enemy combatant. But how can that be? Ramsey offered a redescription of morally legitimate killing in war as being, in the strict sense, "the incapacitation of a combatant from doing what he is doing because he is this particular combatant in this particular war; it is not the killing of a man because he is this particular man. . . . From the proper direction of just action in war upon the combatant and not upon the man flows the prohibition of the killing of soldiers who have been captured or who by surrender have taken themselves out of the war and incapacitated themselves from continuing it."[20]

The important point is that like the civilian, the moral worth of a combatant creature cannot be simply reduced to a political status or function. To say strictly that we aim to kill a person, God's human creature, because of his or her political role is to collapse the former into the latter, and so to lose sight of how that creature remains, as God's own, other to us and to worldly authorities and hence as one whose fellow humanity claims our faithfulness.

No doubt critics can point to what they see to be the withering abstraction of Ramsey's redescription. Yet he saw it as capturing, from the perspective of agape, a critical truth about the logic of Christian moral discourse about war. Its purpose was not to permit some legalistic evasion of responsibility for killing ("I didn't really want to kill him—just to incapacitate"), but to enable a clearer understanding of the moral features of an agape-driven theory of just war.[21] The theory could not morally account for directing killing force at a human being simply considered and as such; one aims rather at that being's materially unjust function in gravely assaulting the needs of innocent neighbors.[22] Of course, one can concede the point and still wonder whether this analysis of moral talk can be anything more than academic chitchat in the life of Christian communities and a wider culture. I address this issue below.

Keeping Faith in Political Ethics

Ramsey's ethics of just war fits the pattern of "love transforming justice" in two respects. First, it affirms and brings to light the relevance of a creaturely, covenant-based natural justice, both in its justifying the defense of rights to fellow humanity and in its limiting the manner in which that defense is conducted. Second, it challenges some widely held norms for the purpose of reshaping alternative notions of political justice. These include accounts of war and killing based on a right of self-defense. Also included for criticism is the approach of Reinhold Niebuhr, within which Ramsey proposed an "extension." He argued that "there was more to be said about justice in war than was articulated in Niebuhr's sense of the ambiguities of politics and his greater/lesser evil doctrine of the use of force."[23] The "more" was the morally unexceptionable canon of loyalty, the immunity of noncombatants from direct attack, an expression of agape that does not and must not rely for its applicability on assessments of greater versus lesser evils.

Ramsey targeted other problematic approaches to politics and justice. He took issue with pacifists who condemned modern war because it is usually fought without limits, and "bellicists" who, for reasons of "justice," thought it tragically necessary to fight in wars—without limits! His answer to both was the theory of just war, which based armed conflict on human moral purpose and limited its direction and extent. "The case for making just war possible" in discourse and practice was important work in service of vulnerable neighbors; pacifists and bellicists fail to keep faith with them by betraying, respectively, the victims of injustice and noncombatants along with an enemy people's common human life as such. "War first became total in the minds of men," Ramsey would write, and he had in mind precisely those folks who advanced from opposite sides the idea of total war. Against them, he defended distinctions internal to just war theory, such as between close, remote, formal, and material cooperation in injustice, or between guilt and innocence as these terms applied only to the presence or absence of close cooperation.[24] Not seeing, moreover, the moral difference between an immoral direct attack on noncombatants and a permissible indirect but foreseen (and proportionate) attack on them could lead back to the dilemma of claiming either that wars must never be fought (because moral noncombatants are killed), or that they must, though without moral restraint.

Ramsey also struggled generally against accounts of political life that failed to reckon with the indivisibility within it of power and purpose, of force and human values. Such views included a "practical pacifism" that used a facsimile of just war theory for the purpose of delegitimating all wars one by one, and the "humanitarian liberalism" that held on to the myth that there is a nonviolent solution to every conflict. Usual American approaches to war—what Ramsey often called the "aggressor-defender doctrine"—wax hot and cold. There is the initial supposition that force can be banished from politics. Any just recourse to war, then, must be as a response to the extraordinary and outrageous employment of violent force against a people.

Thus it happens that war tends to be waged unrestrainedly, because force is deemed to be intrinsically alien to morality in the first place, and because the unlimited end of banishing force from human history invites the employment of unlimited means. Americans wage wars to end all wars, and wars to make the world safe (once and for all) for democracy. Similarly, strategies of total, counterpeople nuclear deterrence would be put in place to guarantee with murderous violence that force be banished from human affairs.[25] This was the cultural and political ethos Ramsey the Christian ethicist opposed. Christian pacifists and realists who bought into it, in one way or another, were to his mind cultural Christians pure and simple.

We now have to ask whether this position is fully adequate on its own terms. Does it drive moral reflection and discernment deeper into the realities of human need and suffering, and, as Ramsey would say, to the meaning of faithfulness as it may be attested in the covenants of life with life? There are grounds for answering in the affirmative. Just war theory, it would seem, does direct us to the evils of injustice. It affirms the faithfulness claims of the innocent, and it fosters moral anguish "over inevitable clashes between justice-reasons for going to war and disproportion-reasons prohibiting it. The sounder our understanding, the more the moral anguish over suffering we ought to let continue unrelieved because to topple the oppressor would bring on as great or greater suffering."[26]

But there are also dangers to just war discourse. Within the context of a narrow nationalism, the language of just war may operate to mask or marginalize realities of killing, injury, and human suffering. Killing the enemy becomes a matter of disarming or incapacitating, and this redescription can remove from view the ordinary citizen, a son or daughter or father or mother, whom we kill for justice's sake. The permissible-because-indirect killing of noncombatants is described as collateral damage deemed proportionate, and so forth. Talk of direct and indirect attack may specify injury as a mere by-product, or as accidental, unwanted.[27] Generally, just war discourse could foster the illusion, useful to sovereign nation-states, that easy judgments of wickedness and rectitude may impartially be made, and that human events may be ordered and controlled always in the direction of the good and the right. This conceit can be a comfort to citizens who are anxious to vindicate their own righteousness.[28]

Ramsey's just war theory, based as it is on the norm of agape, makes no sense if the masking and marginalizing of injury and injustice is constitutive of it. Thus morally indirect attack on noncombatants must be for the theory also the morally regrettable (if permissible) killing of fellow humans; war understood as an "arbitrament of arms" with limited purposes defined by competing "common goods" must be also a contest in which each side seeks to out-injure the other; and the incapacitation of a combatant must be also the killing of one who in some sense must be seen to share with the killer "undiminished fellow humanity."[29] Yet in saying this we have to add that the saying is insufficient for the purposes of Christian ethics. The struggle to refuse abstraction from the reality of war will fail, and abstraction will result, in the absence of certain moral skills and practices which, though bound to the logic of just war theory, go beyond the promotion of it as a ruled moral discourse superior to bellicism, pacifism, and the American aggressor-defender doctrine.

Let me mention five interrelated skills and practices of this sort. First, the people of a warring nation would need somehow to grasp the relative justice of their cause. Somehow it would have to be the case that a sentiment of regretful and chastened resolution, in contrast to nationalistic fervor, had a sure hold on the citizenry. Second, public understanding of war could not be that of either a "crusade" fought for infinite ends (warranting unlimitedly destructive means) or a war of "autonomous national interest" independent of objective moral considerations.

Third, preparation for and execution of war must not be one in which the enemy is demonized, conceived as inhuman or less than human. Here, too, just war theory authorizes the practical implication. The principle of discrimination and the account of incapacitation demand sharp awareness of the human otherness of the enemy, the distance, in and for fellow humanity, at which enemy combatants and noncombatants stand as creatures of God, and therefore as engaged in creaturely activities such as work, citizenship, friendship, and family life. Fourth, a clear sense of victimization in war should be socially present and effective, the apprehension that across the board innocent persons, in a morally broader sense than stressed by the theory, suffer and die on account of the injustices of others. Fifth, critical vigilance toward the conduct of war must be maintained come what may for one's own side; considerations of discrimination and proportion, relative justice and right intention, must come together in an ongoing assessment.[30]

Ramsey would not have quarreled with any of these steps in principle, although he may well have wanted to qualify them in terms of a nation's morally imperative resolve to wage war effectively for the sake of innocent neighbors. He seldom stressed these steps, however, and the practical direction of his political ethics tended elsewhere. He seemed, in contrast, to stress the privileged role of the statesman in applying principles to political practice, and his work can be seen to have encouraged an inevitable and unambiguous deference to the competent authorities, or higher magistrates who make policies on grounds of fact that may well elude the ordinary citizen.[31]

In his time, Ramsey was especially suspicious of "pacifist" uses of just war principles to discredit conduct in war. But these moves, surely, must be included as part of Ramsey's vocation to specify Christian moral discourse in light of the whole idea of God; for they reflect attention to matters of order and the realities of power in a fallen world. By themselves, however, they hardly set afire the heart of the properly prudent moral agent to resist the absolutization of one's cause or the demonization of the enemy. The practical setting for holding in mind and heart the undiminished fellow humanity of the enemy, which as such is not to be exclusively subsumed to membership in any earthly setting, is not a major concern, however much it appears to be demanded by the theory espoused. And this problem is especially telling given the vulnerability of just war discourse discussed above.

If Ramsey is to be held to his own requirement of addressing the whole idea of God in Christian moral discourse, then perhaps a reconsideration of the full bearing of the work of redemptive love on the realities of politics and war is in order. I mean that the ethics may have to reflect this work more than notionally, and be geared to practices that set a context for it and bear promise of it. I will return to this issue, but, at this point, two comments will suffice. First, H. Richard Niebuhr's call for a permanent revolution of heart and mind that turns from defensiveness to trust in the Lord of a universal community is not a bad theological point of departure for this practical task.

Second, in his essay on H. Richard Niebuhr, Ramsey acknowledged how easily the conversionist type of answer of the problem of Christ and culture loses its dynamic character. It may become static by the implicit practice of synthesizing Christ with a culturally conditioned form of the moral law. If that happens, Niebuhr said, the Christian "will be required to turn to the defense of that temporal foundation for the sake of the superstructure it carries when changes in culture threaten it." And so Christ is transformed "into a cockpit from which to defend a culture that is withering away" before God.[32]

Does Ramsey's defense of just war lose its dynamic character in something like this way? From defense of a love-informed theory that would realistically serve the neighbor over against alternatives that jettison, in one way or another, the moral limits to war, Ramsey may have moved to a defense of the "law" of just war that tends to neglect the problems covered in this section. The problems cut to the root of the meaning of neighbor love and love of enemy as these witness to the redemptive righteousness of God and turn from the sin of self-justification. One consequence of this tendency could be a sort of cultural Christianity that ironically leaves to the state the embodiment of "Christ," the highest ideal feasible among the options in political life. In that case conversion, a conversion that Niebuhr saw rooted in repentance and faith, may be given up.

Medical Ethics and the Conditions for Covenant

In this section, I argue that portions of Ramsey's writings in medical ethics are covenant-ridden in ways he did not always acknowledge or helpfully signal.[33] In these works, the language of covenant generally refers to the loyalty to be shown a person in need of special protection, who stands before us as a child of God, a brother or sister for whom Christ died. The loyalty, as always, images the righteousness of the faithful God. Specifically, however, Ramsey implicitly uses Barth's formula on creation and covenant to reflect on the external conditions of covenant in the creaturely relationships that bear on and make up the practice of medicine.

Recall that the argument in *Christian Ethics and the Sit-In* concerned social arrangements that require moral attention and protection insofar as they secure, on the one hand, a differentiation of partners as irreducibly other, and, on the other, a sphere of common ground within which partners may stand together. That innkeeper and patron may be with and for one another presupposes both a right to property that resists the merger of persons and respects a proper distance, and an intersubjective space defining goods to be shared (in this case, the use of property for the public provision of services in response to basic needs of food and shelter). The individual right and the common space comprise external conditions of the possibility of mutual benefit and assistance in a relation of fellow humanity.

Ramsey's portrayal of free and informed consent as a canon of loyalty in the practice of medicine is strikingly similar to this earlier venture into social ethics. Consent is a condition of "man's capacity to become joint adventurers in a common cause" of the advancement of medicine and benefit to others, or of healing the consenting patient.[34] Because fellow humanity is precarious in us, because there exist pressures that might endanger medical recognition of the free differentiation of would-be partners (e.g., the temptation to see only the future benefit promised by technology and present research, or to view informed consent as excessively cumbersome in therapeutic contexts), protection of the patient-subject's right to consent is enormously significant. It is, perhaps, because he is so struck by these pressures that Ramsey does not quickly endorse a general duty of fellow humanity to participate in research—although he surely seems to move in that direction. The basic point, however, is clear. As a central feature of current medical practice, as an instance of natural justice, and as a proper curb to sinful exploitation, informed consent is an external condition of a covenant of mutual assistance between human creatures.

In making special reference to children involved in medical investigation, Ramsey provides a "prismatic case" in which to understand more clearly how the moral claims of any fellow man rule out treatment reducing one to the status of property—that is, the mere extension of the will of another.[35] How much more precarious is the fellow humanity of the vulnerable child unable to consent? Not ever a presumed volunteer in the cause of progress, his or her needs for unimpaired life and growth frame the only legitimate possibility of partnership with medical investigators. The needs set the terms of distance, in and from which may be found the condition of participation in a common therapeutic cause. They also figure centrally in establishing the common cause constitutive of the bond between parents and children. The power of parents and mistaken ideologies of presumptive consent, together with the promise of medical benefit to future persons, render fellow humanity precarious with regard to those terms of relation. To secure social arrangements in various quarters that honor these terms is also to honor an external basis of creaturely covenant.

In covenant, there is distance in the relation; otherwise creatures cannot be partners, but are absorbed into and endangered by lofty visions of little and larger communion. There is also relation in the distance; otherwise, partnership is again impossible, because nothing is found to be common in the situated social realities of our lives. Ramsey's ethic of only (but always) caring for the dying is in part an attempt to display the common ground between medical healers, members of an ongoing tradition of practice, and dying patients whose uttermost need is the comfort of a faithful human presence. Medicine's work is not exhausted when curative measures no longer offer a reasonable hope of success; nor is medicine's work inexhaustible, overwhelming human need by the incessant effort to maintain life whatever the cost.

Abandonment of the person to his or her dying, even perhaps to the point of direct killing, is a confession that no more can be shared between professional and patient. Abandonment to life-saving (and dying-prolonging) technology presumes as well an absence of mutual partnership, at least in the absence of the patient's explicit will to hold on a bit longer. Both errors consign the dying to their solitude without a caring response, and heap isolation upon itself. The delineation of a shared good captured in the medical-moral practice of care for the dying shows how there is relation in the distance of self and other, and shows as well how the denial of common ground can lead to the denial of the other in his or her need; without the former, the patient is present only to be left alone or absorbed into some unilateral cause (e.g., vindicating the power of life-saving technology).[36]

Consider another example of Ramsey's interest in preserving social arrangements that acknowledge terms of relation that externally anticipate a covenantal realization. His criticism of the 1976 Supreme Court decision in *Planned Parenthood v. Danforth* includes a vigorous attack on the manner in which a statutory requirement for spousal consent to abortion was struck down. Acknowledging that there may be good Christian reasons for thinking a consent requirement to be too strong, he argues that the logic of the Court's decision jeopardizes a proper social understanding of marriage as a relationship that bears constituent elements neither dictated by the state nor resolved into the free choices of forever separate, autonomous individuals:

> It has been the law's assumption that marriage entails the conveyal to one partner of access to the possibility of having children of one's own. Reproductive capacities are not withheld, as may rightfully be done so long as persons remain la femme seul or l'homme seul. These powers are given over not so much to the other party as to the marriage union itself.[37]

Surely husband and wife also remain individuals, whose reality is not completely comprehended by their existence as spouses; nonetheless, Ramsey contends, the "specific difference" in marriage refers to "mutual bodily lovemaking and access to the possibility of a fruit of that union." The Supreme Court in *Danforth*, however, simply atomized the relationship of marriage into a matter of projected conflict between the private and seemingly separate rights of husband and wife. The opinion of the Court contains no whisper of the idea that a certain sort of relationship needs and is rightly owed state protection. Only individuals stripped of such relations qualify.

Hence, a valued conception of a distinctive human relationship wins no legal support, and the outcome is that spouses are depicted in the law as isolated choosers, unbound by the relation they entered, as free as before. There is no relation in the distance—such is the "omnivorous influence of a personalistic, individualistic notion of privacy."[38] The notion obscures in principle what husbands, as a matter of justice, may be due—the prospect of having some knowing relationship to the reproductive decisions of their wives, especially as they concern the fruit of conjugal union.

In all of these cases, Ramsey attends to the external conditions of covenant present in various natural and social situations. These are worthy of preservation in their own right. Although their preservation does not necessarily lead to relations of genuine creaturely covenant, such a fellowship is their internal meaning. Agape may work both to safeguard the conditions and to redirect and transform thought and action regarding the covenantal fulfillments themselves. They may, that is, signify more than the features of differentiation, fellowship, and mutuality. In Ramsey's hands, the relation between investigator and experimental subject is projected to be the opportunity for faithfulness in mutual partnership, and not merely contract for mutual benefit. Keeping children from nontherapeutic trials is to be a mode of cherishing the most vulnerable in their need and need only. By neither directly dispatching nor ceaselessly prolonging the dying of patients in their final passage, caretakers for the dying may yet find with them reconciling meaning in the face of suffering and death.

In sum, Ramsey's view that "faithfulness claims and canons of covenant loyalty may be the profoundest way to understand all of our concepts of justice and fairness"[39] may suggest that these concepts of justice and fairness, establishing patterns of both human differentiation and human terms of relation, are permeable to practical fulfillments that realize moral dispositions—gratitude, care, loyalty, mercy—expressive of the divine pattern of righteousness in Jesus Christ. Now recall that the concern with human covenants and their conditions is itself a concern for the needs of the neighbor, channeled through reflection upon social rules of practice, norms of professional conduct, the state of the law, and so forth. In these ways, Ramsey's "care and feeding of Christian moral discourse" would coincide with the approach of "love transforming natural justice."

But Ramsey has a problem in his medical ethics analogous to the difficulty I pointed out in his case of just war. He will, as I said, project the fuller inner meaning of covenant in his work. He will seek to describe and discern human bonds in the light of God's creative, preserving, and redeeming activity. As Stanley Hauerwas has cautioned, however, a liberal society like our own can dangerously deform these descriptions by resolving them into approximations of isolated personal autonomy on the one hand and undifferentiated community on the other. Ramsey saw and knew this, but we do not have much help from him, apart from the critical articulation of norms, about how to address the language of fellow humanity to a world that may be lacking the moral skills needed to appreciate them.

For Ramsey, medical ethics bears promise of being a social practice of faithfulness, reconciliation, and care for the vulnerable. But from the standpoint of a liberal society, Ramsey's medical ethics may appear to defend the primacy of the individual (which from that standpoint is good), or the paternalism of the physician (which is not), or the imposition of Christian notions of parental responsibility or the meaning of dying upon liberal citizens (which is worse). How can the conditions for creaturely covenant be named and witnessed in a world whose lived context (call it liberal individualism) tends to distort recognition of the depth and goodness of these conditions? This is similar to asking how the creaturely otherness of the enemy in war can be named in an address to a nation that has enormous resources at its disposal (including just war discourse) for denying it. Similarly, too, the question prompts us to consider the significance of specific moral skills and practices that offer a fitting context of intelligibility for the Christian moral discourse that Ramsey so carefully analyzes and develops.

Conclusion: Conversion and Context

Paul Ramsey sought to interpret H. Richard Niebuhr's thought away from moral relativism, which makes no place for objectively valid norms, and toward "relational objectivism." Niebuhr invites this interpretation; "the discovery of the absolute within the relative," he says, "is the discovery of the real within the apparent, of the permanent character in changing relations."[40] Ramsey took his point of departure from an account of this permanent character that relied formally on an argument for "canons of loyalty" and materially in a rendering of the covenantal character of human bonds. He incorporated these themes within a tranformationist understanding of Christ and culture, or love and natural justice, which made prominent the distinction and indivisibility of God's creating, preserving, and redeeming activity in the world. Christian ethics, the critical explication of Christian moral discourse, should respond and witness to this activity as it addresses the moral problems of Christian and human creaturely life.

As I argued in the previous chapter, Ramsey also builds on Niebuhr's understanding of the one God's sovereign activity as Creator, Judge and Preserver, and Redeemer. Such activity is for conversion and transformation, and for Ramsey this emerges in the lived expression and social embodiment of agape or neighbor love in human affairs. Expression and embodiment for him typically involved the ways genuinely human creaturely existence is covenantal or fellow human. Ramsey's development of these themes of universal love, human sociality, and their basis in the whole idea of God point to the essential features of a Christian ethic of faithfulness.

It further illumines Ramsey's project to consider its connection with two other features of Niebuhr's theological vision. First, in "The Christian Church in the World's Crisis," written in 1941, Niebuhr claimed that the responsibility of Christians included "helping the nation to become morally fit either to stay out or to enter into war." They needed most of all to point out that the real issue concerned the context of either action, and specifically whether that context is nationalist or "universalist," prompting a decision of "American peace or peace of God," or "American war or acceptance of the judgment of God."[41] "Actions," he wrote, "are like words. Despite all efforts to discover the 'real' meaning of a word by contemplating it long and thoughtfully, it reveals its meaning only in a sentence or paragraph in which the full intention of the speaker is made manifest."[42] In the Christian case, the context of actions is the kind of faith that places words and deeds within a pattern of continuous action that is in some measure redemptive or defensive, more or less universal or exclusive, more or less grounded in trust in God.

Now Ramsey implicitly follows Niebuhr's dictum that acts differing greatly in material content may still be evaluated similarly when placed in similar contexts in the argument for morally legitimate resistance. Resistance on behalf of the innocent neighbor is warranted, and the context of nonresisting love focused entirely on the neighbor's need establishes the theological warrants. Also, Ramsey's defense of just war theory, and his criticisms of pacifism, amoral realism, and the American aggressor-defender doctrine were intended in part "to help the nation to become morally fit to stay out or to enter into war."

Second, as Richard Miller has claimed, Ramsey's just war theory may be read as an expression in normative ethics of Niebuhr's general reflections on war and God's activity in the world. The latter's focus on innocent suffering and the need for Christians to foster a people's repentance of egoism and injustice finds parallels in Ramsey's principles of discrimination and relative justice.[43]

These themes, however, also frame critical questions to be put to Ramsey. Niebuhr's theology of permanent revolution requires deep and deeper probing into the context of our actions before God. He insisted that "whatever particular action we have chosen as our moral duty, our greater duty is to make that action conform to the context of our universal or our nationalist faith."[44] We should ask whether Ramsey sufficiently attended in his ethics to the practical differences between just war as an instrument of nationalism and just war as an instrument of a more universal outlook.

We may also question the degree to which Ramsey in his medical ethics successfully distinguished his covenantal defense of the individual from a prevailing liberalism that gave priority not to conditions of trust and fidelity but to the mutual accommodation of individual interests. Recall, finally, that Niebuhr's writings on war urged repentance of self-defensive self-righteousness; in this posture, wars are fought and judgments passed in order to preserve "our" values, or democracy, or country, or religion. In its place, we may be free for trusting and loyal service of neighbors.

Ramsey's translation of these themes in defense of just war leaves in the background Niebuhr's account of the moral dispositions that would lend intelligibility to his normative theory. He does not address, therefore, how a dynamic response to self-defensive ideologies can be communally sustained when the normative theory is co-opted or eroded by them. We are brought back to Hauerwas, who reflects on this sort of issue again and again.

Notes

1. Note, however, that the theme of "love transforming natural justice" is crucial to Ramsey's argument in *War and the Christian Conscience* (Durham, N.C.: Duke University Press, 1961), xix, 20.
2. Paul Ramsey, *Basic Christian Ethics* (New York: Scribner's, 1950), 40.
3. Paul Ramsey, *The Essential Paul Ramsey*, ed. William Werpehowski and Stephen D. Crocco (New Haven, Conn.: Yale University Press, 1994), 45–46.
4. Ramsey, *War and the Christian Conscience*, xvii–xviii.

5. Paul Ramsey, Letter to Byron Johnson, February 17, 1961, Ramsey papers, Duke University Archives, Durham, N.C.

6. See Reinhold Niebuhr, *Moral Man and Immoral Society* (New York: Scribner's, 1932), 242–52. Cf. David Attwood, *Paul Ramsey's Political Ethics* (Lanham, Md.: Rowman and Littlefield, 1992), 40–46.

7. Ramsey, *Essential Paul Ramsey*, 37.

8. Attwood, *Paul Ramsey's Political Ethics*, 124.

9. Reinhold Niebuhr, *The Nature and Destiny of Man*, vol. 2, *Human Destiny* (New York: Scribner's, 1943), 265–69.

10. Ramsey, *Essential Paul Ramsey*, 92–93.

11. Paul Ramsey, *Christian Ethics and the Sit-In* (New York: Association Press, 1961), 48.

12. Ibid., 49–50.

13. Paul Ramsey, "Force and Political Responsibility," in Ernest W. Lefever, ed., *Ethics and World Politics* (Baltimore: Johns Hopkins University Press, 1972), 61–62.

14. Ramsey, *Essential Paul Ramsey*, 62–63.

15. Ibid.

16. Paul Ramsey, *Speak Up for Just War or Pacifism* (University Park: Pennsylvania State University Press, 1988), 89–90. Cf. Richard Miller, *Interpretations of Conflict* (Chicago: University of Chicago Press, 1991), 14, 66–67.

17. Ramsey, *War and the Christian Conscience*, xxi.

18. Ramsey, *Essential Paul Ramsey*, 82.

19. See, e.g., Ramsey, *Essential Paul Ramsey*, 81, and Miller, *Interpretations of Conflict*, 153.

20. Paul Ramsey, *The Just War* (New York: Scribner's, 1968), 502; see also 465–78. Cf. ibid., *War and the Christian Conscience*, 39–59, for an earlier view, and *Speak Up for Just War or Pacifism*, 102.

21. John Finnis has argued that the "fundamentals" of the Roman Catholic natural law tradition implicitly entail the rejection of the belief that "war must involve intending to kill." John Finnis, "The Ethics of War and Peace in the Catholic Natural Law Tradition," in Terry Nardin, ed., *The Ethics of War and Peace: Religious and Secular Perspectives* (Princeton, N.J.: Princeton University Press, 1996), 33.

22. For an extended use of a functional interpretation of killing in cases of "therapeutic abortion," see Paul Ramsey, "Abortion: A Review Article," *The Thomist* 37, no. 1 (January 1973): 174–226.

23. Ramsey, *Just War*, 260. Cf. Attwood, *Paul Ramsey's Political Ethics*, 42ff.

24. Ramsey, *Essential Paul Ramsey*, 68–83. An excellent contemporary discussion of the principle of cooperation is James F. Keenan, "Prophylactics, Tol-

eration, and Cooperation: Contemporary Problems and Traditional Principles," *International Philosophical Quarterly* 29 (1989): 205–20.

25. Ramsey, *Just War*, 48, 51, 69.

26. Ramsey, *Speak Up for Just War or Pacifism*, 72.

27. Elaine Scarry, *The Body in Pain* (New York: Oxford University Press, 1985), 60–160.

28. Jean Bethke Elshtain, *Women and War* (New York: Basic Books, 1987), 156–59.

29. Ramsey, *Essential Paul Ramsey*, 70–71.

30. Cf. Miller, *Interpretations of Conflict*, 14.

31. See, e.g., Paul Ramsey, "Does the Church Have Any Wisdom for the 1970's?" (unpublished manuscript, Princeton University, Princeton, N.J., 1972). This long text apparently includes Ramsey's 1972 lectures at the Perkins School of Theology. Cf. the published excerpt in *Perkins Journal* 26, no. 1 (fall 1972): 29–40.

32. Paul Ramsey, *Nine Modern Moralists* (Englewood Cliffs, N.J.: Prentice-Hall, 1962), 219–20.

33. Here I draw from the longer discussion in William Werpehowski, "Christian Love and Covenant Faithfulness," *Journal of Religious Ethics* 19, no. 2 (fall 1991): 103–32.

34. Ramsey, *Essential Paul Ramsey*, 180–81.

35. Ibid., 186–94.

36. Ibid., 113–64, esp. 144–57.

37. Paul Ramsey, *Ethics at the Edges of Life* (New Haven, Conn.: Yale University Press, 1978), 15.

38. Ibid., 13–14.

39. Ramsey, "The Case of the Curious Exception," in Gene H. Outka and Paul Ramsey, eds., *Norm and Context in Christian Ethics* (New York: Scribner's, 1968), 119.

40. H. Richard Niebuhr, *Moral Relativism and the Christian Ethic* (New York: International Missionary Council, 1929), 10.

41. H. Richard Niebuhr, "The Christian Church in the World's Crisis," *Christianity and Society* 6 (summer 1941): 16–17.

42. Ibid., 11.

43. See Miller, *Interpretations of Conflict*, 142–43.

44. Niebuhr, "The Christian Church in the World's Crisis," 15.

CHAPTER FIVE

Keeping Faith in Good Company

Here are the very last words of Stanley Hauerwas's very first book:
"The task of Christian ethics is to help keep the grammar of the language of faith pure so that we may claim not only to speak the truth but also to embody that truth in our lives."[1] The word "pure" indicates for some of his critics an ethic that is ecclesiologically sectarian, ethically tribalist, and epistemologically fideist.[2] Let us sum up these accusations in order. The sectarian intention to keep the Christian community pure of a Godless culture by withdrawing from it is irremovably present in his writings. Prescriptions for maintaining the integrity of the distinctively Christian tribe reflect the belief that the Christian life may go on unadulterated, with a purity that excludes and ignores the moral lives of folks on the outside who know not God. Attention to the purity of the grammar of Christian language suggests that the norms for understanding are unmixed and unmixable with other, non-Christian languages and their rules. Christian talk is sealed, alone for Christians adept in the language of faith.

I think the criticisms are unhelpful and improper, and Hauerwas has always held this. The quotation, however, can help us to understand Hauerwas as long as we see his work as a continuing process of presenting and revising a way for Christians to do what the quotation in its entirety says. Christians are "not only to speak the truth but also to embody that truth" in their lives. The embodiment is important. Too much attention can be given to the relation between fundamental Christian beliefs and ethical conclusions derived from them. That focus can make the Christian religion look like just another worldview for personal choosing than what it is in fact: a people summoned to live a certain manner of life together before God. Christian ethics is an activity of articulating the grammar of Christian language so that the task of embodying truth in social life comes clear. In this sense, the grammar or norms or measures of a language must be the norms or measures of a particular form of communal life, and the goal of Christian ethics is somehow to get that right, to have the grammar contain all that does and nothing that does not properly belong—to keep it pure.

Contrast Paul Ramsey's "care and feeding of Christian moral discourse." Hauerwas is less occupied with framing and specifying the character of Christian moral talk within the larger context of basic theological convictions than he is with the social context and location of Christian existence today. Christians are a people gathered and summoned to witness in a particular way to the being and rule of God. The church's first task, as the Body of Christ, is to be itself and, indivisibly with this, "to make the world the world," to show it to itself in its nature and need. The "grammar of the language of faith," again, is not so much a set of rules for discourse but a set of communal skills, nurtured in practices such as Baptism and the Eucharist, that enable and enact a truthful existence in responsibility to God and in service of the world. Christian living is keeping faith in good company.

I intend to explicate Hauerwas's positive recommendations about ethics and the Christian life. I cannot do that without also discussing his criticisms of political liberalism, the moral ideal of personal autonomy, American Christianity's Constantinian accommodation to an ethos of democracy, and violence as an instrument of nationalism. Hauerwas's theological stance challenges and corrects a position such as Ramsey's while being in its own right, as a kind of Christian pacifism, an honorable if perhaps not exclusive form of Christian discipleship.[3] Yet Hauerwas's ethic permits a sort of Christian witness that is not utterly out of touch with Ramsey's just war ethics properly understood. In connection with this and other possibilities of witness in the world, I will critically explore in the next chapter Hauerwas's views about the meaning and interrelation of the divine activities of creation, preservation, and redemption in light of Ramsey's effort to give a conversionist account of the "whole idea of God."

I will also distinguish five lines of convergence or divergence between Hauerwas's thought and the theology of H. Richard Niebuhr. First, Hauerwas explicitly credits to Niebuhr's influence his early interest in the nature of the self, moral agency, and the ethics of character.[4] In retrospect, we can see how Hauerwas established a research program that moved from analysis of these three categories toward a consideration of the social and communal context necessary for the development of Christian character. There are marks of Niebuhr's work on human sociality and the unity of the self in this program and movement. Second, even though Hauerwas somewhere says that Niebuhr's distinction between internal and external history (or "history as lived and as seen") is "more trouble than it is worth," there remain instructive parallels between Hauerwas's appeals to narrative or story and features of that very distinction. Moreover, the narrative focus resonates strongly with the interpretive dimension of Niebuhr's ethics of responsibility. Third, the background of Hauerwas's pacifism is partly illuminated by connecting it with Niebuhr's 1932 essay, "The Grace of Doing Nothing," and the subsequent exchange with his brother Reinhold over Japan's invasion of Manchuria. Here and elsewhere, Hauerwas endorses and transforms Niebuhr's challenge to change the question of ethics from "what should be done?" to "what is going on?"

In comparison with these themes, the last two, respectively, draw Hauerwas and Niebuhr closer together and farther apart. As a great admirer of Niebuhr's 1935 essay, "Toward the Independence of the Church," Hauerwas may fairly see it as a precursor to his own call to liberate the church from its bondage to a corrupt civilization dominated by capitalism, nationalism, and liberal humanism. But he will also save his harshest words for Niebuhr's *Christ and Culture*, viewing it as doing great damage to a church and church ethics condemned always to compromise its integrity by being a transformer of culture. This sort of critique will receive a good bit of attention in chapter 6.

In this chapter, I propose that Hauerwas, whether he likes it or not, takes up Richard Niebuhr's legacy in a number of ways; moreover, his work is instructively about the business of orienting the language of Christian faith to its social location. Here Ramsey's care and feeding of Christian discourse plays out in the claim that what nourishes it is its concrete placement in a gathered community of disciples that is constituted by practices that faithfully bear witness to God in Jesus Christ—in, for, and against the world.

I see four interconnected moments in the development of Hauerwas's thought. Much of the dynamism of his work derives from his continually rethinking the meaning of Christian ethics in terms of human sociality, concrete life in the church, and the relation between Christian communities and a "world" distinguished by political liberalism and violence.

Character, Virtue, and Vision

In *Character and the Christian Life*, Hauerwas defined a person's character as "the qualification of a man's self-agency through his beliefs, intentions, and actions, by which a man acquires a moral history befitting his nature as a self-determining being."[5] He argued that Christian sanctification may be grasped in terms of Christian character, "the formation of our affections and actions according to the fundamental beliefs of the Christian faith and life. To have Christian character is to have one's attention directed by the description of the world that claims it has been redeemed by the work of Christ."[6] The virtues are moral skills and dispositions that orient Christians to discern and pursue the good as it is defined by the person and work of Jesus Christ and, following from that, the fundamental symbols of the language of faith. Discernment and pursuit go hand in hand with a "vision" or a "seeing" of the world that truthfully reflects the nature of our existence.[7]

Hauerwas's defense of this triad of moral categories was aimed at versions of theological ethics that focused one-sidedly on the rightness or wrongness of acts (not virtues or dispositions to act), on the event of moral decision making (not character as what makes decision making intelligible), or on patterns of human obedience and divine command (not the given power to see the world with the mind of Christ). In making these challenges alone, his early contributions were important. But Hauerwas was also about the business of deepening his own constructive position. In the epilogue to *Character and the Christian Life*, he wrote:

> Our character can be formed only because we are fundamentally social beings. . . . The kind of character we have is therefore relative to the kind of community from which we inherit our primary symbols and practices. The variety of the descriptions in any social setting is one of the reasons character can be and is remarkably different. However, an

intentional community can provide a range of symbols that create boundaries for an ethics of character by suggesting the fundamental symbols that should give each man's character its primary orientation.[8]

By placing his analysis of character within the terms of human sociality and the symbols and practices of intentional community, Hauerwas anticipates his later studies of the role of Christian community and narrative in depicting a social ethic of the Kingdom of God in Jesus Christ. He also raises a set of questions about the moral life that is continuous with Niebuhr's explorations. These questions address the communal provenance of moral agency, and how agency emerges from responsive interpretations or attentive "seeings" of the world that are learned through communal practices grounded in loyalty to a particular cause.[9]

Narrative and Truthfulness

Hauerwas initially defined character as "the qualification of self-agency." He later acknowledged that this formulation "still suggests a kind of dualism insofar as a 'self' seems to stand behind our character." But once character and vision are framed by the communal activities that nurture them, the path is clear to describe character not as the qualification but as "the form of our agency."[10]

If character nurtured in community is the form of our agency—and if character refers to a central orientation or loyalty pursued through moral skills or virtues that capacitate us to see the world aright—then moral action, emerging from moral character, is constituted and made intelligible by vision. If also character conditions the agent's acquisition of a moral history, then vision, with which character is correlative, might properly refer not so much to a set of controlling symbols or images as to a master story that historically orders our lives and equips us to see the world truthfully. The need to account for the intelligibility of action and the acquisition of the self's moral history naturally lead Hauerwas to embrace narrative as a concept that complements his ethics of character. Finally, if his is a Christian theological ethics of character, then, he believes, it must serve the activity of the church's faithful witness to God in Jesus Christ. But that God is identified through a particular narrative involving Israel and Jesus.

There are three points here, concerning the intelligibility of action, the historical nature of the moral life, and the identity of God. Narrative is implicated in each one. First, the identification of a human action is always of action of a particular sort; action-description and understanding rely on determination of historical or narrative context. When I find my seven-year-old son outside our house breaking up the earth and lifting it with a shovel, I ask him "What are you doing?" When he answers, "Digging for gold," there is, logically speaking, a story to be told that makes sense of this action and the act it refers to. It is a story about young children and the dreams they have about great adventure, to be sure; but it is a story that discriminates what is being done (subject as such to assessment regarding its prospects for success) from, say, the act of hunting worms for bait or planting flowers. Narratives also underlie these acts.[11]

Second, narrative is the characteristic form of our self-understanding as accountable historical beings. We pursue the end or telos or central orientation of our life in time. The unity of this pursuit can only be a narrative unity that admits of both unpredictability and teleology; "like characters in a fictional narrative we do not know what will happen next, but nonetheless our lives have a certain form which projects itself towards our future."[12]

Third, "God has revealed himself narratively in the history of Israel and in the life of Jesus. . . . Scripture as a whole tells the story of the covenant with Israel, the life, death, and resurrection of Jesus, and the ongoing history of the church as the recapitulation of that life." Loyalty to God includes learning how to "grow into the story of Jesus as the form of God's kingdom." Here Hauerwas orders vision to narrative: For Christian ethics, the "first task is to help us rightly envision the world. Christian ethics is specifically formed by a very definite story with determinative content."[13]

Appeals to narrative and the Christian story, then, are connected to notions of "seeing the world rightly" and "embodying the truth in our lives." Yet how are narrative and truthfulness or truthful existence related? A basic point is that there is no strictly neutral standpoint from which the agent, who would accept the Christian story as his or her own, may impartially assess the truthfulness of the life it enables. One learns to live truthfully through the development of virtues that dispose us to desire rightly, and to describe and discern what is going on without egocentric distortion or self-deception or recourse to violence.[14] The defense of the relation between truthfulness and the Christian narrative, then, is paradigmatically enacted rather than argued for apart from that virtuous way of life.

This is a difficult theme. Perhaps the best way to understand it is to follow the sorts of examples that Hauerwas gives. I will discuss one example at this point and turn to another below.

Why do people have children? Whatever reasons we may give in response to this question, a common background presumption in our culture is that we choose to have them. What else could responsible parenthood mean other than placing our will through free choice behind this project? To see things this way, Hauerwas contends, is a mistake. When we put our choice to assume responsibility at the center of the moral reality of having children, we are tempted also to assume that our children's well-being is fully our responsibility and subject to our control. In that case, we risk making our children, through the sacrifices we make for them, our product—or at least a mere predicate of our desires for them. We do not doubt that our children had better cooperate with us in this grand and costly enterprise.

I will assume that this pattern of responsible choice, parental control, commodification, and excessive demands upon children is recognizable to the reader. How does Hauerwas address it? He begins by attacking the background presumption that we do, after all, choose our children in the way we think we do, and argues instead that parenthood is better understood as an adventure in which we discover more and more how our children are gifts. Any interpretation of parental choice within Christian communities must be qualified and controlled by this more fundamental notion. "For only when we understand that our children are gifts can we have an intelligible story that makes clear our duties to them and the form our care . . . should take." Christians are called to have children as a witness to God's patient care of a world and a people called church who remain faithful to him. By having children, Christians attest to a God whose faithfulness establishes a continuing faith that children may yet be welcomed into the world that is God's, and also into the life of a people formed by God's story.

It could appear that this stance is a recipe for the worst parental domination of all, in which children have their lives plotted in advance as the "good Christians" their parents will see that they become. That way of putting things, Hauerwas thinks, gets everything wrong. First, parents hope that their children will "carry the story of God in the world," but the hope derives from a God who would "give us and them grounds for hope." Second, parenthood is a calling in which faithfulness to God is embodied in the corporate witness of the church. It turns out that the church makes it possible for children to maintain independence from their parents; for "unless the child has a community that also provides him or her with symbols of significance beyond the family, then in fact the child is at the mercy of his parents." Children "are not ours for they, like each of us, have a Father who wills them as his own prior to our choice of them."[15]

Hence, children are gifts in two senses. They are not under our control, and they create needs in us to love them without the need to control them. As parents, we find ourselves blessed or gifted with the opportunity to learn how to love nonpossessively. The story of God and of a people vowing to trust in God makes the description and the seeing intelligible. Indeed, that narrative makes a proper claim to truthfulness to the extent that it directs us to have children without telling ourselves destructive and self-deceiving stories about the meaning and importance of parenthood and parental sacrifice. Hauerwas in this way renders an account of how the truth to be embodied in Christian lives challenges alternative claims to the truthfulness of central human practices.

Compare this theme with H. Richard Niebuhr's contrast between the internal history or story of our lives and the external history as seen or impersonally observed. In an internal, lived history of "selves" in community loyal to some cause,

> social memory . . . is our own past, living in every self. When we become members of such a community of selves we adopt its past as our own and thereby are changed in our present existence. So immigrants

and their children do, for whom Pilgrims become true fathers and the men of the Revolution their own liberators; so we do in the Christian community when the prophets of the Hebrews become our prophets and the Lord of the early disciples is acknowledged as our Lord. . . . In our history association means community, the participation of each living self in a common memory and common hope no less than in a common world of nature. . . . Hence we may call internal history dramatic and its truth dramatic truth, though drama in this case does not mean fiction.[16]

The external point of view, in contrast, sees society as made up of individuals related to each other by external bonds. It is "a vast and intricate organization of interests, drives or instincts, beliefs, customs, laws, constitutions, inventions, geographic and climactic data, in which a critical and diligent inquiry can discover some intelligible structures and moving patterns of relation."[17]

Hauerwas's category of narrative not only parallels functionally the dramatic nature of Niebuhr's internal history, but does so over against what Hauerwas calls the standard account of post-Enlightenment moral rationality. That account intends to free the moral life "from the peculiarities of agents caught in the limits of their particular histories." Alienation becomes the central moral virtue, empowering rational agents to treat their own lives as outside observers with generic desires and interests that could belong to just any other rational agent.[18] Thus has Hauerwas carried forward Niebuhr's positioning of Christian ethics within internal history. What is more, his emphasis on the Christian story includes the claim that Christians respond to moral reality first of all by interpreting it in a particular way. Truthful vision of the world in terms of the Christian story depends on an interpretation of what is going on, just as Niebuhr held in his view of agency as responsibility.

Community, Practices, and the Critique of Liberalism

The use of narrative could take on an individualistic cast, as when persons pay closer attention to stories and their purely personal religious meaning than to the distinctive story of the church. It could also refer primarily to the historic character of human experience, and become part of a general theory of human nature to which theological claims were subordinated or correlated. This approach is compatible, for example, with a generic characterization of religious truth that has different historical and social expressions. The kernel of general religious truth becomes separable from the socially necessary storied husk. Neither direction finally appeals to Hauerwas; for him the notion of narrative had to stay connected to both its social basis and its theological authorization.[19]

The upshot of the former connection for Christian ethics is a keen focus on the role of moral practices in a tradition-based Christian community. Participation in these practices may give rise to the virtues of Christian character. The latter connection, between narrative and its theological authorization, takes the form of a commitment to a common life that specifically practices nonviolent peacemaking in conformity to Jesus Christ. These two themes now will be taken up in turn. Both imply in distinct ways a critique of the moral and political ideology of liberalism.

Liberalism construes personal freedom and individual consent to be the bases for moral and political life. It "presupposes that society can be organized without any narrative that is commonly held to be true. As a result it tempts us to believe that freedom and rationality are independent of narrative—i.e., we are free to the extent that we have no story."[20] Another way to say this is that this type of thought tends to place all particular, tradition- and narrative-dependent visions of reality normatively at the mercy of the free and rational will, eroding their substance for the sake of individual, autonomous validation. Autonomous validation is deemed a great good, and this valuation enables, according to Hauerwas, the self-deceiving belief in freedom as individual independence. Life in liberal culture deforms our experience of core moral relationships and strips us of the moral skills needed to describe and make sense of these realities.

Christians may recover the skills they need by placing their talk about the bonds of moral life within the context of the church. This is a community in that it is constituted by a tradition, a "memory sustained over time by ritual and habit."[21] The church hands down the Christian narrative from generation to generation; its adherents are accountable to one another in terms of that shared narrative and through the practices that distinctively witness to its end, the Kingdom of God in Jesus Christ.[22] Liberal culture and politics, in contrast, view bound-edness to tradition as antithetical to individual freedom. They limit accountability to respecting that freedom in others, and consider social practices to be instruments, created by contracts of mutual self-interest, to the pursuit of individual desires. Rather than distancing themselves from tradition and history in freedom's name, the concern of Christians "must be to understand better how to live appropriately to the God whom we find in the narratives of Israel and Jesus, and how these stories help provide the means for recognizing and critically appropriating other stories that claim our lives."[23]

A reflective emphasis on the practices of the Christian community captures the right level of social concreteness and guards against idealistic interpretations of the church. Social practices are historical activities governed by standards of excellence and relations of authority conforming to these standards. They are defined with reference to the internal goods pursued within them, and thus virtues are the moral skills enabling more or less excellent pursuit of these goods.[24]

Let me risk a trivial example for the purposes of illustration. In the history of the game of basketball, defensive strategies have developed over time in a way that qualifies what it means to play "man-to-man" defense. One player has primary responsibility for guarding one opposing player (rather than for policing an area, as with zone defense); but each defensive player is also responsible for helping teammates when other opponents are in a position to score or otherwise advance his or her team's play. Learning how to be in a position to help requires a good sense of the spacing and movement of players on the basketball court, and of one's own place in the midst of that spacing and movement. It may involve stepping off the player one is guarding when he or she is in poor position to do much (e.g., when he or she is out of shooting range). Helping itself is a matter for careful judgment and fitting anticipation; you do not want to overcommit away from the player you are guarding, risking an easy pass to that player for a score. Skills of discrimination and justice are required in that you need to know what your opposition is due. Is your immediate opponent, for example, a good long range shooter? (If so, then beware of stepping off!) A weak shooter and strong rebounder? (Then don't lose track of his or her whereabouts and be sure to keep him from the "boards" when a shot goes up!) Moreover, you cannot worry exclusively (and perhaps selfishly) only about keeping your designated player from scoring. That misses the point, for you all are responsible to one another on defense for keeping the other team from scoring.

A player can, needless to say, be better or worse at this activity. One learns from coaches and other players who are presumed to be good at teaching and doing what is to be done. Hence, good performance requires acceptance of the relevant authorities and the standards they realize. Finally, though you may get to be so good at this and other related skills that you end up making a lot of money, the basic good involved here is internal to the practice. The idea is to learn to play defensive basketball well.

According to Hauerwas, a life of Christian discipleship should be comprehended along the lines of respect for authority, mutual accountability, habituation, and the attainment of virtues enabling realization of goods internal to the practice at hand. There are practices to be learned about resolving disputes among the faithful, teaching the tradition, reading Scripture, participating in Baptisms and the Lord's Supper, marrying and raising a family. The last is a favorite example. Prevailing liberal accounts of human sexuality tend to be either realistic or romantic. In the first case, you assume that people will decide to have sex with one another along their varying purposes and commitments. The moral task is to recommend realistic ways to handle this fact and the possible damage accompanying it (e.g., unintended pregnancies, the transmission of disease, and betrayed expectations). In the romantic view, you normatively build sexual expression on the love that exclusively authorizes it. These approaches only ratify individualism; sex, whether demystified or romanticized, remains a private matter governed by individual choices and feelings. Conservative sexual ethics (heterosexual spouses only!) falls flat in challenging these positions without the right sort of community and community practices to make that ethics intelligible. To see Christian marriage and family as a practice is to see it above all as a vocation to which one is called. It is neither a mere choice nor a mere natural necessity. Christian affirmation of the vocation to singleness underwrites this claim. For the sake of the Kingdom, one may not marry, and this possibility is a reminder that marriage and family themselves are neither our destiny nor our salvation, but acceptable forms of discipleship among others.

In the Christian community, the commitment to faithful partnership with one's particular spouse in marriage points to God's faithful commitment to Israel and the church. All will be brought to the Kingdom through this divine covenant, and Christians may learn something of this sort of fidelity in their married life.

Children may be welcomed in the trust that God's faithfulness does not flag, with the hope that his world continues to embody his sovereign, gracious rule, and with the patience that lets us take time to serve the vulnerable and dependent in unconditional love. If the family is deemed a school of virtue, it is not so as the backbone of liberal society. Against the background of other practices in the church, it teaches us to be not independent but bound within history in the service of one's fellow creatures. Also, practices and the virtues they teach call for authoritative expressions and exemplars that are accepted as such. But just this context of guidance and support within the Christian community tends to question the privatizing distortions of marriage and family in liberal culture. Thus these practices are a prototypically political venture.[25]

Three implications of the emphasis on the practices of the Christian life are important. First, the practices enable the development of virtues that in turn make possible the fuller understanding of the language of Christian faith. This is not to deny that Christians are constantly tested by preaching and hearing the Christian message. But preaching and hearing are themselves Christian practices interrelating with others. "The preached word's power is its capacity to create a people receptive to being formed by that word."[26]

Second, participation in these practices may display to the world its own limitations while rendering the church a "real option." The church is not to provide "an ethos for democracy or any other form of social organization, but stands as a political alternative to every nation, witnessing to the kind of social life possible for those that have been formed by the story of Christ."[27] As I will discuss, that kind of social life is identified crucially with the practice of nonviolence.

Third, moral discernment in the Christian community may commend, clarify, and complete some particular understanding of practices undertaken in cultural life outside the Christian community. Although Hauerwas speaks of the church as a contrast model, he also at times suggests that the church is not bound to model strict opposition to a world that still does not fail to belong to God. He sees the practice of medicine as morally significant for embodying the refusal to abandon embodied, mortal creatures who suffer among us. Medicine does this while struggling to maintain itself against the liberal dissolution of this commitment into one value preference among others. Hauerwas thinks that "medicine needs the church" to assist in this struggle; at the same time, "the fact that we believe that we have a common Creator provides a basis for some common experience and appeals."[28] One has to test these appeals in terms of the new life made possible in Jesus Christ. Now our author is not perfectly clear about this theme. I will return to it in chapter 6 by comparing it to his deep suspicion that theological appeals to creation are ideological concessions to prevailing culture.

Principalities, Powers, and the Peaceable Kingdom

Christian living is marked by peaceableness. It presupposes a people trusting in God's forgiveness and loyal to the divine cause of reconciliation and loving fellowship enacted through mercy's power. Discipleship is a community's faithfulness to Jesus Christ, who enacted God's rule through suffering nonviolent love.[29] Virtues of Christian character—forgiveness, patience, gratitude, hope, courage, justice—thus have a distinctive shape. The biblical narrative of Jesus sets a pattern to be extended in Christian common life; it sets the terms of narrative vision and defines and measures its central practices. The standpoint of discipleship, moreover, qualifies theologically the critique of liberalism, which refers not just to its erosive effects on narrativized ethics but also to its complicity in the dominative and idolatrous pretensions of the nation-state sustained by threats of violent power. Hence, this theological account governs more general categories in his ethics of character while also securing their social reality in the company of faith living in, with, for and against the world of unbelief.

Jesus Christ is "the presence of the peaceable Kingdom." "Possessed by the power of God," which "does not serve by forcing itself on others," Jesus "knows that the form of power which results from our being dispossessed of the powers currently holding our lives can come only as we freely give up those things and goods that possess us. But we do not dispossess ourselves just by our willing, but by being offered a way of selfless power."[30] The Kingdom of God, eschatologically proclaimed, is then "present insofar as his life reveals the effective power of God to create a transformed people capable of living peaceably in a violent world." Our true end is found in cross and resurrection, utter dispossession and humble rest in trust of God. It is a matter of learning to live "out of control," learning to be forgiven and to participate in God's community of peace. This is necessarily an education in nonviolence because violence "derives from the self-deceptive story that we are in control—that we are our own creators—and that only we can bestow meaning on our lives, since there is no one else to do so."[31]

Disciples seek justice nonviolently in patience and hope, but their strategies and judgments must emerge out of a common life constituted by prayer, preaching and hearing, mutual upbuilding and correction, and the practices of Baptism and the Eucharist. These last two fundamentally "are our effective social work. . . . It is in baptism and eucharist that we see most clearly the marks of God's kingdom in the world."[32] In fact, Hauerwas thinks that it is only by shaping theological ethics liturgically that we can recover it "as a tradition determined craft" or practice. "Insofar as ethics has a task peculiar to itself, that task is to assemble reminders from the training we receive in worship that enable us to rightly see the world as well as how we continue to be possessed by the world."[33] The practice of Baptism is an education in how our lives are not our own, but that we are members of the Body of Christ gathered to love and serve one another. Practices of suicide that deny the former lesson and paeans to the nuclear family that overturn the latter are challenged accordingly. The unity discovered through the Eucharist offers alternatives to community based on individualistic notions of ownership or the threat of violent force. "The peace of the eucharist is not the absence of violence or the violence that often appears as order, but rather it is the peace that comes from being made friends with God and with one another."[34] Thus Christian worship can develop skills of discriminating judgment about state and society.

Christians understand that the injustice that fails to answer to human needs and that perverts proper relationships among God's creatures should be resisted; however, the form of such resistance must not subvert but may only issue from the common life of the church. Nonviolent resistance is conditioned by hope that faithful witness to God "will be of use in God's care for the world," and by the patience that resists the temptation "to make history come out right" by our efforts apart from the way of discipleship.

Hauerwas's case for a discipleship of nonviolence sharpens his typical political critique. Liberalism does not merely dilute or reduce the integrity of faith by subjecting it, along with other particular traditional visions, to the abstract criteria of autonomy, rationality, and universality. By doing this, liberalism also masks the violent, dominative character of political relationships in societies like our own. For at least three reasons, it is an error to try to justify a politics founded on state coercion on the grounds that "we, the people" have somehow consented to that politics in the name of democracy, toleration, respect for pluralism, and so forth. First, genuine politics is not founded on coercion but on the nonviolent discovery and pursuit of goods commonly held and shared.

Second, the language of consent deludes us about our self-sufficiency and denies the extent to which our violent political ideologies hold us in their grip. Third, appeals to democracy, toleration, and pluralism tend to cover up struggles for ascendancy among powerful classes in society equipped with disproportionate amounts of economic, political, and cultural capital.[35] Or alternatively, such appeals limit motivations for social action to versions of autonomous self-interest, because no other basis can be found in a pluralistic society where citizens disagree so thoroughly about the full meaning of the good life. As a consequence, the citizens of liberal democracies "quite literally live off our wars because they give us the necessary basis for self-sacrifice so that a people who have been taught to pursue only their own interest can at times be mobilized to die for one another."[36] A truthful Christian social ethic has to be able "to sustain a people who are not at home in the liberal presumptions of our civilization and society."[37]

The very opposite has occurred in Christian thought and life. More and more Christian convictions "have lost their power to train us in the skills of truthfulness, partly because accounts of the Christian moral life have too long been accommodated to the needs of the nation state, and in particular, to the nation state we call the United States of America."[38] Hauerwas thinks that Paul Ramsey, for all of his criticism of cultural Christianity, was guilty of accommodation. Through espousal of normative positions like just war theory, he followed the path of Constantinianism, or the effort to preserve broad cultural significance by fitting the values of the nation-state into a loosely Christian framework. The tendency here is to water down Christian ethics, as in the case of the "democratic policing of Christianity," in which American Social Gospel thinkers (e.g., Walter Rauschenbusch) and their critics (e.g., Reinhold Niebuhr) adapt their theologies to the presumption that "democratic social processes are the most appropriate expression of Christian convictions."

Constantinian strategies sacrifice Christian identity for the sake of social empowerment; but they turn out ironically to have contributed to the disempowering of Christians in a world where religious convictions have either become irrelevant to or mere images of the liberal and nationalist convictions of the powers that be. But Hauerwas sees an opportunity to be grasped. "Since no one expects Christians to make the world safe, since Christians are no longer required to supply the ideologies necessary to 'govern,' because Christians are not expected to be able to provide philosophical justifications to insure the ways things are or the way things should be, we are free to be Christians."[39] And that freedom is nothing less than to witness as a peaceable people formed by Jesus Christ. It is a freedom that may, by accepting "the grace of doing nothing," make "the independence of the church" more a reality. Its captivity to nationalism, capitalism, and liberalism may be overcome.

This last description of Hauerwas's position puts him in direct contact with a set of remarkable writings by H. Richard Niebuhr in the 1930s. Reflecting on American and Christian responses to Japan's invasion of Manchuria, Niebuhr argued for a Christian inactivity of rigid self-analysis, the renunciation of self-interest, repentance, and faith. The inactivity involves the building of "cells of those within each nation who, divorcing themselves from the program of nationalism and of capitalism, unite in a higher loyalty which transcends national and class lines of division and prepare for the future." The move might make possible a vision of what is going on that itself could contribute to the creation of conditions under which a genuine "reconstruction of habits" may take place. The Christian way of doing nothing is not pessimistic or politically realist or indignantly pacifist or a purely historicist or Marxist preparation for what is inevitably to come in time. It does not pretend to greater righteousness but waits patiently and hopefully, fully cognizant of Christian complicity in the suffering of the innocent and of the need for works of mercy to ease present pain "while the process of healing depends on deeper, more actual and urgent forces."[40] Niebuhr's stance presupposes a fundamental trust in the reality of the sovereign God who judges human iniquity yet brings human history to its fulfillment through the call to repentance and the offer of forgiveness.[41]

I think that the alignment between Niebuhr's account and Hauerwas's ethic of discipleship is considerable. The latter stresses the virtues of patience and hope as necessary to sustain inactivity amid the violent alternatives presented by the world. The development of these virtues requires a spiritual discipline nurtured in the practices of the church, and through them "we are slowly recalled from the world of violence that we might envisage how interesting a people at peace might be."[42] Hauerwas also fears the situation of the captive church that Niebuhr described in his 1935 contribution to *The Church against the World*, coauthored with Francis Miller and Wilhelm Pauck. Bound to a "faith in wealth . . . as the savior of man from his deepest misery," to confidence in the nation as a supreme value, and to an affirmation of the utter sufficiency of humanity, this

is a church which seeks to prove its usefulness to civilization, in terms of civilization's own demands. It is a church which has lost the distinctive note and the earnestness of a Christian disciplines of life and has become the teacher of the prevailing code of morals and the pantheon of the social gods. It is a church, moreover, which has become entangled with the world in its desire for the increase of its power and prestige and which shares the worldly fear of insecurity.[43]

Summing Up

These resonances can be acknowledged without overlooking Hauerwas's sharp criticisms of Niebuhr's conversionism; I will consider them in the following chapter. Nevertheless, Niebuhr's legacy includes not only a theological program directing attention to the nature of the moral self and its temporal life in an internal narrative history, but also to substantive claims regarding the possibilities and limits of engagement between church and world. Assuming the necessary qualifications, we can say that Hauerwas takes up that legacy.

His work, as we have seen, dynamically orients the language of Christian faith to three fields of social location: (1) His early writings on moral character initially relied on an explication of human agency that he later dismissed as individualistic, and an account of vision that made epistemological sense but lacked social concreteness. The sociality of the human agent is more effectively affirmed with Hauerwas's stress on community as the context for development of moral character, and on narrative as the social and historical correlate to vision. (2) Even the appeal to community is too abstract on its own, however; thus Hauerwas rightly seeks to depict how a life shared and shaped within the practices of the church is the locus of a Christian ethics of character. (3) Finally, he needs to situate this life within the social context of the world, and argues for its distinctiveness over against the false neutrality of liberalism and the idolatrous pretensions of nationalism. Christians who do not recognize this context and accommodate to these ideologies imperil faithful witness. In his Gifford Lectures, Hauerwas more than ever honors Karl Barth's theology for the way it challenges Christians to "relearn the grammar of their faith;" just so his *Church Dogmatics* "with its unending and confident display of Christian speech, is Barth's attempt to train us to be a people capable of truthful witness to the God who alone is the truth." He finds Barth's own example, both theologically imperialistic (from liberalism's standpoint) and antinationalistic, to be deeply compelling.[44]

The project of situating and resituating Christian discourse has continued in Hauerwas's work. For example, he has come to suspect abstract appeals to community on the grounds that they can reflect either liberal presuppositions or a general and self-contradictory counterliberalism that by itself serves too much the claims of the nation-state. That is to say, we have either pluralistic communities that avoid real and important social conflict by appealing to the shared value of autonomy, or "communities formed by alienated selves who are created by liberalism." The second Hauerwas dubs "a kind of fascism"— family values, it turns out, is how Americans talk about "blood and soil."[45] The church is not a community, after all, if these are the going and growing cultural senses of the term; it is, instead, the Body of Christ, "constituted by disciplines that create the capacity to resist the disciplines of the body associated with the modern nation state and, in particular, the economic habits that support that state."[46] This church may be present even as it embodies a cultural Christianity that forms in its members the keen sense that their membership is nonvoluntary, a discipline to which one submits rather than just another consumer preference for a life option.[47]

Recall the criticisms that Hauerwas is sectarian, tribalist, and fideist, and consider how he responds. The work of the church is not to withdraw from the world, but to engage it as such, exposing its falsehood and displaying its conflict with the peaceable Kingdom in relevant respects. If the church is against the world in this sense, it is not for purposes of maintaining internal purity but part of fidelity to and service of neighbors who live in this world.

To say that Christian ethics is for Christians is not to say, tribalistically, that it is not for anyone else. To the contrary, it is for everyone else, every human creature of God, to whom new life has been offered in Jesus Christ. It is a life that may resist the real tribalism of the nation-state, which would command a loyalty so total and so local as to require killing other fellow creatures in its name. Hauerwas's play on the language of the body above, finally, suggests that his is not a strictly fideist ethic unintelligible to outsiders. He relies on a comprehensible contrast between the body as possessed and controlled by an indivisibly individual subject (a liberal view, according to Hauerwas), and the body as given and shared by incorporation into Christ by the power of the Holy Spirit. This incorporation is made manifest in the disciplines and practices of the church that nurture the virtues of Christian life before God.

Notes

1. Stanley Hauerwas, *Character and the Christian Life* (San Antonio: Trinity University Press, 1985), 233. The book was originally published in 1975.
2. For Hauerwas's discussion of these sorts of criticisms, see John Berkman and Michael Cartwright, eds., *The Hauerwas Reader* (Durham, N.C.: Duke University Press, 2001), 90–110.
3. Here I follow Ramsey in his claim that the way of justified-war Christians and pacifists are "equally Christian discipleships"; Paul Ramsey, *Speak Up for Just War or Pacifism* (University Park: Pennsylvania State University Press, 1988), 123.
4. Hauerwas, *Character and the Christian Life*, xiii, xvi.
5. Ibid., 11.
6. Ibid., 203.
7. Stanley Hauerwas, *Vision and Virtue* (Notre Dame, Ind.: Fides Publishers, 1974), 2–3; cf. 11–29.
8. Hauerwas, *Character and the Christian Life*, 231, 232.
9. Cf. H. Richard Niebuhr, *The Responsible Self* (New York: Harper & Row, 1963), 42–68.
10. Hauerwas, *Character and the Christian Life*, xx. Cf. Stanley Hauerwas, "Agency: Going Forward by Looking Back," in Lisa Sowle Cahill and James F. Childress, eds., *Christian Ethics: Problems and Prospects* (Cleveland: Pilgrim Press, 1996), 185–95.
11. Cf. Alasdair MacIntyre, *After Virtue* (Notre Dame, Ind.: University of Notre Dame Press, 1991), 194.
12. MacIntyre, *After Virtue*, 216.
13. Stanley Hauerwas, *The Peaceable Kingdom* (Notre Dame, Ind.: University of Notre Dame Press, 1983), 28–30.
14. Stanley Hauerwas, *Truthfulness and Tragedy* (Notre Dame, Ind.: University of Notre Dame Press, 1977), 15–39.
15. Ibid., 152–53.
16. H. Richard Niebuhr, *The Meaning of Revelation* (New York: Macmillan, 1941), 52–53.
17. Ibid., 51–52.
18. Hauerwas, *Truthfulness and Tragedy*, 16–17, 23.
19. I question whether Hauerwas completely avoids the latter direction in "Narrative and Ethics in Barth," *Theology Today* 43, no. 3 (October 1986): 334–53. I now think that he moved farther away from this tendency in more recent writings.

20. Stanley Hauerwas, *Community of Character* (Notre Dame, Ind.: University of Notre Dame Press, 1981), 12.

21. Ibid., 92.

22. Hauerwas, *Peaceable Kingdom*, 45–46.

23. Hauerwas, *Community of Character*, 96.

24. Cf. MacIntyre, *After Virtue*, 186–91.

25. See Hauerwas, *Community of Character*, 155–95. Hauerwas extends this line of reflection in "Resisting Capitalism: On Marriage and Homosexuality," in his *A Better Hope* (Grand Rapids, Mich.: Brazos Press, 2000), 47–51.

26. Stanley Hauerwas, *Christian Existence Today* (Durham, N.C.: Labyrinth Press, 1988), 60.

27. Hauerwas, *Community of Character*, 12.

28. Ibid., 106.

29. John Howard Yoder has had great influence on Hauerwas's development as a Christian ethicist. See, e.g., Hauerwas, *Better Hope*, 129–36, and the essays listed in *Hauerwas Reader*, 10 n. 13.

30. Hauerwas, *Peaceable Kingdom*, 80–81.

31. Ibid., 83, 94.

32. Ibid., 108.

33. Stanley Hauerwas, *In Good Company* (Notre Dame, Ind.: University of Notre Dame Press, 1995), 156.

34. Ibid., 162.

35. Stanley Hauerwas, *Dispatches from the Front* (Durham, N.C.: Duke University Press, 1994), 98–107.

36. Stanley Hauerwas and William H. Willimon, *Resident Aliens* (Nashville: Abingdon Press, 1989), 35.

37. Stanley Hauerwas, *Against the Nations* (New York: Winston Press, 1985), 12.

38. Ibid., 6.

39. Ibid., 17.

40. H. Richard Niebuhr, "The Grace of Doing Nothing," in Richard B. Miller, ed., *War in the Twentieth Century* (Louisville: Westminster/John Knox Press, 1992), 6–11.

41. H. Richard Niebuhr, "A Communication: The Only Way Into the Kingdom of God," in Miller, *War in the Twentieth Century*, 19–21. Here Niebuhr responded to his brother Reinhold's criticism of "The Grace of Doing Nothing." The criticisms of "Must We Do Nothing?" are also found in the Miller volume.

42. Hauerwas, *Peaceable Kingdom*, 150.

43. H. Richard Niebuhr, "The Church against the World," in Sidney E. Ahlstrom, ed., *Theology in America* (Indianapolis: Bobbs-Merrill, 1967), 608; H. Richard

Niebuhr, Wilhelm Pauck, and Francis P. Miller, *The Church against the World* (Chicago and New York: Willet, Clark, and Co., 1935).

44. Stanley Hauerwas, *With the Grain of the Universe: The Church's Witness and Natural Theology, Being the Gifford Lectures Delivered at the University of St. Andrews in 2001* (Grand Rapids, Mich.: Brazos Press, 2001), 176, 179.

45. Hauerwas, *Dispatches from the Front*, 158.

46. Hauerwas, *In Good Company*, 26.

47. Stanley Hauerwas, *Sanctify Them in the Truth* (Nashville: Abingdon, 1998), 157–73.

CHAPTER SIX

Politics, Creation, and Conversion

In this chapter, I pose some critical questions regarding Stanley Hauerwas's Christian ethics. I begin by looking at his criticism of just war theory, and then take up his approach to liberalism, the church's "double wrestle" with Christ and culture, and H. Richard Niebuhr's book of the same name. It is easy to jump to conclusions on each of these themes. Because he is a Christian pacifist, Hauerwas could be taken to disavow responsibility for a world governed by authorities that have to employ force, and perhaps violent force, to secure some justice and peace in political society.[1] Because he says that liberal justice is "a bad idea for Christians,"[2] inferences may be drawn that at best he has nothing to say, and cares to say nothing, about the moral responsibilities that citizens have to one another in civic and political life.

One way to summarize this line of analysis is to look at *Christ and Culture*, and derive from that book the challenge that Hauerwas is an adherent of the "necessary and inadequate"[3] model of Christ against culture. These conclusions are not fair to Hauerwas; but he can make clearer how they are mistaken (1) by complementing his critique of Constantinianism with continuing acknowledgment and probing of a Christian responsibility to witness to the state; and (2) by developing the way his ethics refer substantively to human creaturely life. *Christ and Culture*, a book that Hauerwas seems to love to hate, offers a number of theological cautions and convictions that he might well heed without compromising his core criticisms and commitments.

Speaking Up about Just War

Hauerwas's response to just war consists of two general arguments. First, he opposes the theory insofar as it underwrites Christian loyalty to the order of violence rejected and overcome by Jesus Christ and,

specifically, to the idolatrous claims of the nation-state as it is constituted by the use of violence. As a Christian theory of responsible involvement in politics, just war becomes a mode of Constantinian accommodation to secular power. Following John Howard Yoder,
Hauerwas takes Constantinianism to denote "the identification of the
church's mission and the meaning of history with the function of the
state in organizing sinful society"; but "the meaning of history is not
what the state will achieve in the way of progressively more tolerable
ordering of society, but what the church achieves through evangelism
and through the leavening process."[4] Thus Paul Ramsey's defense of
just war, Hauerwas says in one essay, "becomes a blanket justification for the 'states' that exist and the present configuration of these
states in the international arena." Hence "it is difficult to see how just
war might actually function to tell a state it could not go to war."[5]

Second, Hauerwas qualifiedly endorses just war thinking if and only
if it is embedded within the common life of Christian discipleship. "It
has long been my suspicion," he writes, "that if we could force just
war thinkers (and churches) to recognize the kind of communities necessary to sustain the discourses and practices necessary for just war, it
would make it increasingly difficult to accuse pacifists of being hopeless 'idealists' and/or 'sectarians.'"[6] He admits that "just war can be
understood as an attempt to discipline the power of the state" as long
as just war Christians are able to use their theory "with integrity exactly to the extent they assume a position of resistance to the state not
unlike that of their pacifist sister and brother."[7]

The arguments depend on a commitment to the dual character of
Christ's redemptive work for church and world. Hauerwas takes his
cue here from Yoder, who conceives of present history in terms of the
coexistence of two ages or "aeons." The old aeon of sin, already overcome but futilely resisting the kingdom's supercession of it, is ordered
to Jesus Christ in the use of violence against itself for the purpose of
its limitation. The cycle of vengeance answering vengeance maintains
peace so that all persons may have access to the witness of the Gospel.
The state is part of the old aeon in its external ordering to Christ; it
does its job when it protects the innocent, punishes evildoers, and preserves the fabric of society. In contrast, the new aeon is the common
life of discipleship founded in Christ, "who is God's agape—self-giving

nonresistant love."[8] Its task is evangelization and witness. Although both aeons fall within the realm of redemptive grace, the meaning of history lies only in the creation and work of the church.

Thus Christian responsibility is marked by a necessary duality that corresponds, respectively, to the audiences of faith and unbelief. What the Christian takes as finally normative, following the way of Christ, cannot apply to the unbeliever; but Christian witness to the world may include addressing the state in terms of its proper police function of limiting violence. For example, democracy, though liable to criticism as an ideology luring folks to believe self-deceptively in the people's authorship of government and in the full moral appropriateness of autonomous self-interest, might more modestly refer to the least oppressive oligarchy. It contains the greatest number of controls to mitigate the oppressiveness of coercion (e.g., procedures approaching consent of the governed, checks and balances, and guaranteed personal rights against the government).

Christians should hold the democratic state accountable in these terms and for this reason, recognizing that coercive control is essential to the state and as a fact comes before any justification of it. Christian witness to the democratic state can also include defense of the "dignity of dissent," "the ability of the outsider, the other, the critic, to speak and be heard."[9] The responses presume both that the state be held to its rightful role of containing violence to a minimum, and that the state tends of its nature to make illegitimate religious claims to loyalty in the very act of placing "the authority of its police arm behind its pretension to represent an ideal order."[10] No exercise of violent dominion is very far from self-glorification, and for this reason Hauerwas and Yoder reject Christian theories of the state or of the ideal political society—they can serve idolatry while deflecting attention from the fundamental contrast between the sword and the self-giving, nonviolent love of discipleship.

Christian pacifists may call for eliminating specific abuses and injustices in the social and political order. They may try to advance human values that are "somehow subject to Christian formative influences." These concern the "entire fabric of human togetherness," and include honesty, mutual respect, hard work, unselfishness, and tolerance. Through moral osmosis, nonbelievers may dwell within this normative fabric; yet Christians will also seek to protect this fabric from the idea that it is subject to state control or valuable only or mostly in the service of the state. They will speak out on behalf of widows, orphans, enemies, "those categories of persons . . . excluded from the economic and social privileges of the strong."[11] Always and everywhere, the most just and least violent policy is commended, and the pattern of critique and realistic commendation finds no bottom, no stopping point. The life of witness extends to envisioning nonviolent alternatives in social life and to participation "in the many activities in societies and states that do not involve violence."[12]

Christian pacifist discipleship seeks to draw a strong contrast between war and the domestic police function. The latter "can distinguish the innocent from the guilty and maintain a semblance of order, whereas war cannot."[13] Yet "a continuum of increasing tolerability, leading from total disorder to the Kingdom of God," applies to pacifist witness even in wartime. The primary concern, again, is to restrain violence as much as possible, and to this end just war criteria of proportionality, discrimination, last resort, right intention, and the like work to distinguish wars as more or less unjust.[14]

The duality of Christian witness is perhaps most evident here, because a logic of recommending the lesser evil does not govern the lives of disciples. But it is also the case, according to Yoder, that the recommendations to representatives of government are a sort of evangelization. "What we ask of him does not cease to be gospel by virtue of the fact that we relate it to his present available options. It is rather the gospel itself in relation to his present situation," so that a commitment to reverse direction and honor the principle of discrimination, for example, may be seen as a step of obedience, an act of repentance, a leap of faith made possible "in the strength of the Holy Spirit and in the name of Jesus Christ."[15] And as for the disciples themselves, efforts at protest or civil disobedience "will be most appropriate when it is most possible to distinguish between their witness function and a self-seeking participation in the power struggle. The difficulty of making this distinction . . . cannot justify avoiding such channels of witness entirely."[16]

Hauerwas put his dual understanding of just war to work in a critical commentary on the Persian Gulf War.[17] On the one hand, he claims that just war thinking "made it more difficult for Christians to distinguish their story from the story of the United States of America." Elements of "political realism" and the American penchant for fighting crusades, or wars waged with unlimited means for unlimited ends, were covered up and not corrected by just war ideology. During the war, Hauerwas charges, U.S. leaders used just war criteria to serve national interests more than justice; spin control and disinformation ran rampant to thwart the citizenry's acquisition of information necessary to render moral judgment on just war grounds; and the illusion that just war embodies a universal moral rationality supported the exercise of imperial power at the same time that it blinded the imperialists to what they were, in fact, doing.

On the other hand, Hauerwas appeals to the theory, explicitly and implicitly, in the course of his critique—to the demands that wars be fought for limited ends and with limited means, that they not be identified with crusades or wars of national interest *simpliciter*, and to the requirement that wars be prosecuted discriminately and proportionately, even if this requires that more American combatant lives are placed in jeopardy. The crucial factor for Hauerwas (and for Yoder) is the social and moral credibility of the theory—which can only be advanced by rooting it within a community committed to practices of nonviolence, forgiveness, and peacemaking. The challenge applies to Christians across the board. "Are there people," Yoder asks, "who affirm that their own uncoerced allegiance as believers gives them strength and motivation to honor the restraints of the just-war tradition and to help one another do so? . . . Would believers commit themselves, and commit themselves to press each other, to be willing to enter the political opposition, or to resign public office, or to espouse selective objection? Does any church teach future soldiers and citizens in such a way that they will know beyond what point they cannot support an unjust war or use an unjust weapon?"[18]

The same pattern of ideological critique and selective reorientation is present when Hauerwas takes on Paul Ramsey. On the one hand, Ramsey's just war theory is Constantinian. It presupposes that there is yet and should in any case be a Christian civilization. It represents an unstable compromise with realism, the view that "violence is the character of our relations, both individually and in groups."[19] On the other hand, the Christian community, constantly exploring the depths of human violence and the possibilities of conversion from it, may perfectly well "use just war theory to communicate to those whose language it is (Christian or not) to call them to their own vision of their integrity as well as making them less violent."[20]

How shall we assess this approach to just war? I agree that the theory is liable to distortion, and that its Christian employment requires something of the social rootedness in nonviolence that Hauerwas describes. My criticism of Ramsey in chapter 4 indicated how Hauerwas's vision is a corrective to the tendency to distance the care and nurturance of Christian discourse from the social contexts of distinctive Christian practices. However, Hauerwas's recurring charge of Constantinianism against Ramsey and others can oversimplify, and maybe even distort, the sort of defensible Christian vision that animates some just war stances. In fact, I think that vision overlaps with Hauerwas's Christian pacifism, as it also stands in clear contrast to it. Both the overlap and the contrast establish a basis for fruitful exchange between these "equally Christian discipleships."[21]

Recall that Ramsey's approach to the political order is in relevant respects similar to the shared stance of Hauerwas and Yoder. Government, or the state, is conceived theologically in terms of the use of violence against itself to protect the innocent, restrain the wicked, and make for a kind of peace. Now Ramsey counts this as a divine order of preservation, which Christians may have a vocation to serve and which is not separate from love's transforming impulse. The conflicts within the life of a people may also be present between peoples, when different "combinations of will over the necessities of life" run up against and threaten one another.

Here also the Christian may find himself or herself called to participate in the *ultima* ratio of war, in loving service of neighbor through a resistance that he or she would not pursue solely for oneself. Hauerwas and Yoder, of course, cannot agree to this, and even in the case of the domestic police force there remains a degree of doubt about the legitimacy of such a call.[22] But the gap between them and Ramsey may be explained in terms of an Augustinian ethic of the two cities that also makes room for some agreement.

According to Saint Augustine's ethic, the love of God and self-love define the *civitas dei* and *civitas terrena* respectively; the life of secular political order, however, includes citizens of both. The Christian makes fitting use of the earthly peace of this order. He or she "finds his own life and will bound up inextricably with such a common agreement among men as to the objects of their political purposes, and he is bound to foster the combination of men's wills to attain the things which are helpful to this life."[23] This means that political society is a site in which the two cities—with their competing allegiances socially expressed in practices and institutions directed toward a temporal peace—intermingle.

The meaning of responsibility to God's "preservative ordinances" may come clear in terms of this intermingling. Christian activity for an acceptable common creaturely good regarding what is helpful in this life, or in response to the genuine needs of the neighbor, finds itself shot through with alien purposes and presumptions, above all the threat and use of violent force. He or she lives by trust and also lives in a system of distrust, serving the neighbor.[24] Hence love may be expressed in the "alien work" of violent resistance to oppression or exploitation of the innocent; and if we have a real intermingling of cities rather than a normative subordination of one love to another, or a mere compromise, underwritten by violence, between trust and distrust, then two far-reaching consequences follow for Christian life. The first is that the use of coercive or lethal force must evoke horror in the bearer of it. The same act "is at once inhuman and terrible, and it is an expression of love." Resistance is "a duty which can only be done with a shudder."[25] Second, the goods of political activity are always for the Christian caught up with the recognition that they are fleeting, transient, the barely comforting marks of a life that is invariably loved too much and doomed to final judgment.

The logic of Ramsey's argument for just war and Christian political responsibility permits and requires these two qualifications. His acknowledgment of the first is uncertain at best; yet some of his later work implies that the explication of wartime killing as "functional incapacitation" is to be taken with the greatest moral and spiritual seriousness. In a theologically important sense, such killing must not be the same as the killing of a human creature *simpliciter*, no less than that killing should be motivated out of hatred or the lust for revenge. The analysis makes a place for the "shudder," and from Ramsey's Augustinian standpoint both pacifist and strictly realist political critiques fail to take the intermingling of the two cities seriously enough. Ramsey referred to the second qualification in his last writing on just war:

> The intermingling of the Two Cities is through the heart of every just war Christian. We live in the midst of a people—whose history and future are ours also—who cannot vividly imagine that democracy, freedom, as we know it, America, the Constitution, are among those tragic empires, built and upheld while we dreaming weep, haunted by a future when all these things, too, shall have passed away. We belong to this temporal city and are engaged in the continuance of it, yet our citizenship is also in another city, not made with hands, whose builder and maker is God and his Christ.[26]

An implication is that Christian involvement in political life to serve the neighbor always coincides with a readiness for recoil, a disposition to draw back in discovery of how some needed and valuable work is complicit in the vain efforts of states to glorify themselves. The stance of the Christian citizen may oscillate between withdrawal and engagement. Thus, in the final book of *The City of God*, readers are urged to keep watch in the midst of this miserable life "to make sure that we are not deluded by plausible suggestions, or deceived by clever talk, or immersed in the darkness of error, for fear that we may believe evil to be good, or good evil, that fear may distract us from doing our duty, that 'the sun' may 'set on our anger,' that hostility may provoke us into returning evil for evil, that dishonorable or immoderate sadness may overwhelm us, that an unthankful heart make us sluggish in doing acts of kindness."[27] We might add: Keep watch in the midst of the turmoil of political life, lest our acquiescence leave some possible good undone, or lest our citizenship give comfort to vanity, manipulation, and tyranny. If this was not Ramsey's view, it should have been.

Hauerwas's critique of Ramsey's Constantinianism can tend to miss or cover up these matters. Disclosing them points to some overlap between Hauerwas's pacifism and Ramsey's just war theory. Both acknowledge ways that violence is alien to Christian discipleship, and both explore strategies for limiting violence in common life. Both are suspicious of the idolatrous tendencies of violent political order. Yet in their contrast, each also poses hard challenges to the other. One has to ask of the two-cities just war position what sort of common Christian life, with its practices and disciplines, could possibly maintain an integrity of witness that rules out hatred of the enemy and idolatrous nationalism. And pacifist discipleship must attend to how exactly creative responses to a violent world can emerge from that common life, without close attention to the meaning of just war theory and to the avenues of citizenship that enable and open up a grasp of the moral character of statecraft and political relationships among peoples. Note here Ramsey's suggestion that pacifism is a doctrine addressed to the church, whereas just war theory applies to states. I believe that the overlaps and the tensions as I have presented them permits constructive conversation between just war and pacifism, as the former looks anew to the disciplines of the church that give it life, and the latter takes with appropriate seriousness its faithful witness to the state.

Christ and Culture

The vigor with which Hauerwas goes after just war is matched by his challenges to liberalism. The two inquiries are connected. He wants to expose liberalism as an ideology of domination that masks itself as a sweetly reasonable philosophy of pluralism, justice, or respect for persons. Adherence to the first notion tends to sacrifice distinctive Christian convictions; the second advances the tendency while importing unacceptable assumptions about the primacy of the individual and his or her rights. The third extends the individualism by dangerously stripping moral analysis of any substantive norms save those that identify personal autonomy as the ground of respect. Thus we have the legitimation of both the all-encompassing bureaucratic state, equipped to protect individual rights, and an all-encompassing theory of citizenship whose reality is conditioned by the duty of military service.[28] The acceptance of liberal presuppositions and projects breaks the integrity of Christian witness and the ability of disciples to address state power truthfully. Correlatively, the powers of the state to control life and demand allegiance are given a friendly face and proceed unchecked.

Hence Hauerwas is suspicious of theologies of creation and preservation because they so often are, or so readily can become, Constantinian accommodations. Ramsey's stress on the principle of informed consent and the primacy of the individual in medical ethics seems only to prop up liberal assumptions, for example. Hauerwas ignores Ramsey's commitments to fellow humanity as developed in chapter 3; but even if he had not his point would be that that account of the human creature, if split away from the radical demands of the Gospel, would be an overly formal portrayal that in our social context can seem to owe more to Kant and contracts than it does to the life of faith. Certainly Hauerwas sees just war theory, evidently a reflection on the meaning of God's preservative ordinances, as playing into the hands of the idol state's claim on our lives.

The same kind of criticism is applied to other Christian ethicists. Oliver O'Donovan's suggestions that, in relation to modern reproductive technology, Christians affirm the natural order as God's good creation, divine providence in history, and the norm of fellow humanity are found to be inadequate because "O'Donovan seeks an account of natural law that is not governed by the eschatological witness of Christ's resurrection." Though not denying "that we are creatures of God's good creation," Hauerwas is "simply suggesting that as Christians we know nothing about what we mean by creation separate from the new order we find through the concrete practices of baptism and Eucharist, correlative as they are to Christ's resurrection."[29]

Dennis McCann, David Hollenbach, and similarly minded Roman Catholics are also chided for too quickly commending political virtues and bonds that buy into American liberalism. McCann's pleas for public civility in the church in the name of human sociality appears only to serve the "forces of modernity that grind all genuine disputes into calm conversations." Civility in our time and place simply puts the name of virtue to the separation and "bureaucratization of private affect and public demeanor." Hollenbach's call to respect human dignity by seeking "justice as participation" and appreciating "new possibilities . . . for expressing love of one's neighbor by engaging in the march of cultural transformation . . . turns out to be another way to say Catholics should be good Americans."[30]

These criticisms are overstated. O'Donovan's claims on behalf of "created order" depend explicitly upon God's self-revelation in the resurrection of Jesus Christ. He wants to say both that there is a certain natural knowledge of morality that is part of humanity's created endowment and that "only in Christ do we apprehend that order in which we stand and that knowledge of it with which we are endowed."[31] Roman Catholic reflection is put aside here without guarded attention to the way McCann and Hollenbach can rely on working understandings of creaturely flourishing grounded in Christ's vindication of humanity in Incarnation, cross, and resurrection.[32] Of course, the criticisms do pose the proper question of what creation, preservation, and redemption can and ought to mean in Christian ethics. Hauerwas relentlessly reminds his readers of the corruptions accompanying so much Christian use of "creation talk";[33] but is there no fitting and articulated employment of the whole idea of God, no usage that inevitably and by its own logic corrupts?

In fact, and as I mentioned in chapter 5, Hauerwas affirms the possibility and necessity of fitting employment throughout his work. His ethics often refer to moral realities that are meaningfully described as creaturely or as part of an order of preservation. To the degree that he shares with Yoder a qualified acceptance of the police function of the state, ordered to the work of Christ and Christian evangelization, he falls in line with the second category. If he concedes that by moral osmosis a realm of human values may be built up in non-Christian communities by way of contact with disciples, he seems to be relying on some common creatureliness to which the osmosis, and even its status as a sort of evangelization, refer. He intimates reliance in one of his very best essays, a study of the virtue of peaceableness and the time it takes and makes for us. The university in this account, for example, is not a means to peace but

> a form of peace. . . . Universities are dedicated to continuing the conversation across centuries of the hard-won wisdom of people who often sharply disagree. The university is committed to exposing these disagreements, believing that by so doing our lives will be lived more honestly and richly. The university, therefore, stands as an activity that thrives on disagreements while believing that such disagreements can never be resolved by violence.[34]

Christians have faith that in following Jesus Christ, the peace of God, they may learn to "make the peace around us more fully ours. Such a theological appeal, however, is not extranatural but rather the means through which we come to see the naturalness of peace."[35] Here are the rudiments of a theology in which common goods of creation are valued in their integrity at the same time as they are taken to be ordered Christologically.

By his own admission, Hauerwas's *Suffering Presence*, a study in medical ethics, is a corrective to his tendency "to fail to do justice to contingent 'points of contact' between Christian convictions and the world."[36] Much of the book's argument presupposes an appreciation of the moral practice of medicine, according to which practitioners teach the "wisdom of the body" to the sick while always never abandoning them in their illness and accompanying aloneness. Clearly, this analysis is based on Hauerwas's vision of charity-informed virtues as they arise in the life of discipleship; but it is just as clear that it also depends on a positive view of the goods proper and available to God's human creatures as such. He holds that the practice of medicine needs the church to bring to it (by moral osmosis?) something of the faithfulness to the suffering that it requires; the external condition of this holding, however, is some notion along the lines that human creatures are made for this kind of fidelity in the relevant medical relationships.[37]

My claim is not that Hauerwas's arguments require a view of creatureliness that is separated from an account of the person and work of Jesus Christ or the witness of the Body of Christ; nor would I deny that in an important sense the disciple's new life in Christ crucially affects the Christian's understanding of what God's restoration of human creatures means. I am proposing that Hauerwas's ethics include and require a substantive reference to human creaturely life, to forms of human relationship that in their goodness cut across the distinction between Christians and non-Christians. They involve shared goods and solidarities in areas of human activity that obtain even while that distinction is appropriately maintained. Hauerwas's sense of urgency about the problem of the church's accommodation to the world may lead him to find this kind of reference untimely or secondary. But how could he rule it out or not welcome it, bearing as it does on the whole idea of God?

In fact, Hauerwas's most recent work seems to offer a theological basis for a creaturely reference in Karl Barth's view that all human beings exist and stand in the light of Jesus Christ.[38] But his continuing reluctance would be based, I think, on a conviction that Christian ethics in the United States just does use languages of creation and preservation to support Constantinianism, or, to make matters more concrete, "America" itself.[39] The conviction is fueled by a severe assessment of H. Richard Niebuhr's approach to the problem of Christ and culture. In *Resident Aliens*, Hauerwas and William H. Willimon present the case:

> We have come to believe that few books have been a greater hindrance to an accurate assessment of our situation than *Christ and Culture*. Niebuhr rightly saw that our politics determines our theology. He was right that Christians cannot reject "culture." But his call to Christians to accept culture (where is this monolithic "culture" Niebuhr describes?) and politics in the name of the unity of God's creating and redeeming activity had the effect of endorsing a Constantinian social strategy. "Culture" becomes a blanket term to underwrite Christian involvement with the world without providing any discriminating modes for discerning how Christians should see the good or the bad in "culture."[40]

More specific criticisms are made quickly and hit hard. Niebuhr's rigging of his typology to create a stark either/or between world affirmation and world denial obscures Christian history and theological insight. His pluralistic approach, in which his preference for the fifth type comes clear but with a disavowal regarding *the* Christian answer, gives a "theological rationale for liberal democracy," which also claims this pluralism while simultaneously rejecting "narrower" views of the Christian life. "*Christ and Culture* thus stands as a prime example of repressive tolerance"; points of view are ruled out in the name of a stance putatively opening out to difference. This is a book that justifies the self-congratulatory church transforming the world as it is tamed by it. It implicitly denounces alternative approaches as sectarian, and suggests that the church should be willing to suppress its peculiarities in order to participate responsibly in the culture.[41]

The attack reflects Yoder's influential study of *Christ and Culture*.[42] He has (at least) four sorts of problems with that book that relate to Hauerwas's own. First, he thinks that Niebuhr combines excessive typological solidity with nonfalsifiability. His five types (Christ against culture, Christ of culture, etc.) seem to dictate the character of different Christian stances in an exclusive way; "you are either a radical or not, and therefore an accommodationist, synthesist, and so on." Thus Yoder complains that *Christ and Culture* puts so-called radicals of his Mennonite faith "in a box in which they do not recognize themselves," and Hauerwas adds with him that Christian history is distorted accordingly. The problem is made worse because Niebuhr does not show how to test his typology critically (e.g., by showing how it might in fact limit descriptions of historical phenomena in a helpful way, or bring proper attention to the diversity of the phenomena, or display a logic of historical development). "The charm of *Christ and Culture* on the superficial level is its flaw on the fundamental level; it can hardly be falsified by any kind of test which Niebuhr could suggest. Thereby its power to convince by seeming to project great clarity is spurious."[43]

Second, for Yoder Niebuhr speaks as a partisan of one of the types (conversionism), but distances himself conveniently from criticism by claiming a humble appreciation of pluralism in Christian life and history. The strategy leads to the repressive tolerance of delegitimizing theologies that do not measure up to the same humility and respect for difference. It also seems both to authorize and be authorized by a parallel strategy in liberal democratic politics in which communal particularity is constantly undermined by appeals to find some tolerant and abstracted common ground in our pluralistic society. It turns out that the transformationist type fits the strategy precisely; it would combine the strengths of each type without the troublesome (and in the case of the radicals, the divisive) weaknesses. Oddly, pluralism comes to be overwhelmed by a single position that postures as the most inclusive.[44]

Third, Niebuhr treats culture monolithically. It is "assumed to be a single bloc, which an honest and consistent approach would either reject entirely or accept without qualification; you must either withdraw from it all, transform it all, or keep it all in paradox." This material difficulty underlies the formal problem of typological solidity, and affords grounds for dismissing the Christian radicals as inconsistent for failing to take exactly the same attitude toward every single aspect of human cultural achievement. The move also explains Niebuhr's so-called inability to come up with the necessary discriminations "for discerning how Christians should see the good or the bad in 'culture.'"

Even more problematic is the implication that the state, or even the violence of the state, is "preeminently representative of culture, so that the pacifist who rejects that is described as being against culture 'as such' or as a whole." Generally, Niebuhr confused in the reader's mind the createdness and fallenness of society. "He puts the goodness of nature as the work of God and the destructiveness of the sword as man's rebelliousness all in one sack."[45]

Fourth, according to Yoder it is "a necessary presupposition of the entire argument that the value of culture is not derived from Jesus Christ but stands somehow independently of him, in the orders of both being and knowing, prior to his criticism of it." Culture is autonomous of Jesus, though not of God. "Jesus is very important; Lord he is not," because nature and history are also, as works of the Father and the Holy Spirit, separate channels of divine revelation and moral insight.[46]

Hauerwas's (and Willimon's) and Yoder's criticisms are unquestionably instructive. They signal matters that compromise the adequacy of Niebuhr's analysis of Christ and culture insofar as they apply to it. Even if they do not apply, a question persists regarding whether Constantinian and other "misuses" of H. Richard Niebuhr can be avoided by analyzing more carefully his basic theological intentions and their continuing relevance. The following four points are geared toward reaching greater precision while admitting the force of criticism.

First, on the one hand, *Christ and Culture* sometimes presents the types, especially Christ against culture, in a way that appears to force either–or choices. What seems to explain this is the grounding of typological solidity on the monolithic view. Thus even the radicals' modified use of an inherited cultural language is taken by Niebuhr to establish self-contradiction; the radical type "affirms in words what it denies in action."[47] For Yoder and Hauerwas, this is a caricature dangerously kept in place because Niebuhr gives no basis for verifying or falsifying the typology as a whole.

On the other hand, Niebuhr concedes that his constructs are artificial and historically inadequate, and that strictly speaking they represent at best typical partial answers that help us to follow more intelligently the great conversation about Christ and culture. The irony here is that Niebuhr does, at least implicitly, offer a sort of criterion of falsifiability: If the types operate to freeze the conversation for Christians in the church, they fail to be true to the phenomena. Think about Niebuhr's views on the reality of God and relativity. The sovereign God in Christ cannot be captured in any typology. The answers given by Christians in their double wrestle are always from a creaturely point of view and to that extent partial. Niebuhr also conceives the relevant terms to pull in different directions. Christ does direct persons away from culture, but culture directs them toward the conservation of human achievement, and to that extent away from a reliance on grace; yet the Son of God also "sends his disciples to tend the lambs and sheep, who cannot be guarded without cultural work."[48] These maneuvers suggest an irremovably dynamic dimension in the analysis.

To the extent that Yoder is right, Niebuhr stands condemned also by Niebuhr, because I think he means it when he says that on the matter at hand "an infinite dialogue must develop in the Christian conscience and the Christian community."[49] Far from demanding either–ors, at his best he insists that whatever position one takes on Christ and culture be perennially tested by the problem's prominent motifs as they are expressed in the attempts at faithfulness in Christian history. The typology would expose those motifs and in some measure sketch the movement of the dialogue.

Second, the point I have just made can be used in defense of the criticism that *Christ and Culture* privileges one type over others because it is both most inclusive and most respectful of difference. The idea of infinite dialogue may conjure up the image of wishy-washy Christians constantly second-guessing themselves, first with one thing, then with another; tolerating all other partners in the conversation; and generally congratulating themselves for their high-mindedness while selling out to a culture they claim they are transforming. Over against these contented folk, radicals are burdened by imposed definitions that question their reasonableness, openness, or realism about the necessities of pluralism. In this scenario, the transformationist type is preferred because it is a sublime synthesis containing all the voices of the dialogue—the rejection but also the affirmation of culture, its judgment but also its redemption, and so forth. To Hauerwas and Yoder, this dialogue looks suspiciously like a monologue.

This scenario does not get the story exactly right. Niebuhr states that responsible Christians must assume "the burden, the necessity, the guilt and glory" of arriving at their own final conclusions "in present decisions and present obedience."[50] Presumably these conclusions would emerge from an internal dialogue in which themes of rejection, affirmation, synthesis, dualism, and conversion are considered in an interpretation of what is going on. But then it is not entirely clear whether the conversionist type has to be seen as normatively overwhelming or internally corrective with regard to the other types.

If the former is true, then Niebuhr violates his own basic intentions not to offer the Christian answer. If the latter is true, then conversionism amounts to a persistent reminder that in Christian response to cultural achievement the dynamic character of God's work in Christ be acknowledged in word and deed across the realities of creation, judgment, and redemption—and that, in line with this, certain errors of stasis and dualism be avoided.

I offer this reading well aware of the following serious ambiguity in *Christ and Culture*. When Niebuhr talks about history, he allows that a process of mutual correction can, does, and ought to go on among Christians and Christian communities. Radicals keep conversionists from going soft on culture, for instance, whereas conversionists challenge any radical substitution of a new law of cultural life, as if any human attainment is not liable to sin, or as if there is nothing of God's good creation to be found in the world that has been rejected. But in his theological construction, Niebuhr treats the conversionist or transformationist type as preeminently self-correcting. It comes across as equipped independently to avoid the overvaluation of culture, the dualistic division of creation and redemption, and so on.

The ambiguity is captured perfectly in a discussion of the conversionist F. D. Maurice. His theology appears, on the one side, to avoid all the errors of the other types on its own; but on the other side, Niebuhr supposes that he needed in his time the association of "synthesists and dualists and radical Christians" to keep him honest in his work for church and world. Placing the words in Maurice's voice, Niebuhr concludes with "the reflection that no Christian thought can encompass the thought of the Master, and that as the body is one but has many members, so also the church."[51]

If we lean in one direction of this ambiguity, we will, with Hauerwas and Yoder, see Niebuhr effectively abandoning his claim that he is really just offering five "typical partial answers" to the problem of Christ and culture. He is simply about converting nonconversionists to conversionism by definition. If we lean in the other direction, we will pay special attention to his reflection that "the seeking of an inclusive theory is of great practical importance," because it "might enable one to see more unity in what is now divided, and to act in greater harmony with movements that seem to be at cross purposes."[52] I plead that this second point not be lost, and that, indeed, for the purposes of theological ethics, it have a kind of priority. The abiding value of *Christ and Culture*, I believe, is its delineation of a set of theological considerations regarding creation, judgment, redemption, grace, and sin that rightly condition the infinite dialogue among Christians as they seek faithfully to witness to God in Jesus Christ.

Third, if the charge about a monolithic approach to culture is on target, then Niebuhr runs the risk of confusing creation and fall. But this is just the sort of mistake he tried to expose and avoid in his discussions of the radical and dualist types. Although Yoder's criticisms of *Christ and Culture* on this score may be defensible, they do not rule out of court what I called above the book's abiding value. That value brings to the forefront the cautions (1) not to deny or fail to articulate in specific terms the goodness of creation in culture, (2) not to deny nor fail to articulate the thoroughly fallen character of cultural life, (3) not to pursue strategies of replacement or substitution in Christian ethics in a way that undermines the force of the preceding two criteria (as if what is to be replaced is not created and what replaces it is not fallen), and (4) not to reduce Christian ethics to utilitarian accommodation or dualistic withdrawal (in its various guises). Christian social ethics may proceed along these lines in response to historical circumstances and to the dual requirement of Christians to be in the world but not of it.[53]

Nothing found in Hauerwas, Yoder, or Ramsey denies the force of these cautions and convictions. Indeed, all attend to them in one way or another. Yoder, in particular, has, as we have seen, written with power about the faithful and responsible pacifist witness of the church to the state. This witness will change in different times and will meet inescapable limits and boundaries. So I am proposing that if monolithic speech about culture cuts off activities of careful discrimination and dialogue, the continuing validity of Niebuhr's general theological analysis as I have interpreted it enables us to correct these difficulties.

Fourth, on its face, the view that Niebuhr separates out the authority of culture for Christians from the authority of Jesus Christ is false. Conversionism is based upon both "the participation of the Word, the Son of God, in creation" and "the redemptive work of God in the incarnation of the Son." "Not that the conversionist turns from the historical Jesus to the Logos that was in the beginning, or that he denies the wonder of the cross in marveling at the birth in a barn; he seeks to hold together in one movement the various themes of creation and redemption, of incarnation and atonement."[54] There may be tremendous disagreements about Niebuhr's execution of this tensive movement, about the balance he strikes within it, or about the theological adequacy of Niebuhr's Christology. It does not help to point to these disagreements in a way that fails fully to reckon with what the man says.

No doubt *Christ and Culture* has been used in the ways presented by Hauerwas and Yoder. But Niebuhr was fiercely anti-accommodationist within a framework that approximates Saint Augustine's theology of the two cities. He could not give up on the responsibility to defend innocent neighbors by force of arms, but he could also say in the aftermath of World War II that utilitarian Christianity was guilty of "killing the Son of God in the effort to preserve our civilization."[55] He was anti-accommodationist within an approach that stressed moments of withdrawal and engagment for Christians in cultural life. He was anti-accommodationist in his critique of what he called direct action, in which the Christian community's service of human needs was separated from what should be the incessant Christian call to repentance and faith across the entirety of cultural life.[56] The theological analysis of *Christ and Culture* is fully compatible with these positions.

Conclusion

The upshot is that a critique of problematic uses of the doctrines of creation and preservation does not exclude the legitimate attempt in theological ethics to make sense of the reality of these divine activities. One may focus on the common vulnerability and interdependence of all creation, locating human life within that sphere. Human creatureliness may be comprehended, as Barth, Ramsey, and O'Donovan try to do, in terms of the normative determination to fellow humanity, which itself witnesses and corresponds to Jesus Christ. One may offer an interpretation of God's preserving work that has implications for Christian ethics. Hauerwas cannot do without interpretations along these lines, as I have tried to show. His Christian ethics may become more complete and may avoid misunderstanding if he makes his commitment to them more explicit.

Hauerwas's suggestion "that as Christians we know nothing about what we mean by creation separate from the new order we find through the concrete practices of baptism and Eucharist, correlative as they are to Christ's resurrection," can be made more concrete by working out the moral shared goods and solidarities between practices witnessing to God's Kingdom and spheres of creaturely activity. Working them out may contribute, on Hauerwas's terms, to witnessing to Christ's Lordship in the world. He could rightly say that human creatures as such in their communities may attain partial insight into the truth of the moral life; however, this insight would be tested in the light of Christ and the practices of discipleship.

O'Donovan, then, is correct when he says that an "unbeliever or non-Christian culture does not have to be ignorant about the structure of the family, the virtue of mercy, the vice of cowardice, the duty of justice. Nor does such a one have to fail entirely to respond to this knowledge in action, disposition, or institution." However, "if the Creator is not known, then the creation is not known as creation; for the relation of the creation to its creator is the ground of its intelligibility as a created universe. . . . But this means that the order of reality is not truly known at all."[57] Partial knowledge is also deep misunderstanding:

> Thus St. Augustine in the *City of God*, with an inconsistency that is only apparent, explains the success of the Roman Empire in terms of the traditional Roman virtues and, at the same time, denies that they are virtues at all, since there is no virtue without true religion. . . . From which we conclude that revelation in Christ does not *deny* our fragmentary knowledge of the way things are, as though that knowledge were not there, or were of no significance; yet it does not *build on it*, as though it provided a perfectly acceptable foundation to which a fur-

ther level of understanding can be added. It can only expose it for not being what it was originally given to be.[58]

Hauerwas should accept the corrections I suggest in this chapter. In his discussions of the university, medical ethics, the demand that injustice be resisted, and the Christian witness to the state, he displays a readiness to do so. Consider, too, his claim that "as Christians we may not only find that people who are not Christians manifest God's peace better than we ourselves, but we must demand that they exist. It is to be hoped that such people may provide the conditions for our ability to cooperate with others for securing justice in the world. Such cooperation, moreover, is not based on natural law legitimation of a generally shared natural morality. Rather, it is a testimony to the fact that God's Kingdom is wide indeed."[59] Hauerwas can and should say all this at the same time as he drums home the refrain that "the grain to which the universe itself witnesses can only be dimly known if the church does not exist: for if the church did not exist how would we know that we were created to be at peace with one another? . . . The witness . . . that unites all Christians is that found on a cross by which God restores the peace of creation."[60] In this distinctive way, he therefore may move closer to Ramsey's effort, following H. Richard Niebuhr, to embody the whole idea of God in Christian ethics.

Notes

1. Reinhold Niebuhr, of course, is the classic modern source for this challenge to Christian pacifism. See, e.g., Larry Rasmussen, ed., *Reinhold Niebuhr: Theologian of Public Life* (Minneapolis: Fortress Press, 1991), 237–53. Cf. Paul Ramsey, *The Just War* (New York: Scribner's, 1968), 259–78.

2. Stanley Hauerwas, *After Christendom?* (Nashville: Abingdon Press, 1991), 45.

3. H. Richard Niebuhr, *Christ and Culture* (New York: Harper & Row, 1951), 65.

4. John Howard Yoder, *The Original Revolution* (Scottdale, Pa.: Herald Press, 1971), 83. Cf. Stanley Hauerwas, *In Good Company* (Notre Dame, Ind.: University of Notre Dame Press, 1995), 231 n. 15, where he suggests that the label has only a limited usefulness.

5. Stanley Hauerwas, *Dispatches from the Front* (Durham, N.C.: Duke University Press, 1994), 127.

6. Stanley Hauerwas, "Epilogue," in Paul Ramsey, *Speak Up for Just War or Pacifism* (University Park: Pennsylvania State University Press, 1988), 152.

7. Hauerwas, *Dispatches from the Front*, 128, 134.

8. "Epilogue," 159. Cf. John Howard Yoder, *The Christian Witness to the State* (Newton, Kans.: Faith and Life Press, 1964).

9. John Howard Yoder, *The Priestly Kingdom* (Notre Dame, Ind.: University of Notre Dame Press, 1984), 159, 167.

10. Yoder, *Christian Witness to the State*, 37.

11. Ibid., 40.

12. Hauerwas, *Dispatches from the Front*, 134.

13. Yoder, *Christian Witness to the State*, 48.

14. Ibid., 49; John Howard Yoder, *When War Is Unjust*, rev. ed. (Maryknoll, N.Y.: Orbis, 1996), 71–101. Typical criticisms of this sort of analysis, originating in this form in the work of Reinhold Niebuhr, are that the pacifist position fails to clarify the relevant difference between coercion and violence, or that its attempt to follow Jesus is inauthentic because it does commend that complete nonresistance that effectively removes pacifists from political responsibility in history. See, e.g., Ramsey's version in *Speak Up for Just War or Pacifism*, 115–19. Hauerwas makes his response in *Dispatches from the Front*, 130.

15. Yoder, *Christian Witness to the State*, 25.

16. Ibid., 55.

17. Hauerwas, *Dispatches from the Front*, 136–52.

18. Yoder, *When War Is Unjust*, 77–78.

19. Hauerwas, *Dispatches from the Front*, 125.

20. Ibid., 128.

21. Ramsey, *Speak Up for Just War or Pacifism*, 123.

22. See, e.g., Stanley Hauerwas, *The Hauerwas Reader* (Durham, N.C.: Duke University Press, 2001), 379.

23. Paul Ramsey, *War and the Christian Conscience* (Durham, N.C.: Duke University Press, 1961), 29.

24. Ramsey, *Speak Up for Just War or Pacifism*, 192.

25. Oliver O'Donovan, *In Pursuit of a Christian View of War* (Bramcote, England: Grove Books, 1977), 5.

26. Ramsey, *Speak Up for Just War or Pacifism*, 123.

27. Saint Augustine, *The City of God*, trans. Henry Bettenson (London: Penguin, 1972), 1069.

28. Hauerwas, *After Christendom?* 56–68.

29. Hauerwas, *Dispatches from the Front*, 175.

30. Hauerwas, *In Good Company*, 103–5.

31. Oliver O'Donovan, *Resurrection and Moral Order* (Grand Rapids, Mich.: Eerdmans, 1986), 19–20.

32. See, e.g., *Vatican II's Pastoral Constitution on the Church in the Modern World* (Boston: Daughters of Saint Paul, 1965).

33. For a general statement see Hauerwas, *Dispatches from the Front*, 111.

34. Stanley Hauerwas, *Christian Existence Today* (Durham, N.C.: Labyrinth Press, 1988), 261.

35. Hauerwas, *Christian Existence Today*, 264. Cf. more recent discussions in Stanley Hauerwas, *A Better Hope* (Grand Rapids, Mich.: Brazos Press, 2000).

36. Stanley Hauerwas, "Epilogue," in Ramsey, *Speak Up for Just War or Pacifism*, 176.

37. Stanley Hauerwas, *Suffering Presence* (Notre Dame, Ind.: University of Notre Dame Press, 1986), 1–83.

38. Stanley Hauerwas, *With the Grain of the Universe: The Church's Witness and Natural Theology, Being the Gifford Lectures Delivered at the University of St. Andrews in 2001* (Grand Rapids, Mich.: Brazos Press, 2001), 173–204.

39. Stanley Hauerwas, "Christian Ethics in America (and the JRE): A Report on a Book I Will Not Write," *Journal of Religious Ethics* 25(3): 57–75.

40. Stanley Hauerwas and William H. Willimon, *Resident Aliens* (Nashville: Abingdon Press, 1989), 40.

41. Hauerwas and Willimon, *Resident Aliens*, 39–41.

42. John Howard Yoder, "How H. Richard Niebuhr Reasoned: A Critique of *Christ and Culture*," in *Authentic Transformation: A New Vision of Christ and Culture*, ed. Glen Stassen, D. M. Yeager, and John Howard Yoder (Nashville: Abingdon Press, 1996), 31–89.

43. Ibid., 45, 47, 51.

44. Ibid., 52–53, 79–82.

45. Ibid., 54–55, 51–52, 64.

46. Ibid., 55, 43. See also Yoder on Niebuhr on the Trinity, 61–63.

47. H. Richard Niebuhr, *Christ and Culture* (Harper & Row, 1951), 69.

48. Ibid., 39.

49. Ibid.

50. Ibid., 233.

51. Ibid., 229.

52. Ibid., 232.

53. See D. M. Yeager, "The Social Self in a Pilgrim Church," in *Authentic Transformation*, 91–126.

54. Niebuhr, *Christ and Culture*, 192–93.

55. H. Richard Niebuhr, "Utilitarian Christianity," *Christianity and Crisis*, July 8, 1946: 5.

56. Yeager, "Social Self in a Pilgrim Church," 113–18.

57. O'Donovan, *Resurrection and Moral Order*, 88.

58. Ibid., 89; italics in orginal.

59. Hauerwas, *The Peaceable Kingdom* (Notre Dame, Ind.: University of Notre Dame Press, 1983), 101.

60. Stanley Hauerwas, "With the Grain of the Universe." Draft manuscript for 2001 Gifford Lectures. This passage does not appear in the publication of these lectures, but in personal conversation Hauerwas says that he regrets having removed it.

CHAPTER SEVEN

God Will Be God

One of the questions that I am considering in this book is how the church ought to be related to the world. My previous discussions lead me to draw two lessons pertaining to the question. First, Christian moral discourse should be significantly rooted in the practices of the Christian community. It tends to become abstract and ill-defined apart from the social context that locates, inspires, and embodies it. We saw in Paul Ramsey's case how just war theory seems to require a background set of Christian practices that helps to preserve and exemplify its critical edge; in this case, Hauerwas's glance back from just war applications to these peacemaking practices seems right. Similarly, Ramsey's medical ethics call for fostering conditions of covenant, but these conditions are liable to lose their power unless they are tied to a certain set of virtues in medical practice. A basic source for reflection about these virtues in Christian ethics is the practice of a church that refuses to abandon the suffering. Here also Stanley Hauerwas is on target. Christian ethics, then, works out the meaning of Christian agape for the entirety of the moral life, so long as the meaning of love is integrally related to the life of a people who would be faithful to God in Jesus Christ.

The second lesson is that Christian ethics must include reflection on and witness to the divine activities of creation, preservation, and redemption. Placing Christian ethics in constitutive connection with practices of the Christian community enables this reflection and witness. It does not rule them out. Hauerwas's hesitancy about creation talk is acceptable only as a critical suggestion about possible perils; Ramsey's insights on just war, creaturely covenant, and love transforming justice continue to be important even as they are qualified along the lines of the first lesson.

The lessons lead me to say, simply enough, that Christian ethics emerges out of the life of the church in faithfulness to God in Jesus Christ, and that faithfulness includes discernment of and conformity to what God is doing in the world as creator, preserver, and redeemer. As responsible to God, the church, H. Richard Niebuhr argued, "is not a corporation with limited liability. All beings existent in the world are the creatures of this creator and the concern of this redeemer." And the content of the church's responsibility is, finally, mercy, "the conservation, reformation, redemption, and transformation of whatever creatures its action touches. . . . Nothing belongs to its present responsibility for which it cannot answer to the one who gave his life as ransom and whose whole activity was a seeking and saving of the lost."[1] The worldly church, therefore, is irresponsible because it accounts not to God but to some form of human society itself, whether it be a nation, a cultural group, or even humanity as such. Hauerwas's challenges to Constantinianism and the like are reminiscent of Niebuhr's examination of the false prophecy and false priesthood of the Christian community that views itself as responsible to society. It tends to give society the assurance that "its form of organization and its customs are divinely ordained, that it enjoys the special protection and favor of God, that it is a chosen people."[2]

If in worldliness the church fails in its responsibility to God, in isolationism it responds to God only for itself. The isolated church is occupied most of all with "the intense development of its own life and the careful guarding of its holiness. . . . It rejects not only nationalism but nationality, not only worldliness but the world."[3] The church's responsibility to God for the neighbor as a self among other selves in society must be sought, instead, through what Niebuhr calls its apostolic, priestly, and pioneering functions. The apostolic church preaches repentance and announces the good news of God's reconciling work not only to individuals but to the societies, groups, and governments that make up their lives and being. The spiritual dimension of human and social need must be named—the specific forms of idolatry and the sorts of fear, mistrust, and despair that ground them—in the Gospel's light. As a pastoral community the church is the shepherd and seeker of the lost; it must attend to the social circumstances that bear on their well-being and dignity. As pioneer and representative, the church is charged with responding to God on behalf of human societies. It not only denounces nationalism, racism, and so forth, and not only preaches repentance and good news. It must also lead in the social act of repentance in its own internal relations, turning to God and the divine mercy within a Christian common life that "functions as a world society."

On the one hand, Hauerwas proposes that the proclamation of the Gospel to liberal culture risks severe distortion; Ramsey's appeals to just war and covenant illustrate the perils of even unintended worldliness. On the other hand, Ramsey saw clearly that the love of neighbor extends to all who bear the human countenance. Isolationism in the strict sense is impossible. Niebuhr's formulation of the "highest form of social responsibility in the church," the church as pioneer and representative, defines the challenge to both thinkers nicely, I think; for it bases Christian ethics in the internal life of the Christian community as it witnesses to the reality of God's universal promise. The apostolic and priestly functions cannot be separated from that internal life; but the internal life is also that of the revolutionary cell or anticipatory world society called to convert the terms of justice in the world. As circumstances require, this task may be accomplished through a rhythm of critical withdrawal from and positive identification with the world.

I do not think that James Gustafson would likely disagree with the Niebuhrian description of the church's responsibility to society. Yet we have already surveyed, in chapter 1, his serious differences with Ramsey and Hauerwas. In contrast to both of them, Gustafson's theological ethics highlight general human experiences rather than notions of divine revelation, appeals to insight from the natural sciences, and the priority of God as that is distinguished from what he might call Christocentrism, ecclesiocentrism, and biblicentrism.[4] On this last point, he writes: "The theologian addressing many issues—nuclear war, social justice, ecology, and so forth—must do so as an outcome of a theology that develops God's relations to all aspects of life in the world, and develops those relations in terms which are not exclusively Christian in a sectarian form. Jesus is not God."[5] My efforts here are devoted to an exposition of Gustafson's theocentric ethics that both displays his appropriation of Niebuhr's radically monotheistic call to responsibility and conversion, and accounts for his distinctive critical vision.[6] The chapter drives toward a tension between a Christian ethic of faithfulness rooted in the particular, traditioned language and practices of the church and Gustafson's challenge to any particularisms unfaithful to God.

Consent to the Primacy of God

In the circumstances of contemporary culture, religion, theology, and ethics, humanity has become the measure of all things. Cultural life is occupied with efforts to control our environments to free human beings from the sources of insecurity and anxiety. More and more, religion is instrumental to human needs, offering its consumers assurances of psychic health, communal support, and moral energy; but the uses of piety for its tactical effect in the service of a moral cause are, "no matter what the moral cause . . . simply wrong."[7] Theologians too often build their systems around the prospects for salvation or the hope for "humanization in history." Modern moral philosophy tends as well toward exclusive reflection on what constitutes human well-being.

The attack on anthropocentric instrumentalism or functionalism, on making "man the measure of all things," is a distinctive mark of theocentric ethics. God, not humanity, ought to be the proper object of theology; anthropocentrism implies a denial of God as God, "the power and ordering of life in nature and history which sustains and limits humanity, which 'demands' recognition of principles and boundaries of activities for the sake of man and of the whole of life."[8] Theocentric ethics surmises that "if the Deity is not bound to our judgments about what is in our interests, then theological ethics is radically altered. . . . Man, the measurer, can no longer be the measure of the value of all things. What is right for man has to be determined in relation to man's place in the universe and, indeed, in relation to the will of God for all things that might dimly be perceived."[9] Gustafson here creatively develops Niebuhr's idea of radical monotheism, which both "dethrones all absolutes short of the principle of being itself" and "reverences every relative existent." The human existent is revered relative to its relations to other created existents as these all are related to God.

Method

The theological basis of theocentric ethics presupposes a set of three methodological convictions and procedures that Gustafson presents with considerable care. First, he holds that "human experience is prior to reflection"; it is not easily reduced or divided either into component parts (e.g., its affective versus cognitive versus volitional moments) or into a differentiation of kinds (e.g., aesthetic, moral, and religious experience). The priority and unity of lived experience resists to some extent our efforts to order it reflectively. When a lover discerns the beauty of her beloved in his performance of a kind deed performed utterly without guile, she may well suggest that in that experience and not utterly divisible from it, she felt a thankfulness and a sense of direction akin to the holy. Similarly, an experience of being exploited includes being moved by a sense of injustice, a judgment about unfairness, and the motivation to rectify the unfairness if we can.[10] Theology and ethics has to refer not only to ideas but also to the lived experiences where they are found and that tend to elude the conceptual frameworks we devise.

Second, experiences are social. Their articulation, meanings, and explanations are shared socially, interpreted socially, and tested socially within communities that have common purposes, interests, concepts, symbols, and tests for adequacy. There are a variety of these communities of interpretation, and they interact with each other and change over time. So "any organized community that freezes its requirements for membership according to the symbols and explanations adequate at a particular time is bound to have difficulties, especially in the modern world."[11] And there is no escaping the ways experience must be socially tested in light of objective realities apprehended within, between, and across our various lived communities. For example, a religious viewpoint need not be determined by the findings of biology, but it will have to be developed "with reference to the most accurate body of facts about that to which it pertains," and these facts may well include what biology has to teach us.

These convictions about the prior unity and sociality of experience help to explain Gustafson's approach to religion. Certain "aspects of piety" evoke and sustain a religious outlook. Prior to theological reflection, which construes experiences through categories, explanations, and practical implications, there remain various "senses." These include a sense of dependence on forces and powers beyond our control upon which we rely; a sense of gratitude for the "benefits that are

ours as a result of the objects on which we rely";[12] a sense of obligation to persons and communities; a sense of remorse and repentance
based in recognition of our failures to acknowledge dependence, gratitude, and obligation; a sense of possibilities for altering one's personal
and social conditions; and a sense of direction, of where one is going
and where things are heading. Religion is naturally grounded in these
senses, and in many other aspects of human experience. They possess
their own integrity, and in relation to them religious people will move
to affirm a sense of the divine. These aspects of piety and the sense of
the divine are social in character and, in the case of a religion like
Christianity, are mediated through particular historical communities
extended through time, or through traditions.

Third, for Gustafson Christian theology, "a way of construing the
world" in light of the Deity, is developed historically by way of a "selective retrieval" of traditional themes culled from the Bible and other
sources. For the sake of a more faithful account of the relation between
God and the world, theological concepts, themes, and principles may
be recombined so that, for instance, divine creation or eschatology
takes on new or deeper significance. Other notions may be discarded
or reinterpreted as a consequence. The processes of recombination and
innovation also proceed "because Christians, and particularly theologians, are themselves participants in more inclusive communities of
scholarly investigation or of the communities that absorb the significance of the results of these investigations."[13] Theologians who say
that you miss the point of the Genesis creation narrative if you treat
it as a causal explanation of how the world began may present good
reasons from the Bible and tradition to make the case; but no doubt
this interpretation was caused in part by the acceptance of a manifold
of scientific evidences and theories, including evolutionary biology.
Moreover, "debates among theologians are partially about what aspects of knowledge are of such authority that they require abandonment of certain aspects of the Christian tradition, or require subordination of certain themes that had formerly been crucial."[14]

A theological tradition cannot honestly isolate itself from relevant
advances in knowledge and understanding attained within human history. Traditions must be tested by these advances in scientific and other
nontheological inquiry. As a consequence, "undue parochialism" may

be exposed, internal criticism becomes a more vital possibility, and "the intelligibility of the particular can be made clearer and to some extent more persuasive by demonstrating that its insights and truths refer to the experiences of many if not all persons and that its justifications can be made clear in nonesoteric language."[15] Gustafson distinguishes his approach of critical, selective retrieval both from a confessional project based on a doctrine of revelation or the historical relativity of the Christian tradition, and from a straightforward apologetic program of systematically arguing for traditional stances from general or universal sources outside of it.

In line with the convictions, procedures, and aspirations discussed above, Gustafson declares and defends "a preference for the Reformed tradition." The tradition of John Calvin stresses "a sense of a powerful Other" or, objectively put, the sovereignty of God. It also makes piety, or an attitude of awe and reverence, central for moral and religious life, and requires that human life be ordered to what can be discerned about God's purposes.[16] Gustafson is explicit, however, in questioning certain characteristic Reformed interpretations of divine agency, the place of the human within the divine purposes, retributive or compensatory ideas of eternal life, the nature of "salvation from sin," and the authority of Scripture as divine revelation. All of these notions can be fatally anthropocentric or can be defended in ways that illegitimately isolate theological from nontheological and especially scientific inquiry.

Affectivity and the Sense of the Divine

In their experiences of nature, history, culture, and society, persons are affected with senses of dependence, gratitude, obligation, remorse, possibility, and direction. We apprehend, for example, the beauty of a sunset or the destructive power of a forest fire or the agents of disease; these experiences evoke affectivities of gratitude, awe, and dependence or contingency. Living through wartime may bring forth responses of both obligation to near and distant neighbors, and remorse for complicity in injustice. The technological and moral activities of culture provide an objective point of reference for a sense of possibilities and direction as well as repentance; thus ambivalence may be a fitting response to a cultural environment that enabled one's own stable, middle-class, happy family life while limiting the opportunities of women like your mother and perpetuating exclusion of races and creeds outside your circle of contentment. In these and other fields of experience people may start asking questions that have religious significance, such as, In what do we ultimately have confidence? To what are we loyal? For what do we hope? What do we love?

Hence, these affectivities can have religious significance, not only by way of a "native religious response," but also through the mediation of a particular religious tradition like Christianity. "The religious language and symbols of one's tradition penetrate one's perception both of the meaning of what is seen and one's affective responses. What one sees may be an expression of the power and glory of God; one's responses might be a quiet expression of praise of God; one's joy and delight may be in the beauty and goodness of God." One may in fact consent to or share in the meaning of the events, persons, and stories that found the tradition; but in doing so one does not sacrifice to that tradition his or her critical faculties. Gustafson concludes: "My perception of the event and its significance as a moment which declares the glory of God is permeated by the religious symbols and consciousness that characterize the biblical religious traditions. *There is no avoiding acknowledgment of a circularity in this*; the experience confirms that which I am predisposed to have it confirm. But confirmation is subject to assessment by me and by the community. . . . A reliance on the tradition is inevitable; but consent to it is not. The larger meaning of the event is experientially confirmed."[17]

The Christian tradition records the theocentric consent of a people to the powers that sustain and bear down upon them. In theocentric ethics the term "piety" is preferable to "faith" to describe consent for several reasons. Piety, unlike faith, is less readily contrasted sharply with reason as an independent and competing source for knowledge about God. Because all knowledge for Gustafson is based in experience, he rejects any such either–or. Moreover, "faith as a measured confidence in God is part of piety, but faith in the benevolence of God to fulfill human purposes as we desire them to be fulfilled in all respects is not part of piety."[18] Faith as fidelity is central to piety, and properly orients humanity's loyalty to God rather than to itself. Finally, faith as a primary response of trust seems to exclude human responses of fear, anger, and enmity toward the God who can thwart or even destroy human purposes and aspirations. The language of piety does not foreclose these from being "honest religious affections." Note here converging themes in theocentric ethics: the rejection of anthropocentrism, the priority of experience, the avowal that "God will be God."

God, Science, and Theology

Theocentric ethics interprets God's relation to humanity and the world by developing the "classic symbols" of God as Creator, Sustainer and Governor, Judge, and Redeemer. An experiential focus is prominent throughout. Hence, Gustafson points out how the creation narratives in the book of Genesis record significant human experiences involving accountability, interrelationship with nature, human interdependence, and the sense of possibilities. The "objects" corresponding to these experiences were responded to in religiously affective ways early in the biblical tradition, "and led to a theological construing of the world that symbolized the power and the powers in the name of God as the Creator."[19] In piety, this is a vivid religious symbol that displays the creative powers on which all things depend, and the way we are dependent upon them and responsible in their midst.

Persons also have experiences of an ordering of the world that may warrant the symbols of God as Sustainer and Governor. There are natural conditions, like the sun's temperature and a food chain, for continued life on earth. There are prerequisites for human survival and flourishing that have biological, educational, social, and political dimensions. From a theocentric perspective, ethics has to do with discerning what the divine ordering requires in a particular time and place. "The vocation of the human community is to consent to the divine governance, to cooperate with it (not merely to be resigned to it) toward those aims that can be discerned. It is to participate in it, while acknowledging dependence upon it, and acknowledging the limits and possibilities of human activity that are consonant with it."[20]

As participants in patterns and processes of interdependence, human persons confront both limits and possibilities for action. They may bring to them a set of trusts, loyalties, and loves that are narrower rather than broader; they may be to oneself, one's family, church, nation, or even ("merely") to the human species. In the name of these loyalties, proper limits may be crossed or constructive possibilities forgone so that the good purposes and relationships for which one is responsible are thwarted or disordered. The symbols of God as Judge and of the wrath of God are meaningful to the extent that something of the divine ordering can be discerned and transgressions of that ordering are seen to carry the costs of "adverse consequences."

Gustafson steers clear of interpretations of divine intentions that are specifically and exclusively geared to human rewards and punishments; nevertheless, "the religious consciousness confronts the judgment and wrath of God on those occasions when the consequences of our commissions and omissions signal a serious disordering of relationships between persons, in society, in relation to nature." Examples include the bad consequences of brutal or neglectful treatment of children, the pain and confusion suffered by a spouse betrayed, the destruction to human and nonhuman life worked by policies and wars of nationalist expansion, and the threats to the earth generated by narrow economic interests. The point is that "God will not be denied; human activity must find proper ways to consent to the divine ordering; without such ways human life and other aspects of the world are put in peril."[21]

Finally, God may be meaningfully construed as Redeemer. The grace of God redeems human persons from conditions of fatedness and sin. In the first case, piety discerns signs of grace in "the power or powers that make possible rectification, renewal, and recombination of the elements of life that contribute to proper human well-being, to the well-being of the ordering of life with which we are interdependent. These powers do not absolutely overcome limitations but create and extend the conditions of possibility" where before there was only a sense of being driven or destined to burdens and limits that threaten well-being. Redemption from sin is release from guilt, which comes only by forgiveness, and which is ascribed to God by way of human experiences of the offer of forgiveness. Such love offered and received "heals the breaches, moves us to fulfill our duties, and reconciles us to others. . . . The gratitude and joy of being forgiven, for being tendered possibilities in the most undeserving circumstances, rests finally on the divine governance."[22]

These symbols are confirmed within piety, have biblical warrant, and are important for a host of practices within the Christian tradition. But they are used not just because they are biblical or because they are of the essence of a particularly Christian way of life. Their use has backing because they "express meanings of human experience in various surroundings, in response to natural and historical events, in social relationships." Theological construal and piety here refer substantially to the way things really are. And in piety it may be claimed as well that the descriptions and explanations of the natural sciences are important for theology. On the one hand, evidence from the sciences provides some general backing for the theological construal of God as the power that bears down upon and sustains us. On the other hand, in piety the desire to learn of God's ordering directs attention toward what science can contribute to our discernment of it.

The substantial content of ideas of God "cannot be incongruous with well-established data and explanatory principles established by relevant sciences, and must be in some way indicated by these." Theology cannot give a scientific explanation of the world, and theological conclusions may not be deductively derived from scientific theories and data. Still, "it is proper and necessary to test what is said theologically in the light of the relevant sciences, and to use indicators from the sciences in what one says substantively about God."[23]

And when tested in this way, Gustafson claims, a number of traditional Christian beliefs do not fare well. Scientific accounts of the development of the universe point out the immense spans of space and time within which human life emerged. In this context, its emergence appears shot through with contingency, so that even if "there were divine 'foreknowledge' of human life, there was no particular merit in bringing it into being through such an inefficient and lengthy process." Anthropocentrism, a "self- and species-interested conviction that the whole has come into being for our sake," is again the target, but challenged here from a piety-sponsored heeding of the relevant sciences.

Gustafson also questions the notion that God should be understood as a personal agent "in ways similar to those of the human agent." Biological science shows the sharp limits and conditions within which human action is exercised. Drawing analogies to God's freedom by analogy to the "radical freedom" of persons is excessive, and the problem is fatally compounded when theology assumes that God's agency attends exclusively to the good of human beings. That assumption could warrant belief in the afterlife, because it would "in part function to resolve the problem of assuring believers that religious piety finally is beneficial." Yet a traditional insistence about divine, not human, sovereignty over all things joins with the absence of scientifically based evidence to warrant giving up the belief.[24]

The upshot is a theological vision that locates humanity as a participant within processes and patterns of interdependence that all fall under the governance of God. These processes encompass the realities of nature, history, culture, society, interpersonal relations, and intrapersonal experience. Free human participation is more about "directing . . . natural impulses, desires, and capacities," rather than any radical independence from nature. Although all of creation can be named good with God as its source, it does not follow that human good as we would have it is for God exclusive, primary, or even guaranteed. In any case, human persons are called to respond to divine governance, to the powers that bear down and sustain us in and through our interactive (not self-initiating) engagement with persons and events.

For Christians, "Jesus incarnates theocentric piety and fidelity. Through the gospel accounts of his life and ministry we can see and know something of the powers that bear down upon us and sustain us, and of the piety and the manner of life that are appropriate to them." These traditional stories can have a compelling power for us because there are basic similarities or resonances between our human experiences, our senses of dependence, gratitude, and so on, and the gospel depiction of the sensibilities of Jesus. And in Jesus' consent to his fate, we gain the insight that "fidelity does not lead to what we ordinarily and immediately perceive to be a human good, but that what is of human value must be sacrificed for the sake of the purposes of God."[25]

Theocentric anthropology is carefully aligned with a doctrine of God. The human creature is first of all understood "in continuity with 'nature' as much as in distinction from it."[26] He or she is a radically dependent and interdependent being; freedom is limited. Human intentions and choices, though involving moments of reflection and the assumption of some degree of critical distance from our given circumstances, nevertheless draw upon and focus our biological natures in their interaction with cultural and social conditions. In this way we can, to be sure, open up possibilities for well-being, and stand accountable for our responses to our situation, for the ordering of our desires, and for the consequences of our actions. It follows that human creatures are also accountable to themselves, to other persons affected by our actions, and to the communities of which we are a part.

The human person is created but fallen. In our lives we realize misplaced trust, wrongly ordered love, the corruption of rationality, and the experience of unfulfilled obligations and duties. We place our trusts and order our loves poorly when we accord them an idolatrous or otherwise excessive or defective importance. Reason is corrupted when in pride or sloth we refuse to see the world as it is, or refuse to consider or be corrected by relevant information, evidence, and argument. In their disobedience, human creatures betray the trust placed in them by others through deception, breaking promises, or injustice. These four features of the "human fault" demonstrate a contraction of the human spirit. "The human fault, then, is our tendency to be turned inward toward ourselves as individuals, or toward our communal interests. . . . It is retiring within the self or the group, either out of the pride that takes the form of excessive confidence in the partialities of our particular ways of life, or out of the sloth that sustains a self-satisfaction in what has already been achieved."[27]

The correction of the human fault is nothing less than an enlargement "of soul and interests, and by a more appropriate alignment of ourselves and all things in relation to each other and to the ultimate power and orderer of life." The creature's construal of the world is expanded to see humanity in relation to the purposes of the divine governance for the whole of creation. There is a conversion of human nature in the "ordering of the heart" that enlarges affections and loyalties along the lines of Jonathan Edwards's "benevolence to being in general." "Most centrally," the correction displaces "the constricted anthropocentric sources of the material considerations of morality" that give pride of place to morality's and piety's utility for human beings.[28]

In the Christian life, prayers of adoration, confession, supplication, thanksgiving, and even intercession can evoke and sustain an enlarged vision of the place of humanity in relation to God. They can expand understanding of the needs of the world. Prompted by piety, prayer can also awaken and sustain it. Similarly, the narratives of the Christian tradition, especially as they focus on Jesus, have an "evocative and sustaining power that is necessary to generate the religious affections or virtues that are commended." The "full dignity" of the Christian tradition is realized in its practical necessity "to effect the sorts of persons we ought to become."[29]

What sorts of persons are these morally? "What is God enabling and requiring us to be and to do?" First, moral agents "are to relate ourselves and all things in a manner appropriate to their relations to God."[30] Second, moral agency is fundamentally a "process of discernment" in which a person may keenly apprehend the morally salient features of circumstances and relationships and respond fittingly. Discernment consists in an evaluative and affective description of the situation at hand that forms the basis for an "informed intuition" rather than "the conclusion of a formally logical argument." Reasons for action are, therefore, not so fundamentally related to a preeminent moral principle as they are to a "final moment of perception that sees the parts in relation to a whole, expresses sensibilities as well as reasoning, and is made in the conditions of human finitude."[31]

Third, theocentric discernment sees through to "the necessary conditions for life to be sustained and developed. There are fundamental requisites that can be perceived and must be taken into account not only for individual and interpersonal life but also for social institutional life and the life of the species; and not only for these but also for the proper relationships of human activity to the ordering of the natural world."[32] A particular "informed intuition" discerns these requisites in the moral situation and orders them in a fitting way. Some actions and relationships may be judged always to be morally wrong, but these often only set the outer limits of moral deliberation and fail to resolve all questions. Indeed, there is an inescapable measure of uncertainty in many moral choices, because these involve comparative assessments of competing values and the recognition of costs to those beings for whom they are valuable. In short, value is multidimensional, and there are tragic choices that simply cannot harmonize all goods. Under the conditions of finitude, "there is no clear overriding telos, or end, which unambiguously orders the priorities of nature and human participation in it so that one has a perfect moral justification for all human interventions."[33]

Fourth, a theocentric perspective considers the proper relations of "parts" to various "wholes" in light of divine governance. It gives a "proper incentive to expand the areas of relationship and interdependence within which particular entities are explained and understood."[34] This point is very significant for human moral agents, because they are participating, interacting parts within various wholes or processes and patterns of interdependence. These may be defined naturally, by kinship, political and cultural affiliation, species affiliation, and the like. To think about persons as parts is not willy-nilly to subordinate them to "the general good," for the well-being of individuals is included in the divine governance; there remains a duty under God to develop in one's own case the required conditions, resources, and strengths to be participants.[35] At the same time, this vision criticizes overblown views of human creativity and "self-making." It places a high values on the common good of various wholes, where parts will relate to that good, usually, reciprocally but not necessarily harmoniously. Thus Gustafson places a definite stress on the need for sacrifice for the sake of the whole.

Fifth, the meaning of human vocation is enlarged. Persons may see and feel themselves as "being called—being given opportunities to participate through our roles in the ordering of life in the world."[36] But the roles tend not to be conceived narrowly. The "whole" that is the family, for example, is itself part of "wholes" of culture and political society. As such they are acted upon by the values of the former and terms of distributive justice that figure in the latter. A participating member of a family should acknowledge how he or she is implicated in the processes by which cultural values are maintained and by which policies of justice are established. And "failure to provide certain necessary conditions is detrimental not only to families as parts of a larger society but also to the common good of society as a whole. Thus the ethics of family life has to extend to the public policy sector; the concern for social justice is essential."[37]

There are tensions as well as overlap in our role responsibilities. The family is a relevant whole in discussions about overpopulation and food shortages for the earth's human inhabitants. Families can act in ways that affect these matters, even if slightly; one may have to question, say, family claims of an unlimited freedom to procreate. Indeed, although voluntary restraints within families are preferable, theocentric ethics may well justify a nation's intensified practice of persuasion, inducement, and disincentive to accomplish a required limitation of population growth. Coercive means of birth control (e.g., mandatory sterilization) would be warranted in only the most extreme circumstances, and the costs of any restrictive measures to other values like family intimacy and the limitation of state power must be taken into account.[38]

Conclusion

In this section, I caution against four kinds of readings of Gustafson's ethics that, short of qualification and further investigation, could misinterpret them. I also note important similarities between his work and that of Niebuhr, and return to the themes of "church and world" that we considered at the start.

Four Risky Readings

First, theocentric ethics takes Christianity simply to be a particular historical expression of universal religious experience. The beliefs and doctrines of historical religions are symbolic expressions of an experiential core that essentially identifies humanity's relation to the divine.

There are grounds for this interpretation. Gustafson holds that what is given in the Bible, the charter document of Christian tradition, "is itself reflection on the meanings of common human experience in light of an experience of the presence of God."[39] The common experience concerns the various senses or aspects of piety. But Gustafson does not rely on a systematic theory of the nature of religion and the universal, history-transcending experience that constitutes it. The sensibilities that contribute to piety are grounded more empirically and less formally. There is no attempt to correlate systematically his phenomenology of religious experience with a general philosophical anthropology that overwhelms religious particularities by ordering them to itself. What is most important for Gustafson is just that we do find the senses of dependence, gratitude, and so forth in our everyday social and historical world.[40]

Second, Gustafson merely reduces the nature of "God" to the powers and processes of nature as these are apprehended by the investigations of modern science. Gene Outka writes that "sometimes . . . the following exhortation seems for Gustafson to exhaust the matter: consent to the divine governance simply by consenting to the order of the universe as science makes it known to us, and exercise to the full your limited human agency along the way in loving interaction with other human agents."[41] Why not leave it at that?

Gustafson reminds his critics that he has tried "to work from piety and the Christian theological tradition, and . . . within that tradition to interpret elements drawn from other sources."[42] Piety and tradition do not exclusively determine the construal of these elements and sources. Theocentric ethics is based on a "composite rationale."

> Like the Coca-Cola sign fishing raft we used on Brown's Lake in Dickinson City, MI, there are four barrels, one in each corner: evidences from relevant sciences (never "science" as one reified whole), human experience, philosophical judgments, and the heritage of Christianity and Judaism as contained in those traditions. All are necessary, and none is sufficient, but the raft tips to one corner or another depending on the weight of the exposition and defense.[43]

The attack on anthropocentrism, for example, contributes mightily to the composite rationale, along with the other elements. And within the terms of that rationale, Gustafson would say that that the following conclusion properly emerges from the stance of piety informed by Christian tradition: "If God is the ultimate orderer of life in the world, and if this ordering is through the patterns and processes of interdependence of life in the world, then knowledge of those patterns and processes is important for what they indicate about God. . . . Our best sources for knowledge of these patterns and processes are the sciences."[44]

Third, Gustafson's doctrine of God categorically excludes the element of personal divine agency. Here we find arguments and proposals that do not hang together with perfect coherence. On one side, Gustafson distances himself from ascriptions of agency by affirming God's purposes rather than intentions. He allies himself with Paul Tillich's position that we may relate personally to an impersonal God.

On the other side, he continues to speak of God as "enabling and re-quiring," which suggests something of personal agency, as well as piety's response of gratitude, which appears to presuppose something like the (personal) giving of a gift.

Robert Audi seems to be on the right track when he says that Gustafson's attack on anthropocentrism makes him understandably wary of conceptions of divinity that accord God agency like ours to serve our purposes. A related criticism is of *assimilationism*, or "a tendency to regard God as essentially like us, only infinitely greater in the degree of his possession of the same virtues."[45] But neither of these salvos requires entirely jettisoning a conception of God as personal. "Indeed, if what God enables and requires us to do is to be sufficiently intelligible to us to help us in making moral decisions, it looks as if we must posit some broadly personal divine characteristics, perhaps most notably a kind of agency."[46] Gustafson shows an openness to the point when he speaks about his wife's family farm in Iowa.

> I can say, whether it is metaphysical or not metaphysical, that God en-abled and required my father-in-law to care diligently for that land for all those years. And I can say for what ends—for the end of the well-being of his family, for the end of assisting others in the human com-munity to have food, for the end of pleasure and the flourishing of being on a farm and going out there and talking to those cows in the morning as if they were his friends. A whole host of ends were enabled. I can talk about God enabling and requiring. If that means I am using personalistic language in a stronger way than I seem to want to admit in my book, I am ready to do that.[47]

Fourth, theocentric ethics is a utilitarian ethics. Gustafson distin-guishes himself from Ramsey for greater appreciation of the conse-quences of moral actions, and he is prepared to recommend self-denial or self-sacrifice for the sake of the common good. He opposes, how-ever, the utilitarian urge to provide a single and first principle of ethics. He rejects outright tendencies to conceive the good of the whole in terms of an aggregate of individual goods. Gustafson relies on the idea of interactive right relations that have naturalist and other bases, not on simpler atomized measures of value in terms of "happiness" or "preference."[48]

The Niebuhrian Legacy

For many if not most Christian ethicists, James Gustafson is more closely associated with H. Richard Niebuhr than with any of the other figures treated in this book. Like Paul Ramsey, he was Niebuhr's student at Yale; he also collaborated with him in his professional writings, and introduced works of his published posthumously.[49] One cannot help noticing how *Ethics from a Theocentric Perspective* takes up features of radical monotheism, an interactive or responsive model of moral agency, and a conversionist approach to redemption.

Gustafson tries to avoid forms of theological one-sidedness, and this too bears Niebuhr's mark. Recall the five polarities I used to characterize the latter in the first chapter. Insisting on the universal reality of God, Gustafson also acknowledges that theology is a construal of reality from a particular standpoint. Through a method that both admits theology's constructive act within the confines of tradition and provides some backing for that act in common human experience, he tries to avoid reducing either of these poles to the other (i.e., become either a fideist or a natural theologian).

He acknowledges the storied character of Christian life and the essential place that Jesus Christ plays within it. But he also works from a "common sense ontology" of interdependence that significantly if loosely organizes a more general philosophical conception of the nature of God and reality (neither Christian apologist nor henotheist). Thus, from the standpoint of piety, he ventures that his theology and ethics may attend to "a community out there that the church is not able to address meaningfully because of its identification with the traditional sources that determine the basic frame of reference of its language. It is not able to tap what I think is their natural piety and their natural moral sentiment and to help them see and clarify that theirs is a legitimate form of life under God!"[50] The confessional dimension of theology must not overrun the universal intent with which it speaks. Theocentric ethics attends to both being and doing and the broader social context of the moral life as well as to the need for specific acts of discernment that are subject to objective assessment. His attack on sectarianism is complemented by an attack on anthropocentrism that distances him in principle every bit as much from the functionalism of cultural Christianity.

Two more resemblances deserve mention. They are connected in a poignant way. Gustafson's insistence that theology take scientific investigation seriously, his appeals to common human experience, and his critical understanding of Christian tradition attest to his aversion to a form of defensiveness that Niebuhr unrelentingly opposed. This was the posture of self-justification in which "we tend to magnify our distinctiveness from others, and to undervalue our similarities and agreements."[51] The critique of anthropocentrism as a form of utilitarian Christianity, of course, reflects another challenge to self-defense in Niebuhr's legacy. The conjunction of these themes leads Gustafson, as we saw in his response to Hauerwas, to suspect some defenses of the distinctiveness of the Christian tradition that isolate it from more general inquiries and that appear to focus functionally upon its language and practice, rather than on God.

For both Niebuhr and Gustafson, moreover, this defensiveness can and does carry over into types of Christian henotheism that are justified on Christocentric grounds. They resist Christocentric theologies at least because of their opposition to a narrow social faith. This is the second resemblance, and what is poignant is that both theologians have had the authenticity of their Christian belief challenged because of their seemingly weak Christologies. Niebuhr wrote in 1960: "In my confession of faith, as in that of many men I know, the expression of trust in God and the vow of loyalty to him comes before acknowledgment of Christ's Lordship. I realize that it is not so for all Christians but I protest against a dogmatic formulation that reads me and my companions out of the Church."[52] Thirty-three years later, Gustafson remarked: "I will never attribute to Jesus 'ultimate status.' Ultimate status . . . is given only to God. If my theological critics claim that I have to adhere to the Chalcedonian formula to be a Christian, I do not agree."[53]

Church and World

In the introductory section of this chapter, I said that Christian ethics ought to be rooted in Christian communal practice and ordered to responsibility before God in God's work as Creator, Preserver, and Redeemer. These simple claims correct, on the one hand, weaknesses in Ramsey's and Hauerwas's ethics. On the other hand, they suggest a positive view of the Christian community as above all pioneer and representative, functioning in its particular life as a world society. Neither worldly nor isolated, the church may convert terms of justice or the character of right relations in the world. Gustafson affirms all of this in a theology that he believes corrects his critics radically. He claims that his conversionism runs deeper than that of either Ramsey or Hauerwas in part because neither attends nearly enough, if at all, to nature and the natural processes and patterns of interdependence in which we participate. Without such considered attention, Christian ethical reflection cannot answer the question, What serves the divine purposes? But Ramsey "radically separates nature and history," and Hauerwas's failure to entertain the theological and ethical significance of nature (and thus creation) makes him a twentieth-century version of Marcion.[54]

However else Christian ethics emerges from piety and tradition, for Gustafson simple identification with Jesus and the church as its base of historical identity is not enough. That is not an acceptable way to be a pioneer and representative, or to function as a world society. It cannot be the case that "only Christian faith, history, and tradition are theologically important." It cannot be the case on theological grounds that "God" is known as "the tribal God of a minority of the earth's population."[55] The work of Christian communities is pathetically constrained thereby, and not least with the "community out there" who yet live under God.

> I am concerned that we recognize a certain kind of authenticity, a religious sensibility and moral profundity and sensitivity. At least some of us should find a way of talking to and nurturing that, of helping that become self-critical, and not building barriers that in my judgment are not essential to the ultimate thing that life is about—which is not preserving that damn tradition, but it is service to God.[56]

How shall the conversation proceed?

Notes

1. H. Richard Niebuhr, "The Responsibility of the Church for Society," in K. S. Latourette, ed., *The Gospel, the Church, and the World* (New York: Harper & Brothers, 1946), 119–20.

2. Ibid., 123. Niebuhr suggests that worldly religion is likely present whenever worship is aimed at effecting socially desired changes in the worshiper, or when education involves "an effort to create 'good citizens' or 'effective revolutionaries.'"

3. Ibid., 125.

4. James M. Gustafson, "Making Theology Intelligible: An Interpretation of H. Richard Niebuhr," *Reflections* (summer–fall 1995): 2–8.

5. James M. Gustafson, "The Sectarian Temptation," *Proceedings of the Catholic Theological Society* 40 (1985): 93.

6. Gustafson has written that his theocentric ethics "is the product of at least thirty years of 'homework'" and "also the product of fifty-five years of living"; James M. Gustafson, *Ethics from a Theocentric Perspective*, vol. 1, *Theology and Ethics* (Chicago: University of Chicago Press, 1981), ix–x. Some may find his position at odds with a good portion of his earlier work in Christian ethics. See, e.g., James M. Gustafson, *Christ and the Moral Life* (New York: Harper & Row, 1968), and *Can Ethics Be Christian?* (Chicago: University of Chicago Press, 1975). I am not able to consider this issue here, and I will leave it to others to trace an intellectual biography should they so choose.

7. Gustafson, *Ethics from a Theocentric Perspective*, vol. 1, 23.

8. Ibid., 84. Compare Richard Niebuhr's criticism of the defensive social pragmatism of "utilitarian Christianity."

9. Ibid., 99.

10. Ibid., 119.

11. Ibid., 124.

12. Ibid., 130–31.

13. Ibid., 142–43.

14. Ibid., 143.

15. Ibid., 151.

16. Ibid., 163–64.

17. Ibid., 228, 233–34; italics in original.

18. Ibid., 203.

19. Ibid., 237.

20. Ibid., 242.

21. Ibid., 246, 247.

22. Ibid., 249–50.

23. Ibid., 257–58.

24. Ibid., 17, 267.

25. Ibid., 276, 278.

26. Ibid., 282.

27. Ibid., 306.

28. Ibid., 307, 312, 317.

29. Ibid., 318–20, 322.

30. Ibid., 327.

31. Ibid., 338.

32. Ibid., 339.

33. James M. Gustafson, *A Sense of the Divine* (Cleveland: Pilgrim Press, 1994), 72.

34. Gustafson, *Ethics from a Theocentric Perspective*, vol. 2, *Ethics and Theology* (Chicago: University of Chicago Press, 1984), 15.

35. Ibid., 285.

36. Ibid., 285.

37. Ibid., 17.

38. Ibid., 246.

39. Gustafson, *Ethics from a Theocentric Perspective*, vol. 1, 146.

40. See John P. Reeder, Jr., "The Dependence of Ethics," in Harlan R. Beckley and Charles M. Sweezy, eds., *James M. Gustafson's Theocentric Ethics: Interpretations and Assessments* (Macon, Ga.: Mercer University Press, 1988), 122–26.

41. Gene Outka, "Remarks on a Theological Program Instructed by Science," *The Thomist* 47, no. 4 (October 1983): 591.

42. James M. Gustafson, "A Response to My Critics," *Journal of Religious Ethics* 13, no. 2 (fall 1985): 192.

43. Gustafson, *Sense of the Divine*, 46.

44. James M. Gustafson, "Response," in Beckley and Sweezy, *Gustafson's Theocentric Ethics*, 207–8.

45. Robert Audi, "Theology, Science, and Ethics in Gustafson's Theocentric Vision," in Beckley and Sweezy, *Gustafson's Theocentric Ethics*, 173.

46. Ibid., 174.

47. Gustafson, "Response," in Beckley and Sweezy, *Gustafson's Theocentric Ethics*, 230.

48. Reeder, "Dependence of Ethics," 130–37.

49. Gustafson wrote a lengthy introduction to *The Responsible Self* and collaborated with Niebuhr and D. D. Williams in writing *The Advancement of Theological Education* (New York: Harper & Brothers, 1957).

50. Gustafson, "Response," in Beckley and Sweezy, *Gustafson's Theocentric Ethics*, 239.

51. H. Richard Niebuhr, *The Responsible Self* (New York: Harper & Row, 1963), 150.

52. H. Richard Niebuhr, "Reformation: Continuing Imperative," *Christian Century* 77 (1960): 250.

53. Gustafson, "Response to My Critics," 197.

54. Ibid., 188–91.

55. Ibid., 196.

56. This is Gustafson's response in panel discussion to Paul Ramsey's suggestion to him that his account of the sources of theology "is drawing a line that leaves us out," i.e., colleagues and students and fellow Christians who continue to give primacy to Scripture and tradition and liturgy. The exchange is published in Beckley and Sweezy, *Gustafson's Theocentric Ethics*, 238–39.

CHAPTER EIGHT

Questions for Theocentric Ethics

In the last chapter, I discussed points of contact between H. Richard Niebuhr and James Gustafson. In this chapter, I identify what may be a significant difference in their respective approaches to the confessional task of Christian theology.

Types of Christian Theology

Hans Frei devised a typology of modern Christian theology that analyzes different relations between two theological projects. They reflect Christianity's history as both a privileged institution in the general cultural systems of the West and a distinct religious community.

> (1) *Christian* theology is an instance of a general class . . . to be subsumed under general criteria of intelligibility, coherence, and truth that it must share with other academic disciplines. . . . (2) *Theology* is an aspect of Christianity and is therefore partly or wholly defined by its relation to the cultural or semiotic system that constitutes that religion. . . . In this view theology is explained by the character of Christianity rather than vice-versa.[1]

The first view naturally appreciates philosophy to be a comprehensive mode of inquiry that determines the conditions and possibilities of knowledge about God. The second is more at home in alliance with interpretive disciplines such as anthropology and sociology. "What is at stake . . . is understanding a specific symbol system interpretively rather than inductively." Therefore theology contains both "first-order statements or proclamations made in the course of Christian practice and belief," and "second-order appraisal of its own language and actions under a norm or norms internal to the community itself."[2]

Frei sketches five postures toward these two descriptions of Christian theological work. The first type of theology is a philosophical discipline that takes "complete priority" over Christian self-description, as, for example, Immanuel Kant subordinated the internal language of Christian faith to a rich, reductive analysis bearing on the necessary conditions for the moral life. Type two theologies correlate Christian self-description with structures of meaningfulness discovered in a broader cultural life, such as art or science, but do so under the governance of an underlying philosophical scheme or theory that tends to reduce self-description to itself. Thus Christian language and practice might be interpreted systematically to be an instance of a universal religion or religiousness common to human subjects. The theologian shows how Christianity fits in with a variety of common human experiences and cultural understandings.

Theologians of the third type also try to show the fit between Christian claims and more common human cultural experience, but without the systematic theory ordering both to itself and each to the other. Instead, the idea is to indicate through "broadly pragmatic appeals to human experience" how Christianity makes some sense outside the boundaries of the Christian community; yet "the acquisition of *Christian knowledge* qua Christian self-description is as much a matter of learning a set of practical skills or capabilities as of learning a system of concepts under a general criterion of *meaning*" that organizes *external* descriptions of the Christian religion. Frei sees Friedrich Schleiermacher as the paradigmatic embodiment of this procedure.[3]

The type four theologian, such as Karl Barth, reverses the priority ordering of type two. The practical discipline of Christian self-description governs and limits the applicability of general criteria of meaning in theology:

> There can be no ultimate conflict between them, but in finite existence and thought we cannot know how they fit together in principle. As a result, Christian doctrinal statements are understood to have a status similar to that of grammatical rules implicit in discourse, and their relation to the broader or even universal linguistic context within which they are generated remains only fragmentarily—perhaps at times negatively—specifiable; yet it is important to keep that relation open and

constantly restate doctrinal statements in the light of cultural and conceptual change.[4]

Type five theologians take Christian theology to be pure self-description. External descriptive categories have no relation to it, and general theories specifying knowledge conditions are radically questioned in the name of specific and contextual appreciation of "language games" and the "grammar" internal to them.

The reductive maneuvers of the first two types seem wholly to dismiss the theological significance of Christian particularity for indicating a way of life and belief illuminating the normatively human. The fideism of type five elevates Christian particularity excessively and leads to an utterly insular piety. Pure self-description becomes merely repetition rather than an inquiry into the broader intelligibility of Christian claims.

The other two types respect Christian particularity and more general meanings of the normatively human, but in different ways and with different risks. Type three theologians have to watch that their correlation between Christian discourse and general experience not "give away the independence and practical aim of the church's critical self-description of its language;" and those of the fourth type should beware not to turn Christian theology "into the in-group talk of one isolated community among others, with no ground rules for mutual discourse among them all." As long as philosophy and other modes of nontheological inquiry are not summarily eliminated from theological reflection, and as long as theology is not required to pay "pathetic obeisance to philosophy as the master key to certainty about all reason and certainty and therefore to the shape or possibility of Christian theology," the theologian may proceed aware of the need to cut his or her losses in one direction or another.[5]

One way to think about this framework is in terms of how biblical stories about Jesus are differently interpreted. Frei believes that there has been a sort of consensus in Western Christianity about "the priority of the literal sense in regard to the texts concerning Jesus of Nazareth, chiefly the descriptions in the Gospels but to some extent in the rest of the New Testament. . . . The story of Jesus is about him, not about someone else or about nobody in particular or about all of us; that it is not two stories . . . or no story and so on and on."[6]

Whatever we are to make of the historical claim, we can see how the material position may fare in terms of our typology. The first two types tend to substitute general, comprehensive religious meaning for the specific ascriptive subject Jesus; Jesus at best is an exemplar or paradigm with regard to such meaning. The middle types recognize the ascriptive subject but relate Jesus to historical reality or philosophical inquiry in different ways. Type five theologians merely affirm without further comment the necessary connection between living the unique Christian "form of life" and (truly) understanding scriptural statements about Jesus.[7]

Niebuhr seems usually to be a type three theologian, although some of his most important work in Christian ethics—his analyses of types of relation between Christ and culture—possess type four characteristics. Recall the discussion of confessional theology in chapter 2. He takes its work to include identification of central patterns of Christian self-description in history ("seeking the reason within that history"), the presentation of the grammar of faith, and the criticism of that faith by the experience of the church. But he also often attempts to correlate and mutually interpret Christian self-description with more general cultural understandings and external descriptions. As Gustafson has noted, Niebuhr's project includes displaying, through a practical method of reflection, the wider intelligibility of Christian belief both to a secular audience and to Christians who question the meaningfulness of some self-description given its possible collision with otherwise reasonable nontheological perspectives.[8]

Note three examples of Niebuhr's ad hoc correlation. First, as Gustafson shows in detail, the account of faith often involves reflections on common human experiences of confidence and trust, of loyalty and fidelity, and of their opposites, "which refer to aspects that are comprehensible . . . to secular persons." Discontinuities are also noted that distinguish the religious aspects, but "the continuity makes the point of distinctiveness intelligible, if not credible, to the radical secularist."[9]

Second, in the work toward a definition of Christ in *Christ and Culture*, he analyzes the identity of Jesus, depicted in the Gospels, in terms of both a set of generally commended virtues (e.g., love, hope, obedience, humility) and the insights of historical-critical inquiry. This analysis would go some way toward articulating that identity morally and historically, but it is also completed and corrected by the biblical portrait of the one Jesus who directed all virtues to God as God's Son. In virtue of this Sonship he engages "the double movement—with men toward God, with God toward men. . . . He is a single person wholly directed in his unity with the Father toward men."[10] Niebuhr combines the biblical portrait of Jesus and his meaningfulness in the Christian language of faith with historical studies in a way that exposes the more generic intelligibility of his virtue as well as its particular character in the light and language of Christian tradition.[11]

Third, Niebuhr's Earl Lectures on the symbolic form of Jesus Christ begin from a twofold understanding of Jesus. (1) His moral agency is a unique instance of the general image of the responding person, the person who as a citizen of the cosmos "interprets every particular event as included in universal action." His ethos of universal responsibility has affinities with Jewish tradition, Stoicism, and Spinoza; it is not utterly unique in its opposition to all individualistic and social egoism and narrowness. (2) Jesus is to be understood as Redeemer, the one whose ministry, cross, and resurrection make Christians suspicious of their deep suspicion of the Determiner of Destiny "so that the *Gestalt* which they bring to their experiences of suffering as well as of joy, of death as well as of life, is the *Gestalt*, the symbolic form, of grace."[12]

For Niebuhr, these understandings—the general and the particular form of Christian self-description—are interlocked and therefore necessary for Christians to grasp the being of Jesus. On this point, Niebuhr criticizes Barth's attempt at a "completely Christocentric and solely Christo-morphic form of thinking and acting."[13] It is just as important to stress, however, that the appeal (for both Christian and non-Christian) to a general and perhaps universal conception of responsibility works hand in hand with accounts of Christian self-description and redescription that are not simply reduced to or explained by putatively comprehensive moral or metaphysical standpoints. These accounts possess a distinctive logic and practical force that cannot be whisked away. Thus "Niebuhr trod a delicate path between image- or story-shaped and universal ethics, and between universal and particular story-shaped theology. Unlike Barth, he refused to make a decision between a narrative and . . . a trans-narrative, universal understanding of God's acts in history."[14]

An Ambiguity in Theocentric Ethics

In the last chapter, I argued that Gustafson does not, in the manner of type one and two theologians, systematically reduce or explain the language of Christian faith in terms of universal theory. There is no such view of religion as such in theocentric ethics; it refers to common experiences specifically and empirically described as relevant to religious and Christian piety, not constitutive of it.

Also, Gustafson's ontology of process, order, development, and change is of the common sense variety and has no pretensions to subordinate systematically the Christian tradition's language about God to it. He says that he theologically departs from piety as shaped by the language and practices of Christian tradition. But he is also determined not to subordinate more general human inquiries to the tradition's self-description, because his composite rationale requires that the tradition be subjected to ongoing and thorough testing from outside itself. The relative independence of the Christian religion, its piety and tradition, is conceded. Does not this concession align theocentric ethics with Frei's third category?

Consider the nature of God. On the one side of a postulated non-systematic correlation between traditional self-description and general cultural experience, we have a selective retrieval of the Reformed tradition with its views about the sovereignty of God, the significance of piety, and the ordering of human life to God. Also, "The religious language and symbols of one's tradition penetrate one's perception both of the meaning of what is seen and one's affective responses. What one sees may be a expression of the power and glory of God; one's responses might be a quiet expression of praise of God; one's joy and delight may be in the beauty and goodness of God." Christian piety construes the common "senses" in these ways, and *there is no avoiding acknowledgment of circularity in this*; the experience confirms that which I am predisposed to have it confirm."[15]

On the other side, confirmation is liable to assessment, which relies in part on avenues of knowledge and understanding external to the tradition. Gustafson brings Christian talk about God to scientific inquiries and concludes that evidence from these present warrants for a religious sense of dependence, for a religious conception of creation's ordering, and for the conception of God the power that bears down and sustains us. The religious features and the scientific warrants gain their "full religious significance," however, "only within piety," informed by tradition. This strategy does look pretty much like establishing a theological correlation between the language of Christian faith and more general experience and understanding.

Then that is that? No. Theocentric ethics has an ambiguity that may compromise its treatment of Christian self-description as a distinctive and integral theological resource. This ambiguity has two sources. One jeopardizes the Christian practice of making traditioned claims about the way things really are in the language of faith. The other may subject that language to an overly restrictive scientific criterion of justification.

Gustafson admits that his views on the narratives of Christian tradition tilt more toward their social-psychological significance, the way they sustain and vivify communal memory and a way of life, than toward their impact on delivering "objective knowledge of God":

> To acknowledge that the particularity of the Christian story is more important for our individual and communal "subjectivity" than it is for what we are finally able to say about the powers in whose hands are the destinies of the worlds does not render it meaningless. Within liturgies and preaching, religious communities function to awaken and nourish our religious affectivities, to provide the symbols by which we consciously acknowledge God, and through which we praise God. Their symbols always appropriately point to the reality of the divine powers, but never exhaust them. They help us to discern both the presence of the divine governance in and through particular experiences and events and its ineffable mystery before which we stand in silence.[16]

Gustafson holds generally that historical traditions may be sources of moral and religious insight regarding the reality of God. Yet his definite emphasis on the social and psychological over against the objective raises a question whether for the most part he views Christian traditions as only a "matrix and framework for knowing" that "mediates no realities."[17] Hence, although theology or talk about God has its clearest value and significance within the context of piety, what Gustafson does with his selective retrieval of Reformed tradition is to set up a basic theological framework that will carry and express realities substantively grasped through reflection on extratraditional sources. One might see this project in operation when Gustafson highlights three very general Reformed themes: the sovereignty of God, the centrality of reverent and devoted piety, and the requirement that all human activity be ordered properly to God and God's purposes.

Edward Farley persuasively argues that an assumption "that tradition itself has little or no cognitive status" may animate Gustafson's caution in affirming traditional claims just as much as his opposition to "sectarian" or otherwise uncritical appropriations of the "Christian story."[18] In that case, tradition preserves and forms in us certain convictions associated with natural pieties and affections; but it fails to disclose in its own terms something that is true, perdurable, the way things are. Apart from the fact that a whole lot of Christian folks do intend for their language to make cognitive claims in this way, it seems that a theological style of ad hoc correlation requires acknowledgment of both this intention and the possibility that these claims are successful.

The question of whether Christian traditions lack cognitive force is complemented by a question about how much constraint scientific evidence places on theological work. The preferred warranting relation, again, is that though "piety . . . is a necessary condition for ideas about God to be subjectively meaningful and intellectually persuasive," the "'substantial content' of ideas about God cannot be incongruous . . . with well-established data and explanatory principles established by relevant sciences, and must 'be in some way indicated by these.'"[19] Gustafson shows that the relevant sciences indicate the propriety of his conception of God as the power that sustains and bears down upon us, the radically dependent beings who participate in God's ordering and respond to possibilities and directions divinely provided. And he locates incongruity and hence implausibility regarding certain anthropocentric doctrines of eschatology and salvation, the extent of human freedom, and the personal agency of God.

The scientific criterion, however, tends to control the field of inquiry regarding what we can legitimately say and know theologically. For example, divine redemption appears virtually equivalent to conversion to a sense of renewed possibility as participants in processes and patterns of natural and social interdependence. Notions of divine forgiveness (in Jesus Christ) do not figure or are approximated exclusively to the sphere of interhuman relations. Ideas about resurrection or life after death similarly are given up in the encounter with scientific conclusions and their accompanying construal of anthropocentrism without much attention to the significance that Christian self-description of these ideas might have in their own right. There is also at least unclarity about whether or not theocentric ethics finally treats Jesus Christ as simply an exemplar or symbol of human nature in general who stands for the content of theocentric piety and motivates people to practice it.

Gustafson does not systematically reduce Christian discourse and practice to an instance of universal religiousness, and he does not uniformly reduce God and God-talk to natural social processes. The ambiguity is more complex. A requirement that the content of theological ideas must be indicated in some way by well-established scientific data might by itself be overly restrictive in the manner of Frei's second type; it could mean that Christian claims are invariantly and exclusively to be construed as intelligible in scientific categories.

My point is a little different. It is, first, that Gustafson has at best an unsure commitment to the cognitive status of Christian tradition and the language of faith; and that, second, this weak commitment renders the content of crucial kinds of theological proposals captive to external descriptions congenial to naturalist and scientific reflection. A relation between internal and external descriptions, even for the purposes of correlation, is jeopardized by an approach to the former that tends to give them no purchase on the way things are; the latter, again, is controlling in that area, and theological substance is governed accordingly. This break in the trail of Gustafson's argument, as Farley puts it, seriously weakens or opposes the force of the claim that theocentric ethics works "from piety and the Christian theological tradition, and . . . within that tradition to interpret elements drawn from other sources."[20]

Thus Gustafson's theological ethics, which laudably strives to open up inquiry to sources beyond Scripture and narrow or otherwise sectarian appeals to tradition, may unfortunately constrain legitimate theological investigation in other ways. Let us look at a few examples.

More Questions

Grateful or Lucky?

Gustafson's Christology seems to reflect the ambiguity I developed in the preceding section. On the one hand, he interprets the significance of Jesus Christ to be the materially decisive source for the faith of the Christian community.[21] He relies on the narrative accounts of the Gospels and does not reduce them to the terms of historical-critical or theological or ecclesiastical analysis; in the depiction of Jesus these narratives "bear down on the receptive human spirit with their own compelling power," and "clearly testify to the compelling power of Jesus' unique life and ministry, of his devotion to God."[22]

On the other hand, the substantial content of claims about Jesus appears to be virtually identical to the senses of natural piety. The traditioned Gospel stories "guide and direct," "awaken and nourish," and motivate expression of these religious affectivities. Although they manifest what God is enabling and requiring us to be and to do, what is manifested is presented as having objective status only insofar as the language of faith gestures toward realities decisively described external to it. In this respect, Jesus looks more like a symbolically valuable exemplar or representative of human nature than as himself the unique source of Christian faith.

In any case, the Christology presumably works in ways that cohere with other striking features of theocentric ethics, including the general dictum that, in contrast to Christian anthropocentrism, God, of whom the language of personal agency is to be used cautiously if at all, is honored in piety as the source but not the guarantor of human good. The dictum leaves the possibility, for example, that the powers of God may make one's human life an unbearable burden, and that in such cases one must consent to one's own or another's suicide. There is room for enmity toward God. Yet this possibility and its presupposition Gustafson deem compatible with affirming the religious "sense of gratitude" to God, and a biblical depiction of Jesus in which gratitude is expressed over and over.[23]

With other students of theocentric ethics, I wonder whether all of this can hold together. "We might be awestruck before the order of things," William Placher writes, "but why grateful? . . . Has such a theology left us with enough of a personal divine agent to permit a relation like gratitude?" He contrasts Niebuhr's claim that Jesus Christ makes Christians "suspicious of their deep suspicion of the Determiner of Destiny," turning their reasoning around so that they do not begin with a premise of divine indifference but bring instead to the whole of their lives "the *Gestalt*, the symbolic form, of grace."[24] Niebuhr goes on:

> To some of us it seems that in the cross of Jesus Christ, in the death of such a man who trusts God and is responsible to him as a son, we face the great negative instance or the negation of the premise that God is love, and that unless this great negative instance—summarizing and symbolizing all the negative instances—is faced, faith in the universal power as God must rest on quicksand; in facing it, however, we have the demonstration in this very instance of a life-power that is not conquered, not destroyed. Reality maintains and makes powerful such life as this. The ultimate power does manifest itself as the Father of Jesus Christ through his resurrection from death.[25]

This line of reflection emerging from traditional Christian language of cross and resurrection presents these questions: Is "gratitude," or the fitting response to a giver of a gift, the best term to describe the theocentric response to benefits received from God? Does not the description "being lucky" commend itself instead, or an attitude that expresses in piety a feeling of temporary or at least always cautious relief at having dodged misfortune? Is grace as described above always fatally allied with anthropocentrism, or does a language of faith that emphasizes the cross as Niebuhr does have a salutary effect in this regard?

I cannot imagine Gustafson not taking these questions seriously. But a subjective approach to tradition coupled with a strong appreciation of science and its own construal of anthropocentrism can reduce or eliminate their importance insofar as the latter dominates what we can say theologically.

Theology's Practical Force

Another possible difficulty is present when Gustafson denies anthropocentrism, affirms consent to certain suicides when the deepest despair is in fact warranted, and claims grounds in these cases for enmity
with God. Supposedly, we may respond this way to God the Enemy
when God's purposes oppose our good as we understand it; but if
theocentric consent unleashes our hold on the latter as the basis for or
basic expectation of our piety, then where is the warrant for enmity
that is consistent with consent?

Perhaps Gustafson wants to distinguish consent to certain suicides
and the refusal to consent to the God who conditions a human life
with unbearable affliction. Surely he is right to locate anger toward
God as a proper religious response in certain circumstances. My primary concern here, however, is with the practical force of his ethical
reflections. George Hunsinger proposes that Gustafson's "moral assessment of suicide's possible legitimacy hinges entirely on questions
of rational perception. Is despair a reasonable construal of this person's life circumstances or not? Are there or are there not courses of
action available which can relieve the person's suffering?"[26]

Now are human beings so constituted that this recommended approach to moral assessment anticipates forms of consent that may be
premature, or even be the equivalent of abandonment? Barth's anthropocentric tendencies may be evident when he says that only God's
graciously given permission and freedom to live beyond a law that one
must live stands over against the real burdens of the person contemplating self-destruction. But he also admits the possibility of the deepest human affliction, as well as legitimate exceptions to a stringent
norm against self-murder. He refuses, however, to specify these exceptions, and cautions that theological ethicists be careful never to presume that they understand what affliction in practice really is. "A man
assailed and afflicted is hid from all others and sometimes even from
himself. He is alone with God, and tortured by the question whether
God is really with him and for him."[27]

Thus the sovereign self-judgment of suicide, though categorically
forbidden and challenged by God's gracious "Thou mayest live," is not
identical with the case where the gracious God would help a person in

affliction by telling him to take this way out.[28] Yet these cases ought not to be classified or codified, both because of the reserve we should show in claiming really to understand this assault, and because human energies ought to be directed to discerning vigorously the presence of grace. Because we ourselves are always tempted and burdened by laws requiring us to live, perhaps we are too ready to see these burdens as overwhelming others, and even the others entrusted to our care.

Perhaps Barth is not consistent here, as Gustafson thinks. But he does offer an approach toward suicide that resists moralistic judgment and acknowledges exceptions without for one moment giving up on the call to human creatures to find their freedom in witnessing wherever and however they can to God's grace in Jesus Christ. A moral approach that relies (even within piety) on rational perception of possibilities and their absence, and on the possibility of classified consent to suicide, may—I say may—lose sight of imaginative possibilities for witness, or even fall prey to unfittingly despairing interpretations of the human condition.

If my speculation is valuable, it does not lead to the conclusion that practical efficacy determines the truth of our claims about God. It is, rather, that certain suppositions about human existence, captured by Christian self-descriptions about divine mercy, human limits and presumptions, and the like, could offer theological and ethical insight within those terms. I think Gustafson would find these questions interesting and fruitful to explore; I am not sure that he always construes Christian tradition and its language of faith in a fashion that permits or encourages the relevant inquiries to proceed.

Resurrection and Experience

In a recent essay, Ronald F. Thiemann develops a traditional Christian answer to the question "Is there life after death?" He locates belief in survival beyond the grave to faith and hope in the resurrection of Jesus from the dead. That Jesus now lives is part of the message of the Gospel, which proclaims that a loving and almighty God has reconciled the entire cosmos to Himself. Biblical testimonies to Jesus' Resurrection from the dead also make it clear that Jesus' Passion and its sequel are not to be seen as "simple historical facts, but divine actions directed toward *our* salvation."[29] Affirming resurrection is affirming (with humility and astonishment) that God in Christ brings life out of death for my sake and for my salvation.

Being a matter of faith and not sight, for Thiemann belief in the resurrection requires affirming a continuity of personal identity on either side of death. Yet this is not a matter of "blind belief in a miraculous violation of nature." It "in no way implies a general belief in miraculous resuscitation or communication between the spirits of the dead and the living," and "requires belief in only two instances of resurrection, that of Jesus and that of the dead on the last day." What is "miraculous" here is the overturning of our ordinary beliefs about the finality of death, but our language is utterly inadequate to communicate the reality of "God's saving act of bringing life out of the despairing depths of the grave."[30]

By an uncharitable reading, Thiemann's analysis smacks of anthropocentrism and easy confessionalism, defensively isolates belief in resurrection from empirical testing, and relies uncritically on biblical materials and the language of tradition. It is fairer to say that he intends to qualify claims about human salvation by referring to almighty God and the reconciliation of the entire world, that he wishes to interpret resurrection faith in a way that attends both to particular Christian sources and to the shape of our broader experience, and that he acknowledges the inability of language to grasp a promise and a reality held in faith. The critic who would reassert the criticisms above must do so after exploring these qualifications, construals, and acknowledgments as they reflect an account of the traditioned experience of the Christian life before God.

Thiemann only hints at such an account, but it is safe to say that it centrally involves an experience of one's life as constituted by free, divine grace where this is depicted in the narrative of Jesus' ministry, Crucifixion, and Resurrection. Humble and confident trust in that grace carries with it a sense of helplessness before God and the need to live in Christ, as well as the conviction that that new life in the Crucified and Risen Christ promises a salvation that overturns what we may typically and sinfully count as our good. And it is worth adding that the experience implicit in an analysis such as Thiemann's issues in both a reluctance to affirm construals of life after death that are incongruous with our typical and empirically informed understandings of the reality of death, and a reluctance to offer a purely naturalistic vision of the victory of God's love over whatever opposes it.

Do Gustafson's appeals to the priority of experience and his cautions regarding the inevitably selective project of theology resonate in important ways with a so-called orthodox vision of resurrection and salvation? I think so. That vision, however, presumes that the language of tradition can have cognitive significance, and theocentric ethics, I have argued, does not clearly carry forward this presumption. Does the vision exclude attention to testing from other sources of knowledge and understanding? I think not, as long as the nature of this testing does not exclude from the outset the experience of the reality of God in question. Yet our ambiguity in theocentric ethics risks doing just that. It begs the question to assert that any and every caution about external testing expresses a defensive fideism.

Correction and Overcorrection

Niebuhr once compared movement in theology and all thought to the activity of a bicycle rider, whose progress "is marked by an almost infinite number of variations of the wheel to right and left and by a constant balancing of his body through small inconspicuous shiftings of weight. If the variations of the wheel or of his balance become extreme in one direction, they must be compensated for by extreme variations in the other direction and when the corrections become over-corrections there is catastrophe."[31] This analogy appears in a discussion where Niebuhr explicitly questions whether Barth's corrections to antitraditionalism, subjectivism, and pragmatism in theology have tended to become overcorrections that render traditional theological formulas intact but unintelligible, backed by a revelational objectivism that is but the authoritarianism of some particular group, and explained by a speculative system that leaves ethics as an afterthought.

Gustafson's corrections to theology and theological ethics are in part responses to what he believes to be overcorrections of this sort. He opposes the irrationalist confessionalism of in-group Christianity that at best ignores a "community out there" that possesses a depth of piety putting many Christians to shame. He is suspicious of styles of "faith seeking understanding" that rely so much on divine revelation or appeals to particular placement in history that they eschew testing and enriching theological conclusions by nontheological sources of insight, especially from the sciences.

Acknowledging a measure of biblical authority, the importance of Jesus for Christian faith, and the value of faith community, Gustafson cautions as Niebuhr did against biblicism, Christocentrism, and ecclesialism; all succumb in different but related ways to the sectarian temptation.[32] Christocentrism in particular can reduce to the "henotheism" of the church, the fideism of its internal doctrines, an anthropocentrism that guarantees human salvation and eternal life, and a Marcionite rejection of God the Creator, maker of heaven and earth, and all that is seen and unseen.

Gustafson has helped us to see that the theological and ethical significance of nature cannot be ignored; that a merely tribal Christianity is inadequate; that the wholeness of our cultural experience cannot readily let alone honestly insulate religious conviction from other measures of human understanding; and that "the stark and ambiguous evidence of a deity who is 'in the details' not a guarantor of individual temporal well-being is an important corrective to sentimental longings that reduce God to a safety net under life's mistakes and disasters."[33] But I suggest that the ambiguity in theocentric ethics about the status of tradition and the accompanying elevation of the sciences expresses an overcorrection that secures the universal intent of theological discourse at the price of the integrity of Christian self-description. This overcorrection tends practically to restrict the range of theological projects deemed worthy of serious investigation. When Gustafson, for instance, says that Paul Ramsey carries his separation between nature and history to a "logical but amusing, if not ridiculous, extreme when he justifies monogamy in Christendom on the basis of God's covenant with *one* people, Israel . . . and Christ's covenant with one church,"[34] he relies so much on the critical basis of his point that he ends up ignoring or deriding a particular insight about Christian marital fidelity that emerges in tradition.

Such fidelity may reflect a kind of experience of God in piety that resonates with general religious affectivities while also being irreducible to and even transformative of some of them. When Gustafson charges that "Hauerwas's is an intellectual and moral sectarianism of the most extreme sort" that "forecloses apologetics of any kind and limits the range of the ethical," he runs past the very resources I used in earlier chapters to show both how Hauerwas avoids the sectarian label and how he might do so better. Insisting that attention to nature be part of the upbuilding of a doctrine of creation is fitting; not engaging the full meaning and purpose of Hauerwas's appeals to Christian self-description is not.

Nobody in the field of Christian ethics can surpass Gustafson in the care and critical sympathy with which he addresses the contributions of others. I repeat that in the relevant cases I see a sort of overcorrection that can prevent genuine movement in theological ethics. To return to Frei's typology and the risks that attend types three and four, an overcorrection that could give away the independence and practical aim of Christian self-description ought to be avoided just as much as that of making Christian language the in-group talk of a community isolated from all others.

Conclusion

Christian theology's isolation from nontheological inquiries is neither warranted nor possible. It is not warranted because Christians affirm the reality of the God of all creation who orders all that is. It is not possible because theological interpretations, explanations, and evaluations emerge from investigations that select from, combine, and recombine many sources and contexts broader than the "explicitly Christian." As Kathryn Tanner says, theology is apologetic from the start because it always employs and shapes materials from a broader cultural environment to arrive at its distinctive vision, arguments, and conclusions. This process goes on even while one rightly affirms that that vision is independent because it is not reducible to any other.[35]

Gustafson opposes theological isolation, and distinguishes his theological method from revelational and confessional approaches that affirm or enable it. Yet one should not conflate isolation with independence and irreducibility. It is possible and necessary for an independent theology, grounded in tradition and claims about divine revelation, to use and learn from nontheological sources. It will count contrary evidence—say, regarding the presence of seemingly ineradicable evil in the world—as just that at the same time as it may also witness to God's perfect graciousness. It will acknowledge, not out of defensive irrationalism but from piety, divine mystery and the way that faith involves belief and understanding in some propositions about God without a grasp of how exactly they apply to God.[36] It is important to avoid the conflation and to acknowledge these possibilities lest theological work in the Christian community be excessively narrowed and corrections be turned into overcorrections.

Of course, Gustafson's trouble with an independent theology has a lot to do with his positive concern that theologians do in fact negotiate the traffic between other disciplines and theological ethics so that it flows in two directions. Revelational and confessional theologies can be seen to authorize conclusions exclusively, standing on their own without the need for other disciplines, maintaining always the upper hand. Thus traffic flows in one direction only as theological ethics interprets, explains, programmatically annexes or qualifies, and safely confirms the others.[37]

Independent authorization by revelation or confessional awareness of historical particularity does not need to be exclusive of other materials that shape, interpret, and revise theological proposals. Gustafson welcomes Stephen Pope's conclusions, drawn from his studies in evolutionary biology, that an understanding of God's creative ordering must positively affirm an "order of love" that humans exhibit, especially in their preferential regard for family and other kin. Connected to an analysis of natural selection stressing an organism's inclination to preserve the genetic endowment it possesses and shares, this notion of love's ordering surely can correct views of Christian love that disparage, ignore, or offer no place for moral relations of familial preference.[38]

We can think of other pertinent examples. Social scientific studies of human socialization may illumine or explicate naturalistically the formation of Christian vision, character, or moral identity along the lines of Hauerwas's ethics. Ramsey can rightly borrow authority from strategic theories developed in political science to show how certain optimistic theological interpretations of inter-state harmony in our international system are simply wrong.

Simultaneous with these maneuvers, the Christian ethicist (1) may still argue and demonstrate that the order of preferential love is informed by and aligned with a norm of universal love for all neighbors in Jesus Christ; (2) can show how human sanctification in the Holy Spirit remains a work of grace not specified exhaustively by socialization theory; and (3) can point to overlaps between the insights of strategic theorists and theological visions of politics and human responsibility. As long as Christian self-description is granted an irreducible status and even independent authorization, activities of revision, explication, and borrowing authority will be situated and measured by theological efforts to establish the most coherent critical account of Christian faith. Again: independence is maintained, but exclusivity is excluded, and not least that arrogant misuse of independence that denies, after the fact of creative engagement with other disciplines, that nothing new has been learned because some distinctively Christian account may be found in the Christian web of belief to cover all insights.

An isolated and exclusive theology is often anthropocentric, cutting its portrayal of God to the needs and desires of human persons as they understand these. An independent theology may struggle with its anthropocentric tendencies in powerful fashion. Universal solidarity with the rest of creation, God's good gift, gives reason for stewardship and humility, not controlling pride. Humanity's special distinction through creation in the divine image and the Incarnation, Crucifixion, and Resurrection of Jesus Christ is ordered to God's own project of universal well-being, and does not specify any qualities of human nature as such that earn or deserve it.

In fact, "the distinction of being human, its special value and goodness, can be affirmed appropriately only against the backdrop of human unworthiness for it. . . . God is, therefore, never required to bless those that God does bless. . . . We are all like Jonah in the belly of the whale— enjoying a deliverance from God that desperate straits make an unexpected and unhoped for surprise."[39] Theology and Christology address Christian language and practice in a manner that affirms God's graciousness for humanity as a feature of God's utter sovereignty.

Theocentric ethics, more than anything, intends to honor the full reality of the sovereign God. Like Niebuhr's theology, it would give this reality priority at the same time as it strongly attests to the particular traditioned location of Christian confession of loyalty to this God. For Niebuhr, I think, the language of tradition was "unavoidable and linguistically unsubstitutable;[40] it mediates divine reality and does not only carry forward historical convictions to be tested and rendered intelligible exclusively from extratraditional sources. Sometimes, I have argued, Gustafson's ethics suggests that he is at variance with this view. If so, then I would say that his important criticisms of theologians like Ramsey and Hauerwas go too far because Christian self-description tends to lose any independent (not isolated or exclusive) illuminating force.

Notes

1. Hans W. Frei, *Types of Christian Theology*, ed. George Hunsinger and William C. Placher (New Haven, Conn.: Yale University Press, 1992), 2.
2. Ibid., 2.
3. Ibid., 2–3; italics in original.
4. Ibid., 4.
5. Hans W. Frei, *Theology and Narrative*, ed. George Hunsinger and William C. Placher (New York: Oxford University Press, 1993), 195–97.
6. Frei, *Types of Christian Theology*, 140.
7. Ibid., 5–6.
8. James M. Gustafson, "Making Theology Intelligible: An Interpretation of H. Richard Niebuhr," *Reflections* (summer–fall 1995): 2–8.
9. Ibid.
10. H. Richard Niebuhr, *Christ and Culture* (New York: Harper & Brothers, 1951), 29.
11. Cf. Frei, *Types of Christian Theology*, 143–46.
12. H. Richard Niebuhr, *The Responsible Self* (New York: Harper & Row, 1963), 175–76.
13. Ibid., 158.
14. Frei, *Theology and Narrative*, 229.
15. James M. Gustafson, *Ethics from a Theocentric Perspective*, vol. 1, *Theology and Ethics* (Chicago: University of Chicago Press, 1981), 228, 233–34; italics in original.
16. Ibid., 278–79.
17. Edward Farley, "Theocentric Ethics as a Genetic Argument," in Harlan R. Beckley and Charles M. Sweezy, eds., *James M. Gustafson's Theocentric Ethics: Interpretations and Assessments* (Macon, Ga.: Mercer University Press, 1988), 56.
18. Ibid.
19. Gustafson, *Ethics from a Theocentric Perspective*, vol. 1, 257.

20. James M. Gustafson, "A Response to Critics," *Journal of Religious Ethics* 13, no. 2 (fall 1985): 192.

21. See George Hunsinger, "Afterword: Hans Frei as Theologian," in Frei, *Theology and Narrative*, 261.

22. Gustafson, *Ethics from a Theocentric Perspective*, vol. 1, 276.

23. Ibid., 278.

24. William C. Placher, *The Domestication of Transcendence* (Louisville: Westminster/John Knox Press, 1996), 203.

25. Niebuhr, *Responsible Self*, 177.

26. George Hunsinger, "A Response to William Werpehowski," *Theology Today* 43, no. 3 (October 1986): 357.

27. Karl Barth, *Church Dogmatics* (Edinburgh: T. & T. Clark, 1961), vol. 3, part 4, p. 404.

28. Ibid., 410. Cf. William Werpehowski, "Hearing the Divine Command: Realism and Discernment in Barth's Ethics," *Zeitschrift fur dialektische Theologie* 15, no. 1 (1999): 64–74.

29. Ronald F. Thiemann, "Is There Life After Death?" in Ronald F. Thiemann and William C. Placher, eds., *Why Are We Here?* (Harrisburg, Pa.: Trinity Press International, 1998), 160.

30. Ibid., 161–65.

31. H. Richard Niebuhr, *Theology, History, and Culture* (New Haven, Conn.: Yale University Press, 1996), 8.

32. Gustafson, "Making Theology Intelligible," 6–8.

33. Margaret Farley, "The Role of Experience in Moral Discernment," in Lisa Sowle Cahill and James F. Childress, eds., *Christian Ethics: Problems and Prospects* (Cleveland: Pilgrim Press, 1996), 139–40.

34. Gustafson, "Response to Critics," 189.

35. Kathryn Tanner, *Theories of Culture* (Minneapolis: Fortress Press, 1997), 116.

36. Cf. Placher, *Domestication of Transcendence*, 201–15.

37. James M. Gustafson, *Intersections: Science, Theology, and Ethics* (Cleveland: Pilgrim Press, 1996), vii–xvii and passim. Cf. Tanner, *Theories of Culture*, 147–49.

38. Gustafson, *Intersections*, 101–4, 108–9.

39. Kathryn Tanner, "The Difference Theological Anthropology Makes," *Theology Today* 50, no. 4 (January 1994): 574, 575, 577.

40. Frei, *Theology and Narrative*, 218.

CHAPTER NINE

Transcendence, Culture, and Ethics

One striking characteristic of Kathryn Tanner's theology is its (critical) development of a number of convictions dear to H. Richard Niebuhr: the transcendence and sovereignty of God, the relation between Creator and creation, Jesus Christ as the manifestation of God's total graciousness, the social dimension of human existence, the equality of human creatures, and the dangers of defensiveness. In this and the following chapter, I discuss these issues while analyzing Tanner's work and its connections to Niebuhr and our other theological ethicists. Here I move to an assessment of Tanner's concern that Niebuhr's (and James Gustafson's) appeals to human agency as a response to "God's actions upon you" illegitimately constrain the range of free responsibility. Chapter 10 considers—in keeping with a view of divine transcendence that highlights the interpretive discernment of what God is doing in the world—some valuable contributions that Tanner's theology may make to our understanding of conversionism, the particularity of Christian identity, and the latter's link to a universal society under God.

Transcendence and Agency

How ought we to think theologically about the transcendence of God? Admitting that his analogy is limited, William Placher points us in the right direction:

> In a play the various actors act in the usual mixture of determinism and free will. A character may move across the stage dragged against her will, as eagerly headed toward some goal, or more or less at random. And yet, at another level . . . playwright and director have determined everything. We can debate how many choices Willy Loman had in *Death of a Salesman* and what mix of forces and decisions shaped his

tragedy. If someone interrupts our discussion of the relative importance of his family, the company that fired him, and his own character in his tragic fate, to say, "No, you have it all wrong—Arthur Miller was really the force that determined Willy Loman's actions," we do not feel so much that a new point of view has been introduced as that the interruption has changed the subject. *Of course* the author determined all the characters' actions, but that is irrelevant to our discussion of the characters' motivations.[1]

The example suggests two planes of agency. Obviously, they are not to be identified with one another ("what Arthur Miller and Willy Loman are doing is one and the same"). They should not be contrasted with one another, either, within a plane presumed to be shared.

Tanner, following a venerable historical tradition she sketches and defends, affirms the transcendence of God noncontrastively. "Divinity characterized in terms of a direct contrast with certain sorts of being or with the world of nondivine being as a whole is brought down to the level of the world and the beings within it in virtue of that very opposition: God becomes one being within a single order. . . . A contrastive definition does not work through the implications of divine transcendence to the end: a God who transcends the world must also . . . transcend the distinctions by contrast appropriate there."[2] Transcendence, moreover, accounts for the intimacy, immediacy, and universal extensiveness of God's activity in the created world. Far from being incompatible with these features, it "suggests an extreme of divine involvement in the world—a divine involvement in the form of a productive agency extending to everything that is in an equally direct manner. Divine involvement with the world need be neither partial, nor mediate nor simply formative: if divinity is not characterized by contrast with any sort of being, it may be the immediate source of being of every sort."[3]

God is not a character in the play of creation. God exercises God's transcendent lordship "in the radical immanence by which God is said to be nearer to us than we are to ourselves."[4] Thus a theologian need not (and ought not) oppose the order of created causes and effects, willings and doings, behaviors and motivations, to God's creative efficacy, no more than we should with what Willy and Arthur are doing.

There are two planes of activity, "horizontal" and "vertical"; God's agency is totally and immediately efficacious in the latter, and all created being is totally and immediately dependent upon its Creator at every moment. In the former case, the drama proceeds, and "predicates applied to created beings . . . can be understood to hold simply within the horizontal plane of relations among created beings." The freedom and contingency of created beings, for example, "may simply concern the nature of the relation between created beings and their created effects."[5] No contradiction is present between possession of the qualities and their possessor's absolute dependence upon divine agency. God creates nondivine beings with their own powers, including human freedom, and sustains them directly and completely.

There are two sides to this ruled use of talk about God's transcendence and creative agency. On the one hand (and here let us focus on human creatures), our freedom and self-development may be unreservedly affirmed and celebrated because God grants us our own powers; our exercise of them can be said to be according to the divine will. On the other hand, humanity is absolutely dependent on God; God is not constrained by anything we do or by anything else creaturely. Period. The "positive side" permits an understanding of created causality that is sufficient without intramundane reference to what God is doing (because these causes are established as sufficient in every way by God). The "negative side" of this ruled discourse focuses on divine sovereignty, our dependence on God and even our nothingness without God. Tanner lists a number of factors influencing a theologian's emphasis of one or the other side that need not detain us here. Most important for our purposes (and for her own forays into Christian ethics), the emphasis may be based on assessments of the relative importance of claims about divine sovereignty or created empowerment, given timely circumstance and an interest in encouraging or resisting certain individual or social attitudes, tendencies, or practices.

So there may be a concern to promote a particular vision of Christian life. In one case,

> statements to the effect that we are nothing without God . . . encourage Christian humility. Talk of God at work everywhere and even without us prompts the Christian "to glorify God and magnify his name."

Talk of the unconditioned agency of God . . . may promote a hope in God's saving power despite our moral failings, a trust that God will fulfill what is promised, patience and confidence in the face of adversity.[6]

On the other side, a stress on created capacity may be part of injunctions to act morally, or would promote gratitude and praise for God's great gifts.

Theologians could also intend in their focus on the negative or positive side to warn against or discourage Christian behaviors that are judged unfaithful in certain specific contexts. Talking about the human creature's powers could lead to the loss of a sense of gratitude, or unfitting, even prideful, self-reliance before God. The same talk when combined with a sense of human failure can prompt despair. Now consider how leading with strong claims about God's sovereignty in various circumstances prompts moral laziness, suspicions of divine injustice, or, again, ingratitude (because without talk of God's gifts "one assumes one has nothing to be thankful for"). These corrections are meant to ward off mistaken inferences that lose full sight of the rules for talking about transcendence and creation we started with (e.g., arrogant self-satisfaction over our own powers emerges from the error of presuming our real independence from God). Theological judgments about which perils to Christian life are decisive at some time will depend on how human sin is understood and "the actual dangers that a particular time and place represent"[7]

Tanner concludes that theologies which at first appear opposed may in fact complement one another by presenting a fuller, more ramified picture of Christian life and repelling theological misconstruals. Discourse about God's total efficacy regarding creation should not prompt discourse that denies human empowerment. Talk about creaturely empowerment ought not generate claims that affirm its being separate from God's activity. The positive and negative force of the rules and formalities under consideration protect and correct one another.[8]

Providence and Social Change

A theology of creation may oppose both easy identification of God's will with some personal or social or institutional framework of human willing, and denial of the genuine efficacy of created human activity. Identifications of the first sort impugn the fullness and freedom of divine transcendence by implying that creative reality as such constrains divine efficacy once and for all. The created would then take on the character of the divine. Denials in the second case also can jeopardize transcendence, by making God's efficacy a part of the created world and therefore in competition with created efficacy, rather than directly and immediately sustaining its being on a separate axis. Or these denials can wrongly question the universal divine sovereignty by not including free human willing within the range of God's active Lordship.

These errors can have an impact on Christian social ethics. Defense of "orders of creation" such as patriarchal marriage or "unmixed" racial existence seem to deny human working by setting up an unchanging divine standard that must not be questioned. But "assuming that social orders are fixed, and therefore not the potentially alterable products of human working if they are created by God, violates either God's freedom vis-à-vis creation, by denying the contingent character of a social order God creates, or God's transcendence, by insisting on the immutability of any social order created by an immutable God."[9] Similarly, some ethics of natural law, or divine mandates of social norms or institutional arrangements, restrict God's working utterly in natural or commanded norms or power relations; to that degree they compromise God's sovereignty by illicitly transferring to them a form of divine legitimacy.

For Tanner, "pretensions to ultimate finality for human understandings of what is real, true, or good are destroyed" in the claim that "ultimate truth, value, and reality belong only with the transcendent God."[10] Christian belief in God's creation, furthermore, confirms this critical potential "by relativizing the status of natural and social worlds." These are neither absolutely good nor merely given, but are valuable and contingent in relation to the divine source of all value and every moment of being. The upshot is an affirmation of God's "universal providential agency." God is understood to be "bringing about God's intentions for human affairs, and indeed for the whole world, by working in and through all human agencies and natural events."[11] The main features of this account reflect the terms of our discussion above:

God holds up into existence the whole of non-divine existence, a whole plane or level of nondivine being, inclusive of every item or order that is or happens within the world in every respect. . . . In the same way that creatures are given an existence of their own in dependence upon God's creative will for them, they are given powers and operations of their own, powers and operations that are creaturely and not divine, although they reflect God's creative intention for order within the world.[12]

Because all of creation is ever dependent upon God's creative will, the latter floats free of any natural or social order and establishes critical distance with regard to it. "The stress is therefore on the manifestation of God's will in a moral ordering rather than in a moral order with some static and immutable character."[13] And that ordering, because it is completely extensive and immediately efficacious, logically permits human agents to challenge established norms and institutions apart from the obligations set by a social order that could be taken to be strictly identified with the rule of God.

To offer a simple example, by this account one may directly criticize a system of slavery as contrary to God's will rather than seeing oneself constrained only to criticize various practices in the master–slave relation or institutions (e.g., breaking up families) within that system. Crucially, one cannot passively resign oneself to the powers that be unless one mistakenly exempts oneself from God's working and overidentifies what others have done with that working. In situations of human conflicts God's universal providence is understood to encompass all parties, and God's will is fulfilled "in that, in possible contradiction to the intentions of human agents, the consequences of their acts will eventually, and in the light of a wider context of human action and natural events, conform to God's intentions."[14]

Comprehending God's relation to the world in this way makes possible the exercise of interpretive realism and critical intelligence. A disposition to theocentric realism is appropriate because what God is doing in the world is an open and lively question; God is the object of attention in and through all that is, not some value or idea or theory. Yet the discernment of divine activity, of what is going on in terms of divine intentions, is fundamentally an interpretive task. There is no simple reliance on this or that event, individual, group, community, norm, or institution for capturing these intentions in virtue of God's exclusive or specially mediated working there. In the same vein, because human beings are both finite and sinful, "there is no systematic correlation between divine and human agency with which to simplify such judgments. Because of this lack of systematic correlation, because of the emphasis on contingent events, and because of the intervention of situation-specific interpretation, judgment of what it is right to do as God's agent takes on a fluid and flexible character."[15] The necessary work of human interpretation, reasoned argument, and judgment proceeds without hindrance of arbitrary stipulations that confer on created realities a sacred or near-sacred inviolability.

Tanner has already gone pretty far in blocking characteristic defenses of social injustice. For example, justifications of hierarchy depending on a chain of being or chain of command fail because they place God within a single, all-inclusive sphere of existence and activity. Divine transcendence is not compatible with that. Divine sovereignty that creates and sustains everything directly and universally must lie outside the entirety of created existence and agency. Warrants for an order of superiors and subordinates based either on the facts and functions of social location ("this is my divinely appointed place in which I serve these masters") or differences in created natures ("I am made to be a mother"—primarily or exclusively) also cannot succeed. Social relations and natural classification are not finished facts immune to alteration by God's providential will for creation. "Because any extant human hierarchy is in an ongoing relation of dependence upon God's free will, it cannot be deemed necessary or immutable. For the same reason, role relations (e.g., what a husband owes his wife and vice-versa) are potentially fluid and reversible."[16]

Tanner realizes, however, that these arguments are indirect and limited. They do not explicitly deny that God could intend a human world of superiority, subordination, and thoroughgoing inequality in resources and opportunities for human growth and development. That world could be changeable, of course, and the haves and have-nots might change places from time to time in accordance with God's will. As long as the hierarchical relations are not claimed to be immutable or that nature is destiny before God, and so forth, they could find a place in God's world—for all Tanner has said so far.

What, if anything, is wrong with these social arrangements? How do they fall short of the way human beings ought to relate to one another? From the standpoint of a doctrine of creation, Tanner's answer is that there ought not to be human relations in which large disparities in power and resources leave some without equal or even sufficient opportunities for human fulfillment, where the haves not only leave the have-nots vulnerable but gain their prerogatives at the latter's expense. When relations are oppressive in this way, the oppressed are denied the equal respect due them as creatures of God. Moral respect reflects God's love of human beings in the very act of creation and in willing their good. It is a love that is independent of differences that distinguish us. It is not earned but remains unconditional and indefeasible; and because no human being is any more or any less a creature than any other, there is a sense in which each human creature's well being is equally valuable before God. A defense of equal rights to life, self-development, and "to have one's personal integrity respected" follows.[17]

Jesus Christ in a Theology of Grace

In her brief systematic theology, Tanner sets forth this case in connection with Jesus Christ and his meaning for life in the world. God, the "giver of all good gifts," wills the fulfillment of the world through them, and as they are directed to bringing all that is into closer relations with God. "In union with God, in being brought near to God, all the trials and sorrows of life—suffering, loss, moral failing, the oppressive stunting of opportunities and vitality, grief, worry, tribulation, and strife—are purified, remedied, and reworked through the gifts of God's grace."[18] But Tanner describes the terms of union with God precisely by way of her radical interpretation of divine transcendence. Transcendence grounds a "non-competitive relation between creatures and God" which makes it possible to hold that "the perfection of the creature in its difference from God, increases with the perfection of the relationship with God: the closer the better."[19]

Thus "in Jesus, unity with God takes on a perfect form; humanity has become God's own," and that is the basic meaning of incarnation:

> In keeping with the general idea that unity with God is the means of gift-giving to what is other than God . . . the effect of this perfect relationship with God is perfect humanity, humanity to which God's gifts are communicated in their highest form. . . . By way of this perfected humanity in union with God, God's gifts are distributed to us—we are saved—just to the extent that we are one with Christ in faith and love; unity with Christ the gift-giver is the means of our perfection as human beings, just as the union of humanity and divinity in Christ was the means of his perfect humanity. United with Christ, we are thereby emboldened as ministers of God's beneficence to the world.[20]

And so we may live a graced life of worship, praise, and service in which we struggle to purify and perfect our humanity over against sin and its effects. The cross of Jesus Christ is salvific not as a vicarious punishment or atoning sacrifice but because in it "sin and death have been assumed by the one, the Word, who cannot be conquered by them." As sinful human creatures are assumed by Christ, they may seek to overcome sin, their own and others' self-inflicted blindness to and blocking of the reception of God's gifts.[21] This task is not an offer to God as a condition of God's continued giving. All God's gifts are unconditional and unmerited, and our only fitting response is to remain open in gratitude for them and to give them back, not as payment but as offerings of worship and praise. Throughout, "God obliges, offering gifts for gifts, gifts for squandered gifts, 'rewarding' us anyway despite our inability to make a return, our inability to offer anything besides a willingness to receive more, 'rewarding' us with new gifts that remedy even our failure to offer this non-offering of grateful openness to God's further giving."[22]

The shape of human lives ministering divine benefit is accordingly Trinitarian; "united with Christ, we are called to distribute the good gifts of the Father in the power of the Spirit." As the church, we remain a universal community, in that the whole world at least prospectively is united with Christ through God's universal salvific intentions. Human relations responsible to God should be marked by a corresponding unconditional giving, a universal distribution of God's gifts to persons in need "without concern for anything they especially are or have done" to deserve them. By the route, Tanner confirms the conclusion she reached via the doctrines of God and creation regarding equal rights: "God's giving is not owed to creatures but if these gifts are being given unconditionally by God to all in need, creatures are in fact owed the goods of God by those ministering such benefits. . . . Our good works, in short, are not owed to God but they are to the world."[23]

Finally, even with such rights, before God we ought not to treat what we have as our exclusive possessions; we should share our gifts with others "as those others benefit in community from the effect of these gifts' employment—that is the full meaning of a community of mutual fulfillment." Identifying ourselves as persons in community with others and not just for ourselves, our efforts to perfect our own gifts and talents may enter into and supplement the activities of others and vice versa; but we would belong to others in community, be their own, "only as they make you the recipients of their loving concern, not in virtue of their powers to restrict you, take from you, or do with you as they will. . . . Owning by giving is the way the Son is the Father's own, it is the way humanity is the Son's own, it is the way we are the Father's own. . . . We are to be each others' own in community in this same general sense of possession or property."[24] Although working for communities of this kind is hard and risks failure in the face of enormous resistance, Tanner contends it is a work both realistic and responsible.

Niebuhrian Resonances

There is overlap between Tanner's "universal providential divine agency" and H. Richard Niebuhr's theology of the sovereign God who acts in all actions upon us. For Niebuhr, "the will of God is what God does in all that nature and men do."[25] His interpretation of the biblical story affirms a people's responding faith to what God is doing in the world, such that "no event in nature or social history could be dismissed as accidental, arbitrary, unintelligible, or disconnected, as product of some independent power."[26] God is the transcendent power who "presides over" and "works in all our working," and our working may endure only as it may be included in a great divine work of recreation: "There is no action in the whole extent of actuality in which the universal intention, the meaning of the One beyond the many, is not present."[27] Also for Niebuhr, human creatures carry an irreducible dignity that owes to their relation to the Absolute who creates them and wills their good.[28]

Tanner, however, thinks that this case at least must be made circumspectly with regard to Niebuhr (and also Gustafson). A target for criticism is the moral realism that takes "the primary feature of moral choice" to be "acceptance of and adjustment to givens of reality outside the range of human influence." One is not so much responsible for what one has done oneself but "responsible to realities beyond human control."[29] Niebuhr and his followers may justify moral realism with a view of divine sovereignty as "limiting and constraining us and putting us in our place . . . showing us all the weaknesses of our finite creaturehood—before showing us what we can do and achieve within such limits." Specifically,

> humility before the awesome wonders of a God whose influence is beyond human reckoning becomes humility before the uncontrollable, unbidden forces of this life, before the suffering that breaks up our comfortable repose, before challenges of life that in their inevitability face decision, before forces bearing down on us.[30]

God's priority and governance tend to be identified with the uncontrollable givens of existence; but this restricts the reality of divine governance to these worldly realities alone. "God's action and intentions are displayed only in what life forces us to respond to; our own acts of responsible choice in the face of such forces cannot be themselves within the sphere of God's working in the same direct way." For Tanner, of course, they can; honoring God's universal providential agency requires this affirmation. God is at work in natural and given forces that influence and limit us, and God is at work in human judgment and deliberation and responsible choice. Only the disastrous idea of an "either/or between human working and God's working" can undergird these realist tendencies.[31]

The practical implications for progressive politics are especially troubling because moral realism can justify Christians' impertinent and often self-serving messages to oppressed folks regarding their limitations and corruptibility. Tanner spells this out with special reference to the "limitations" of oppression itself:

> The oppressed are encouraged to see the actions of others upon them as the actions of God, as if they were to respond to such actions in a merely reactive way and were not also to see themselves as agents under God and active participants in the direction of their own lives, as if some of these limits upon their own action could not be the grotesque results of sin on the part of their oppressors, as if the mere fact or apparent intransigence of present social obstacles were good a priori grounds to be resigned in the face of them.[32]

To suggest that the victims of injustice may consent to these realities flies in the face of what respect for these creatures of God requires; but Niebuhr and Gustafson "come dangerously close to suggesting such things insofar as they fail to specify the audience for their remarks."[33]

If Niebuhr and Gustafson are in fact guilty of realism, in Tanner's usage, their ethics should be criticized and, if possible, corrected. There surely may be something to worry about if Niebuhr's pivotal formula—"God is acting in all actions upon you. So respond to all action upon you as to respond to his action"—says that my response is something apart from all these other things happening to me where God is acting. With Gustafson after him, Niebuhr does conceive of his ethic of responsibility as a genuine and preferable alternative to "all the ethics of absolute human freedom, the ethics of man the conquerer of the conditions in which he lives, the ethics of human mastery."[34] Perhaps Tanner's either–or is at work in this contrast.

The criticized themselves are not without resources for an instructive answer. Gustafson acknowledges that his emphasis on various givens, including the demands of policy analysis and the limits to action presented by immediate circumstances, can lead to a loss of critical and innovative moral perspective. But he offers the reminder that theocentric ethics expansively welcomes communities of moral discourse which "break the bounds of limited class interests, ethnocentrism, and other restrictive features." These communities may take part in exactly the sort of constantly self-critical moral conversation that Tanner endorses. Although he does not argue for it, Gustafson also confidently affirms "that the theocentric perspective itself alerts persons to possibilities of radical change. . . . One can see how loves need to be expanded and sensibilities intensified, how class interests, ethnocentrisms, and sexism need to be altered. . . . What should temper aspirations is that proposals for change . . . cannot begin de novo and must anticipate and take into account the inevitable 'costs' that accompany the pursuit of some special goods."[35] The realism of acknowledging moral costs, however, is perfectly in keeping with Tanner's ethic of responsibility.

As for Niebuhr, his radical monotheism and its motto—to dethrone all absolutes short of God and at the same time to reverence every relative existent—push in the same direction as Tanner by according respect to human creatures in the midst of their many creaturely relations while protecting them from ultimate claims made on behalf of any such relation. More than primarily focusing on limits to human decision making, Niebuhr's model of responsibility contextualizes decision making by attending to matters of social location, interpretation, and accountability. It prompts the question, before God: "To whom or what am I responsible and in what community of interaction am I myself?"

Moreover, the notion of response draws attention to the work of interpretation in grasping "What is going on?" in the actions affecting you; recall the example of Jesus, who "interprets all actions upon him as signs of the divine action of creation, government, and salvation. . . . He does that act which fits into the divine action and looks forward for the infinite response to his response."[36] Although we acknowledge in this statement traces of realism's unwarranted either–or, we also see in it the point that human action is accountable, and to that extent responsibly one's own, as it anticipates a reply within "a total conversation that leads forward and is to have meaning as a whole."[37] Thus the dynamic of Niebuhr's model of agency has to do with uncovering the community and communities in whose conversations we play a part, and the causes which give these interactions significance and enlist our ongoing, self-identifying loyalty. It does not by itself appear to imply or require realism. In fact, one practical theological implication of the account is that it may uncover henotheistic loyalties (and conversations) that imprison our actions to social idols.

A stunning example of Niebuhr's best approach to divine governance and human agency is a sermon entitled "Man's Work and God's."
An exposition of Psalm 90, the sermon addresses this prayer within it:
"Let thy work appear unto they servants . . . and let the favor of the
Lord our God be upon us; And establish then the work of our hands
upon us; yea, the work of our hands establish thou it." Niebuhr reflects on our fleeting and sometimes destructive work and points out
how we may be tempted to believe that nothing is being accomplished
by them, that "nothing is going on":

> But for the most part we fundamentally believe that something is going
> on, something is being accomplished; that a mighty work is being ac-
> complished. . . . Yet we desperately desire to know what it is. So we
> make our silent or our public prayers. . . . Show us what you are doing
> with all the things we are doing. Show us what it is that we are work-
> ing on.[38]

And then, the prayer continues, make our human work part of the
great work you are about, establish it, glorify it, use it, preserve it. Parents thus pray for their children, teachers so pray for their students,
and all of us pray this "for our culture, for this whole work of our
hands which we labor all our lives and which is forever threatened
with decay."[39]

The human work that is Psalm 90, Niebuhr concludes, presents answers to the very questions that it asks in prayer. This poem endures
before God. It endures, first, because of the great work of the poet who
labored responsibly over the art. It endures, second, because the work
bespeaks the honesty of the artist who made no pretense but struggled
only with "the honest stuff of life itself," especially the life of authentic emotions, thoughts, and longings. The artist, third, labored carefully and honestly "without reference to his own fame, fortune, or
endurance."

Even so, none of this strictly established the author's work. Indeed,
"much over which he had no control happened to his product." The
psalm was included in larger wholes—the hymn book of the syna-
gogue, the Hebrew Scriptures, the Christian Scriptures. Most important, it was made a part of the very disclosure of what God is doing;
for "by this poem, too, in its setting, with its companion pieces, we are

enabled to see, though dimly still, and more by faith than sight, that this whole story of our human life is the story of a supernal, everlasting creation and a cosmic redemption, of God's own artistry." The author of the sermon draws the lesson that our shabby and slothful work "will but furnish fuel for the world's Gehennas;" but even our best work endures only as God who "presides over and works within all our working includes what we do in its deed," a deed not of "enslavement to futility but of liberation to action, not of death dealing but of life-giving."[40]

I find no faulty realism in this reflection. I see a witness to God's universal providential agency that includes directly our human work within it, and is established as it fits the intentions of God rendered in time and forged in free grace. The witness possesses a modesty reflecting the limits of human powers and their dependence on time, circumstance, other events and forces, and, with all this, God's prevenient action. But it also endorses a responsible self-positioning that is together interpretive and assertive. Should our work be established by our Creator and Lord, there is, by God's grace, something of our own that we must do and for good reason. Tanner's progressive political ethic, in the end, embraces these features. She acknowledges that responsible action for justice may not always or automatically bring change for the better, that the oppressed may be corrected by or learn something from the oppressors with whom they struggle, and that humility is necessary. Final certitude about one's rectitude is impossible. Acknowledging limitation, however, can perfect rather than poison conviction, agency, and accountability.[41]

An uncompromising emphasis on divine agency as the source, governor, and completion of all creation marks Niebuhr and Tanner both. Her corrections fit with his best, and most consistent theology. It is not at all evident, however, that Tanner's extension of transcendence to explain the Incarnation finds a parallel in Niebuhr's thought; moreover, her ideal "community of mutual fulfillment" seems to strike a note distinct from the latter's general normative discussions of a "community of selves," in which the loyalty of each to the other is qualified and perfected by the partners' loyalty to some "third," some cause that transcends them both. Thus mutual responsibility concerns loyalty to one another and loyalty to one another's loyalties beyond I and Thou.[42]

But surely Niebuhr's approach to divine agency is patient of Tanner's Christological elaboration; and his formal view of responsible community can be filled in with a content that takes the third, transcending loyalty to be the Trinitarian God, giver of all good gifts. As we will see below, certain aspects of Niebuhr's theology are pitched in this direction. In any event, in both of these instances Tanner's work coheres with and may advance upon Niebuhr's.[43]

In three other respects, alliance is clear. First, Tanner's ethic of faithfulness follows Niebuhr in taking it to include fidelity to a universal community under God that breaks the "usual boundaries of closed communities."[44] Second, both develop similar theologies of grace. The following passage is worth quoting at length:

> The cross of Jesus Christ is the final, convincing demonstration of the fact that the order of the universe is not one of retribution in which goodness is rewarded and evil punished, but rather an order of graciousness wherein . . . the sun is made to shine on evil and good and the rain to descend on the just and the unjust. To live in this divine order of graciousness on the basis of the assumption that reward must be merited and evil avenged is to come into conflict with the real order of things. . . . If men are to live at all . . . they must begin with the acceptance not of some standard of judgment—not even the standard of graciousness—but of an act of graciousness to which they respond graciously. God's righteousness is his graciousness, and his grace is not in addition to his justice; hence man's righteousness does not lie in a new order of judging justice, but in the acceptance of grace and in thankful response to it.[45]

Here Niebuhr's vision matches Tanner's rejection of retributive accounts of atonement and understandings of divine punishment as "an interruption of God's good favor, in response to our failings."[46] It matches her case for divine gifts as universal, unmerited, and sustaining even in the midst of sin. Justice or righteousness is "defined as faithfulness to those in need and expressed in liberality of giving" to persons who get what they do not deserve, get something for nothing, or receive what they are not owed.[47] Recall, too, Niebuhr's proposal that in its responsibility to God, the content of the church's responsibility for society is mercy, the redemption and transformation "of whatever creatures its action touches. . . . Nothing belongs to its present responsibility for which it cannot answer to the one who gave his life as ransom and whose whole activity was a seeking and saving of the lost."[48]

Third, the two theologians stress that life faithful to God is a permanent revolution of heart and mind by which we "struggle against our own sins as well as those of others."[49] In the presence of the mercy of the Sovereign One who acts in all actions upon us, that life-act of self-reformation humbly and courageously faces up to the blind resistance of self-justification in ourselves and our communities, and extends mercy, "ourselves completely linked to the other with no remnant of superiority."[50] Here again, I suggest that Niebuhr at his best resolutely avoids the dangers of moral realism.

Notes

1. William C. Placher, *The Domestication of Transcendence* (Louisville: Westminster/John Knox Press, 1996), 125; italics in original.
2. Kathryn Tanner, *God and Creation in Christian Theology* (Oxford: Blackwell, 1988), 45–46.
3. Ibid., 46.
4. Ibid., 79.
5. Ibid., 90.
6. Ibid., 113.
7. Ibid., 116.
8. Ibid., 118.
9. Kathryn Tanner, *The Politics of God* (Minneapolis: Fortress Press, 1992), 83–84.
10. Ibid., 68.
11. Ibid., 199.
12. Ibid., 100.
13. Ibid., 101.
14. Ibid., 105.
15. Ibid., 106–7.
16. Ibid., 144.
17. Ibid., 165–80.
18. Kathryn Tanner, *Jesus, Humanity, and the Trinity* (Minneapolis: Fortress Press, 2001), 2. I am not able to give this rich, condensed study its full due in this volume.
19. Ibid., 3.

20. Ibid., 9.

21. Ibid., 29, 46.

22. Ibid., 87.

23. Ibid., 89.

24. Ibid., 92–93.

25. H. Richard Niebuhr, *The Responsible Self* (New York: Harper & Row, 1963), 47–65.

26. H. Richard Niebuhr, *Radical Monotheism and Western Culture* (New York: Harper & Row, 1960), 47.

27. H. Richard Niebuhr, "Man's Work and God's," in H. Richard Niebuhr, *Theology, History, and Culture*, ed. William Stacy Johnson (New Haven, Conn.: Yale University Press, 1996), 214; Niebuhr, *Responsible Self*, 170.

28. H. Richard Niebuhr, *Christ and Culture* (New York: Harper & Brothers, 1951), 240.

29. Kathryn Tanner, "A Theological Case for Human Responsibility in Moral Choice," *Journal of Religion* 73, no. 4 (October 1993): 593.

30. Ibid., 598.

31. Ibid., 599, 601.

32. Tanner, *Politics of God*, 241.

33. Ibid.

34. Niebuhr, *Responsible Self*, 173.

35. James M. Gustafson, "Response," in Harlan R. Beckley and Charles M. Sweezy, eds. *James M. Gustafson's Theocentric Ethics: Interpretations and Assessments* (Macon, Ga.: Mercer University Press, 1988), 253, 254.

36. Niebuhr, *Responsible Self*, 167.

37. Ibid., 64.

38. Niebuhr, "Man's Work and God's," 210–11.

39. Ibid., 211.

40. Ibid., 213–14.

41. Tanner, *Politics of God*, 236–49.

42. H. Richard Niebuhr, *Faith on Earth* (New Haven, Conn.: Yale University Press, 1989), 55ff.; Niebuhr, *Responsible Self*, 73ff.

43. For a classic analysis of Niebuhr's Christology, its context, and its relation to metaphysical questions, see Hans W. Frei, "The Theology of H. Richard Niebuhr," in Paul Ramsey, ed., *Faith and Ethics* (New York: Harper & Row, 1965), 104–16.

44. Tanner, *Jesus, Humanity, and the Trinity*, 88.

45. H. Richard Niebuhr, "War as Crucifixion," in Richard B. Miller, ed., *War in the Twentieth Century* (Louisville: Westgminster/John Knox Press, 1992), 68–69.

46. Tanner, *Jesus, Humanity, and the Trinity*, 86.

47. Kathryn Tanner, "Justification and Justice in a Theology of Grace," *Theology Today* 55, no. 4 (January 1999): 523.

48. H. Richard Niebuhr, "The Responsibility of the Church for Society," in K. S. Latourette, ed., *The Gospel, the Church, and the World* (New York: Harper & Brothers, 1946), 119–20. Cf. Tanner, *Jesus, Humanity, and the Trinity*, 88: "We are ransomed on the cross from the suffering and oppression in which a debt economy has thrown us; taken from the cross we are returned to our original owner God, to God's kingdom of unconditional giving. . . ." The convergence I see here identifies Jesus's life as an act of ransoming, of delivering the lost. In this sense he gave his life as ransom.

49. Tanner, *Jesus, Humanity, and the Trinity*, 56.

50. Ibid., 63, quoting Karl Barth.

CHAPTER TEN

Realism, Identity, and Self-Defense

The conversation this book presents among H. Richard Niebuhr and his heirs shows thus far that a Christian ethic of faithfulness to God involves critical reflection on Christian discourse in light of the sovereign God who is Creator, Preserver, and Redeemer. The care and feeding of Christian discourse risks abstraction and corruption, however, without its embodiment in practices of worship and service among Christians in community. God's narrative or history of relation with creation in Jesus Christ implicates disciples in a life in which they may develop moral and religious skills—such as trust, hope, gratitude, and peaceableness—that constitute a characteristic identity. The particularity of their practices is in and for a church responsible to God for society as, among other things, a pioneer and representative showing works of mercy in neighbor love.

The church bases its responsibility in its internal life as it witnesses to the reality of God's universal promise through repentance and conversion, including a conversion of the terms of justice in the world. Yet even functioning as a world society in its common life through attention to human needs and the insights of other disciplines and communities of moral discourse, the church ought not give up its independence. An independent theological ethic need not be exclusive in its interpretive accounts of God's universal providential agency and the agency it sustains, wills, and graciously perfects in Jesus Christ.

In this chapter, I place Paul Ramsey, Stanley Hauerwas, and James Gustafson in dialogue with Kathryn Tanner. From where she stands, the others may offer, respectively, a conversionism that is too conservative, a Christian identity that is insufficiently open, and a theology that too readily gives up on distinctively Christian modes of discourse.

Ramsey and "Realism"

Ramsey identified himself as a political realist. He wrote about the tendencies of human societies to assert themselves inordinately against the claims of others, to fail to recognize the finitude of their own particular perspectives, and the like. Tanner establishes that this sort of "realism," often associated with Reinhold Niebuhr, is independent of the moral realism she criticizes. One can "take sin seriously" without seriously locking human initiative and responsibility within it. Social ethics may attend to the way justice is built through an equilibrium of power (checking inordinate self-assertion) without forging an iron cage that curtails creaturely possibilities. Political realism is compatible with a vigorous transformative moral project.

Ramsey developed this compatibility through his ethic of "love transforming justice." But how successful was he? How, that is, does he fare in relation to Tanner's criticisms of that other realism? I will ask the question regarding Ramsey's positions on the authority of political office, reproductive technology, liberation theology, and the norm of fellow humanity.

The Church and the Magistrate

Ramsey tried not to fall into the realism of orders of creation or natural law ethics in a number of respects. *Nine Modern Moralists* would make room for a dynamic ethic of redemption that converts (and hence does not ignore or obliterate) creaturely reality. This moral reality was not to be depicted in terms of a "static" natural law, but rather through the attention to sources of injustice and the opportunities for realizing an ideal of fellow humanity. Ramsey's own "orders of preservation," social arrangements that protect persons from one another through certain requirements of order and restraint (e.g., the presence of coercive power in the state), were presented neither arbitrarily nor without a view to responsibility. He did not use orders language to stop argument but to locate it within the divine economy, and effectively offered reasons for his claims and welcomed objections. Of course, an ever more just, love-transformed social order remained his manifest theological intention (however well or badly he may have enacted it).

Ramsey's best arguments for the church's deference to political authority defend a moral division of labor and a community of moral discourse in church and world that respects freedom of conscience. He feared that a Christian ethic built upon specific, dogmatically declared policy decisions usurps the proper role of expert policy analysis in political life, reduces the contributions of Christian ethics in clarifying the moral grounds upon which policy may be made, and threatens both moral liberty and church unity. In Ramsey's earlier work, however, there is a dangerous tendency to render the decisions of our political leaders uncriticizable. Although religious communities "should seek to clarify and keep wide open the legitimate options for choice, and thus nurture the moral and political ethos of the nation, . . . in this they need to stand in awe before people called political 'decision makers,' or rather before the majesty of topmost political agency. Political decision and action is an image of the majesty of God, who also rules by particular decrees."[1]

Special identification of the magistrate and the majesty of God inappropriately privileges creaturely political authority. It hints that the ones who hold positions of power are much more like God than the ones who do not. Moves like this jeopardize divine transcendence.[2] Moreover, Ramsey's analysis distances decision making so far from principled ethos formation that the second appears abstract and the first becomes uninformed. Unless ethical argument seeks concretely to apply norms through the details of policy discourse, political decision making will lose contact with moral values under the pressures of feasibility, the need for compromise, and efficiency.

Ramsey went too far here, and he knew it. "Indeed," he later wrote, "one *must* get into specifics in order to *teach* political principles." So where there are an array of policy options arguably patient of Christian moral reasoning, "let the argument for each be made, along with the reasons believed to be telling against the other(s). Let all the facts and predictions be marshaled on each side, by each side's chosen school of experts, or by someone who has made the one or the other 'practically wise' choice his or her own."[3] This statement, I think, corrects the earlier position, and makes Ramsey less vulnerable to Tanner's objections.

Assisted Reproduction

Defending the "one flesh unity" of the marital bond, Ramsey opposed forms of assisted reproduction, such as artificial insemination by donor and in vitro fertilization using donor gametes, that introduced third parties into the procreative process. The marital covenant, borne toward the love of Christ without whom nothing was made, is to bear and nurture love between husband and wife. Sexual life so directed may also be procreative in a way not divorced from that sphere of embodied covenant love, and image the unity of love and creation in God.

> And in human procreativity out of the depths of human sexual love is prefigured God's own act of creation out of the profound mystery of his love revealed in Christ. To put radically asunder what God joined together in parenthood when He made love procreative, to procreate from beyond the sphere of love (AIDS, for example, or making human life in a test tube), or to posit acts of sexual love beyond the sphere of responsible procreation (by definition, marriage) means a refusal of the image of God's creation in our own.[4]

Bracketing the question of how the identification by definition of responsible procreation with marriage is defended, let us turn to the other side of the one flesh unity and ask: Does Ramsey's case that God's creative will is "to make love procreative," ignore God's continuing providential will? Has he illicitly identified the transcendent God with a norm of relationship that, however Christologically ordered, yet bears the marks of natural law? Is there an arbitrariness that reflects not taking divine transcendence and providential agency seriously enough?

It is difficult to say. Ramsey took a view of human nature that he found well-grounded theologically and drew implications for the meaning of fully human existence. He never paid much attention to the sorrow and desires of married heterosexual couples having difficulties conceiving, nor did he address possibilities of same-sex families formed with the assistance of reproductive technologies. Reading his words more than a quarter century after he wrote them, one can get the impression that too much is taken for granted, and that theological argument is presumed to stop with these pronouncements.

There is lots of evidence, however, that Ramsey did not see things that way. Usually, he made his theological vision of the human spill out into arguments defending what God was doing in the world and how Christians may witness to it. He warned of the real dangers to submitting human procreation to technique or "re-production." He feared that giving aid and comfort to methods of assisted reproduction, especially in vitro fertilization, would lower barriers of resistance to the "design" of our descendants, and to a dehumanization rooted in subjecting all action to criteria of isolated desire and disembodied choice. Assessment of these arguments is not at issue. The question is whether Ramsey gives up on an ethic of responsibility. I submit that in his work arguments go forward that welcome criticism and self-criticism unfettered by a theological strategy that improperly fetters God's universal providential agency.

Preference for the Poor

Ramsey's ethics demonstrate a special regard for vulnerable creatures like civilians in wartime, or handicapped newborns, or children as experimental subjects, or the dying in need of care. He did not regularly focus on the victims of economic injustice or institutional oppression. There are proposals in *Christian Ethics and the Sit-In* that appear to involve undefended reliance on forms of natural human community whose order must be maintained even when it collides with abstract requirements for racial justice. On closer inspection, however, these turn out to be arguments that local bonds of neighborhood and voluntary affiliation protect persons in their fellow humanity by increasing their distance from the dangers of state power. In addition, we find his typical case for "taking all values into account, ignoring none," rather than setting some rule that forever elevates one value (say, justice) as it blinds us to others (say, order).[5]

In a later essay in conversation with Latin American liberation theology, Ramsey (1) affirms that "a Gospel ethic . . . is concerned most of all with the weak and oppressed," (2) cautions that classes of the oppressed may make conflicting claims upon neighbor-love, (3) offers a reminder that cultural Christianity may be found in partisanship for the poor as well as for the status quo, and (4) measures a preferential option for the poor by two tests borrowed from Jacques Ellul. First, love of neighbor must extend to the "uninteresting poor," who may not be classifiable within some prevailing political ideology but still stand in need before us. Second, love must be ready to change sides should the oppressed become oppressors. Now, one can question these reflective moments as delaying movements; but none of them oppose a politically progressive Christian witness at all.[6]

Community

What is the meaning of fellow humanity? Tanner argues for a strong respect for creaturely difference. Communal solidarity is constituted by a "nonunifying love" in which "people are helped . . . to cultivate and unfold the capacities God gave them, helped to be what they can be, in delight at their differences."[7] One must not presuppose that love will invariably lead to bonds based on "consensus or an ultimate identity of ends." On the contrary, the other "has the potential to stop one cold, to turn one's self-understanding and one's projects upside down, by revealing, for example, a fundamental moral fault one has hidden from oneself, or the truth of praise, of which one would otherwise have believed oneself unworthy."[8]

The presence of this potential does not mean that the other is an "affront to the value of the self or its projects." As creatures, each and all are valuable before God and are owed an unalterable respect. "Otherness" may be "noncompetitive." Just so it also enables and may require "a highly conflictual process of individual prophetic rebuke for the sake of a better life together." Across the board, Tanner suspects formal claims about our essential sociality or our necessary fulfillment as individuals in community; for "made into a counsel against efforts at self-respect or assertion of individual rights against the community, it begs the question of what that community is like."[9]

"Noncompetitive others" and "nonunifying love" can gloss Ramsey's dialectic of "relation in the distance" and "distance in the relation"; fellow humanity is never to be identified with a unity that overwhelms otherness or a difference that commands isolation. Still, I can imagine Ramsey locating Tanner's account on the verge of a liberal individualism that, in the name of pluralism or respect for difference, jeopardizes traditional normative understandings of human relations (e.g., between husband and wife, or physician and patient). Marriage may become a contract between strangers instead of a covenant between spouses. Physicians may become mere technicians honoring the difference of their patients, whatever they desire.

Tanner denies the implication of liberal individualism, but makes no specific response to the examples sketched above. It is important also to consider that she stresses individual difference and not individual desire or even choice as determinative of a norm of nonunifying love. Also, and as we have already seen, Tanner argues for an ideal of mutual fulfillment in community in which we may become, as the particular individuals we are, one another's very own as we share our very own gifts. "One perfects oneself by making one's own the efforts of others to perfect themselves, their efforts too being furthered in the same way by one's own."[10] The limit that human community cannot subsume the creature who is fundamentally constituted in a gifted relation with God yet may make way for a communion of this sort. Hence, Tanner may move closer to Ramsey while simultaneously, perhaps, radicalizing the terms of community, its otherness and mutuality. Nonunifying love appears ideally to be nonunifying unity, a self-possessed dispossession, an assertive self-giving.

Hauerwas and Christian Identity

Tanner's book, *Theories of Culture: A New Agenda for Theology*, covers a lot of ground. It is at once a history of the development of the modern anthropological notion of culture, a critique of that notion from postmodern standpoints, a recasting of the nature of theology, and a constructive theological vision that departs from the weaknesses of both correlationist and postliberal accounts. I need to risk oversimplifying the book's arguments for the purpose of comparing Tanner's approach to Christian identity with Hauerwas's ethics.

Begin with the suggestion that Christianity can be described as a kind of culture that contains a specifically Christian way of life. According to a prevailing modern view of culture, the idea directs us to the way cultures identify particular patterns and practices of living with their accompanying rationales, and the dominance of these clearly identifiable patterns and practices for members of any culture in question. Living within a culture is a matter of understanding it "in its own terms," and these enable an internally consistent ordering of social life that is grounded in consensus and bounded sharply. A common life is thereby stable over time, as it must be if living in it is to be accomplished at all.

But cultures are not so neat and crafted as all that. Relying on postmodern challenges that emphasize historical process and the facts of political conflict, Tanner presents the following reconstruction. An anthropologist may offer a view of a culture as an internally consistent whole for summary and comparative purposes; in fact, however, participants practicing it never see it that way, and can get along just fine without perfect consistency among beliefs and practices. They have to get along that way, because social processes and the meaningful actions they include are varied and not naturally connected. Furthermore, defining culture in terms of consensus, order, social stability, and self-contained boundaries runs right past the way "historical struggles precede any clearly defined meaning or organization of cultural elements; and these definitions are never so firm as to stop their flow."[11]

A more accurate picture shows that fixed or taken-for-granted meanings of social life "are more the exception than the rule"; that cultures are at best "contradictory and internally fissured wholes" embodying "sites of resistance" that accompany any consolidation of social understanding; that consensus relates more to common attachment to normative reference points than to common agreement over what these norms mean; and that "cultural boundaries" direct us not to self-contained and self-generated ways of life but to different styles of living that arise from distinctive uses of elements that are shared among cultures.

Here is an example that traces in reverse the exposition above. It will not do, Tanner could say, simply to jettison from Christian life appeals to persons' rights on the grounds that this is intrinsically a category of political liberalism (another culture). One may refer to rights by relating them to his or her view of life before God and by relating that view to other uses outside by way of contrast or reinterpretation. Understandings of the rights of persons (who may now be called creatures, with that change making a difference) may shift, collide, and differ, though what unites them is a commitment to argument and action about the kinds of moral claims folks present to one another. Christians may get along well enough, moreover, by limiting their argument and action to certain social contexts and not others that might seem logically to require them. Consistency and coherence may be goals rightly prized, but not taken for granted. Arguments and contests about ethical behavior, indeed, will most likely include challenges to rights talk justified not by an opposition between Christian and liberal, but by a more piecemeal indication of how, say, appeals to individual moral entitlement corrupt Christian practices of social obligation.

No moral relativism follows from these historicist and pluralist remarks. As Tanner's defense of the rights of human creatures in *The Politics of God* demonstrates, Christian discipleship demands a search for and presumes the possibility of getting the substance of ethics right. A "community of solidarity and hope . . . ruled by humility and not by way of the advantage of superior power" may ponder, investigate, and advance its grasp of what it means to follow God in Christ:

> United in the expectation that a purer witness and discipleship will come of such efforts to work through their disagreements, participants must show a willingness to listen to and be corrected if necessary by all others similarly concerned about the true nature of Christian discipleship.[12]

Christianity "has its identity in the form of a task of looking for one." The task requires courage in presenting visions of discipleship as true and openness to God's free Word as it may correct and surpass these visions in the course of time.[13]

Hauerwas has expressed some worries about the preceding. One criticism is that Tanner's Christian identity is described too abstractly and formally. It does not specify the Word that is Jesus Christ, embodied in communal practices that gain intelligibility by criteria internal to Christian life. These criteria and practices set a sharper cultural boundary over against what Christianity is not than Tanner allows.[14] Let us be clear about the possible sources of disagreement here.

First, Tanner's position on identity is against the idea that Christians are a new people who form their own culture apart from others. As this idea has it, Christianity "is comparable to any other society in its functions but qualitatively different in its principles. The Christian community is one, say, of peace, joy, and fellowship. All others are ones of power, conflict, and violence."[15] But Christians and non-Christians alike share in a solidarity of both sin and the promise of free grace; this solidarity will "blur any difference between Christians and non-Christians on social grounds." To focus on the distinctiveness of a social group appears to deny solidarity and to enable Christians "simply because of their group membership," to "congratulate themselves on the possession of some unique perfection."

The difference between life in Christ and life without him, in contrast, should be "a new relationship with what lies beyond the Christian community itself, a new orientation of standards and values around . . . the free grace of God in Christ."[16] Hauerwas, at the very least, wants concretely to interpose the practices of the Christian community between our believing "new orientation" and free grace: "Salvation . . . is best understood . . . as our material embodiment in the habits and practices of a people that makes possible a life that is otherwise impossible."[17] And the practices, after all, are peaceable, do oppose the world of violence, and can offer an alternative society that lets the church be the church, and the world be the world.

Second, Tanner denies that Christianity is a self-contained, self-originating whole qualitatively discontinuous with other forms of life. No sharp cultural boundary exists marking the difference between "our" independently generated whole and other cultures that, in turn, operate on their own terms. One need not and simply cannot "purify Christian practices from outside influences of their possibly corrupting effects." That move also privileges Christian practices improperly, and likely resists Christian self-criticism in light of the Word of God. An excessive emphasis on what is inside and outside Christian life misses how entirely relational Christian identity is in that it is constituted by a distinctive use of materials borrowed elsewhere, from outside. Christianity is not, if you will, a predicate of a "liberal" ideal of "autonomous self-determination" that sets itself off from other cultures through "relations of indifferent exteriority." Differentiation of identity is set at and not so much by the boundary through active relations with cultural materials shared with others but given a distinctive twist.[18]

At this point, reflect on Hauerwas's proposal that, although the Decalogue applies to all people, "only those that had been given the gift of the Holy Spirit had the opportunity to live out the interrelation of the commands necessary to be a holy people. The church . . . becomes the politics . . . that makes the exhibition of the morality God desires for all people a material reality."[19] Does this passage pose the presence of a boundary between the church and other communities that presumes a self-generating internal logic and, at best, a relation of "indifferent exteriority"?

I think that these contrasts are real and significant. But we must be careful not to make too much of them. Nothing in Tanner's proposals regarding Christian identity excludes a theological case for Hauerwas's vision, rightly understood. His point of reference is the God whose disclosure in Jesus Christ calls disciples to faithful and peaceable community and the particular practices embodied therein. That he believes Christian convictions can make sense only through an understanding of these practices in no way makes the practices theologically primary. That he is convinced that, say, belief in and speech about resurrection finds their "material condition" in a particular people (called church) that eats and drinks with their Lord does not mean that the church is Hauerwas's object of faith. And the idea that Christian folks may have a leg up in seeing the interrelation of the commands of the Decalogue seems only to mean that the people referring these to God possess a unique opportunity to see the connections because of that unifying reference.

In addition, it has never been Hauerwas's style to present Christian identity as self-originating and in no need of borrowed cultural materials. What he is doing is to describe and defend his description of that identity through these very materials. He will employ the language of character, but adjust it; then vision might work, or perhaps narrative does better. Community did some good in the critique of liberalism, but do not confuse his use of the term with what communitarians are saying. And so on.

Believe it or not, there are some impressive affinities between Tanner's and Hauerwas's theological styles. They agree that Christian theology has to do "with the meaning dimension of Christian practices," embedded, for example, "in such matters as the way altars and pews are arranged." Also, "going to church, protesting poverty, praying, and helping one's neighbor" are theologically informed actions "in virtue of being constituted by a sense of what Christians believe and how they should lead their lives."[20] Tanner's words here apply to

Hauerwas's efforts, for example, to do theological ethics via reflection on liturgical practice.[21] Although Hauerwas's ethics have taken on certain characteristic features, he is committed to doing theology like a bricklayer, composing essays "one brick at a time" in a fashion that, true to the craft, requires exploration, experimentation, and adaptation. A situation-specific project is congenial to Tanner, who calls for "artisanlike inventiveness" and "tactical cleverness" in theological thinking.

The two are also defenders of a "holistic" mode of justification in theology. Hauerwas accepts Robert Jenson's analysis that "all loci of theology are interconnected as nodes of an intricate web," and infers that theology is about exploring, repairing, and discovering new connections "in a manner that helps our lives not be distorted by overemphasis on one aspect of the faith."[22] Tanner might like that image because it calls for a task of construction rather than the mere unearthing of a completely intact "logic of faith" commanding consensus. Anyway, she is clear that "in the course of daily life or in theological argument, a particular belief or value will seem right according to how well that belief or value hangs together with others and with the rest of Christian social practices. The determination of rightness is a matter of fit."[23]

What "fits" may be expected to be controversial. Responsible argument is necessary if this or that standpoint is to edify or persuade. Nothing that Tanner says, to repeat, can or does preclude a theological vision of the sort that Hauerwas brings forward. She just requires that the case for it be made without idolatrous appeals to indefeasibly privileged social movements or practices, and without reliance on an idea of a closely guarded and readily defined boundary marking and making Christian identity. She also has a high tolerance for diversity in Christian communities regarding Christian understandings and embodiments of discipleship. To seek the proper mean between diversity and agreement is to acknowledge the positive values of the former in allowing for mutual correction and its reminder to be open to God's free Word by not taking one's own viewpoints for granted.[24]

Finally, Tanner offers a substantive interpretation of the relation of Christian practices of praise and worship to acts of service for others and in struggle against sin that locates her well within shouting distance of Hauerwas. United with one another in the church as we are united with Christ in the Spirit, our lives must be made to conform to Christ and his gifts. We become "new subjects of attribution as we become the predicates of Christ, as our lives, in other words, belong to him; only as subjects in that sense are graced characteristics as much ours as Christ's."[25] Assumption by Christ and working that out in our lives correspond concretely to acts of worship and discipleship, and though they are distinguishable, they "are found mixed up together in fact":

> Works do not so much issue from faith as a psychological state preceding and impelling them, as much as they issue continually from the overflowing of Christ's virtues to us, as those virtues become ours in faith. Works, moreover, achieve their goodness, they become what they are, only as they are so empowered in and through assumption by Christ. A life of service to God's ends becomes itself a form of worship and praise.[26]

Differences between the thinkers remain, of course, and they can afford opportunities for mutual correction. Tanner's Christian ethic of creation is an ethic Hauerwas should heed. She also has a sensibly pluralistic sense of the relations between Christ and culture that can loosen up Christian responses to the latter. Returning to the earlier example, a theological use of the language of rights need not be a sell out to liberalism but an effective and theologically warranted borrowing of cultural materials. On the other side, there are, I believe, two important corrections or correcting emphases. In the first place, Tanner's denial that a Christian way of life is in any way self-originating sometimes appears to set as its alternative how that life is merely derivative of cultural materials that exist outside Christian faith. She cannot mean to say this because that view sends a message that what lies outside is itself fixed and self-originating (e.g., some more general, consensual religious logic). A sense of the distinctive Christian style that is not reducible to these materials may be lost, accordingly. Hauerwas's career-long working over the idea that a Christian way of life is "odd" can help right the course.

Also, Tanner's cautions not to freeze Christian identity in any one form or with any one method may give the impression that a Chris-

tian life is most of all about having a conversation that is forever testing and revising one or another social expression of Christian identity.
Christianity "has its identity in the form of a task of looking for one."
All alone this comment, in directing our attention to one requirement
of faithfulness to God's free grace, diverts attention away from how
faithfulness to grace also frees Christians to worship God and serve
the neighbor through communal practices in which argument or testing conversation takes a back seat.

Tanner recognizes this fact when she affirms generally that a
"clearly defined meaning or organization of cultural elements" is possible and necessary in social existence, and that, specifically, this must
take place through worship and service in the church. She wishes to
emphasize aspects of provisionality and contingency in our historical
lives before God. But to worry over and to explicate critically the details of Christian meaning and practice, as Hauerwas tries to do, reflects how details as lived are often the foreground of discipleship. Although we do not want to say that faithful openness to God's Word
is ever in the background, the embodiment of that openness in conversation or argument among Christians and others often is.

Against Defensiveness

H. Richard Niebuhr issued a standing warning against defensiveness
in Christian theology. An implication of belief in the Lordship of God
and our justification by faith alone, the warning concerns two targets.
First, systematic apologetics can be based on an effort to defend and
aggrandize the Christian religion through the introduction of a principle about what (generic) religion is and how it perfects the human
spirit. Christianity is shown to get things right in service of human fulfillment thus described. These moves presuppose a human sovereignty
over all things for the sake of vindicating the superiority of Christianity. In addition to this reliance on a self-serving universality, theological existence is also corrupted by overemphasizing the uniqueness and
difference of Christian faith and life, its particularity, over against
other faiths. Christian henotheism assures its prominence by protecting itself against or evading points of view that might threaten its

splendid singularity and taken-for-granted intelligibility. The church, its words and practices, take center stage rather than God.[27]

Gustafson and Tanner continue this legacy. Both resist systematic apologetics. Their respective interpretations of the current theological scene lead them to attack more pointedly a defensive Christian particularism.

Recall Gustafson's cautions about the sectarian temptation and his plea that persons' natural pieties warrant theocentric recognition. He worries as well about a postliberal theological approach that would be content to avoid challenges presented by historical and cultural relativity, and Christianity's relation to other faiths and the findings of modern science. Avoidance betrays a cover-up of what might be shared by historical faiths and human persons shaped by scientific worldviews for the sake of preserving Christian tradition.[28]

"Postliberalism" in this context refers to the work of a number of theologians who tend to understand theology as a critical redescription of the language and logic of Christian faith as these are rooted in Christian practices. Postliberals often worry about a worldly church that accommodates or subordinates itself to general cultural and political trends. They prefer to reflect on how the "strange new world of the Bible," especially its narrative portions, gives distinctive and valuable perspectives on the nature and meaning of life. They also claim that the identity of God is decisively, uniquely, and exclusively disclosed in the history of Jesus Christ.[29]

Gustafson asks postliberal theologians to be straightforward on the three fronts mentioned above. Regarding relativity, he wants them to come clean on their Christocentrism, their commitment to the absolute and universal significance of Jesus Christ, the revelation of God. He questions whether and how far they assert the superiority of Christianity on these Christocentric grounds. And he demands clarity about the postliberal injunction to "absorb the universe into the biblical world"; for such a task presents what he sees to be an enormous problem of relating or opposing the biblical world to construals of reality that order our everyday experience and challenge some traditional views of God as, for example, a personal agent who answers our prayers given God's overriding will to advance human good in this and the next life. It is clear that Gustafson fears in postliberalism a hyper-particularism that simply avoids these questions which he, to be sure, tries straightforwardly to answer in his own work.

The questions presuppose another, an honest answer to which is methodologically essential to the theocentric perspective: How ought theologians to understand what it is they do in giving an account of God and God's relations to the world? In distinction from defenses of Christian tradition based on apologetics, on the one hand, and divine revelation or one's (historical, confessional) fate, on the other, Gustafson opts, as we have seen, for a stance of accountability for the critical selection of materials from tradition and other ways of making sense of the world. He believes that, in fact, selection among biblical sources, theological ideas, and other perspectives on reality is what theologians do all the time. Avoiding challenges from what we know about history, human faiths, and the sciences enables avoidance of rational accountability for theological judgments always already being made with respect to them. A source of the avoidance (and the judgments, for that matter) can be a self-justifying defensiveness that protects and elevates Christianity in lieu of giving all honor to God.

Tanner explicitly criticizes a type of postliberalism. Understanding theology as redescription of the language of faith can give the impression of some ready-made logic that is just there to be uncovered and displayed, rather than critically constructed and assessed.[30] In this and other ways, postliberals strongly suggest the "self-contained and self-originating character of Christian identity" that is constituted by a sharp boundary between inside and outside.[31]

Even if postliberalism concedes that cultural ideas and other materials not of Christian origin are borrowed for theological purposes, it appears to hold that "all borrowings, once incorporated into a Christian context, take on a Christian character that is utterly individual, a character that therefore can go its own way, developing by an internal impulsion properly immune from outside interference."[32] The upshot is a tendency (1) to reify Christian differences in relation to other ways of life, (2) "to keep the worldviews of the wider society at bay when explicating the distinctively Christian import of the biblical story,"[33] and (3) to try to keep the upper hand in uses of borrowed cultural ideas and materials through processes of "complete assimilation." The tendencies add up to a posture that answers more to a Christian community and its words rather than to the transcendent Word of God.[34]

The criticisms are bolstered by an essentially relational account of Christian identity that images in several ways Gustafson's method of critical selection. For Tanner, theological activity is a matter of creative and tactful use of "incredibly diverse" materials bearing on the "meaning dimension" of all the social practices in which Christians participate—not just religious ones but scientific and political practices, too. "Theologians take responsibility," she writes, "for interpreting and organizing some selection of these materials. They attempt to show how some body of these materials hang together well or cohere according to a certain interpretation of them. Materials are selected and rejected, and their senses mutually modified, in light of one another."[35] It makes the most sense to conceive of the distinctiveness of a Christian way of life as emerging "out of tension-filled relations with what other ways of life do with much the same cultural stuff. . . . Christian practices are always the practices of others made odd," and

> most significantly . . . the distinctiveness of a Christian way of life is not so much formed *by* the boundary [between "Christian" and "non-Christian"] as at it; Christian distinctiveness is something that emerges in the very cultural processes occurring at the boundary, processes that construct a distinctive identity for Christian social practices through the distinctive use of cultural materials shared with others.[36]

Defensiveness is not a possibility both theologically or logically, because the Christian's only privilege is humbly to witness to God's free grace in Jesus Christ, and through maneuvers that always already "mouth the claims of other cultures while giving them a new spin."[37]

The alliance between our two theologians is clear. My analysis in chapter 8 indicated, however, that Gustafson and Tanner appear to part company in a telling way. I argued that theocentric ethics is ambiguous with respect to the independent force of the language of Christian faith to illuminate our vision of God, self, and world. Tanner contends against postliberals that theology is neither self-originating nor self-contained, and in that sense is essentially dependent on outside disciplines and (borrowed) cultural materials. Nevertheless, she maintains a commitment to the irreducible status of Christian theology as a (critical!) redescription of the language of faith. The commitment carries with it the notion that Christian claims are patient of justification in terms of their coherence with the whole of Christian vision: the rightness of particular theological beliefs and values depends on how well they fit contextually with other beliefs and values that Christians hold.[38]

Her vision is extremely open-ended and pluralistic, but just so Tanner contends that "creative redescription of the logic of Christian belief in dogmatics provides a kind of defense of the intelligibility of the Christian faith" that is not reducible to other faiths and perspectives.[39] She is straightforward in yielding independent cognitive possibility to the language of faith, however much that language depends through and through on interaction with the world outside. So a defense of the faith is possible without defensiveness, and a dependent theology may yet independently have something to say about God. I think Tanner avoids Gustafson's possible overcorrections, and to that degree works well within a Niebuhrian polarity between faith's particular significance and its universal placement and thrust.

Conclusion

Realism about what God is doing in the world rules out moral realism, and one way to sustain the force of the former in theological ethics is to test all accounts of political life, human bonds, normative strategies, and the like with arguments, conversation, and self-criticism based on honest readings of God's universal providential agency. Christian identity before God includes a sense of universal solidarity in sin and grace, self-criticism, and a relational understanding of its social origins that opposes traces of henotheism and the easy division between us and them. Still, the identity is distinctive; it has a fitting internal coherence, intelligibility, and independence even as it stands against all forms of defensiveness.

Notes

1. Paul Ramsey, *Who Speaks for the Church?* (Nashville: Abingdon Press, 1967), 156–57.
2. Kathryn Tanner, *The Politics of God* (Minneapolis: Fortress Press, 1992), 152.

3. Paul Ramsey, *Speak Up for Just War or Pacifism* (University Park: Pennsylvania State University Press, 1988), 136, 137.

4. Paul Ramsey, *Fabricated Man* (New Haven, Conn.: Yale University Press, 1970), 39.

5. Paul Ramsey, *Christian Ethics and the Sit-In* (New York: Association Press, 1961), 40–98.

6. Paul Ramsey, "Tradition and Reflection in Christian Life," *Perkins Journal* 35 (winter–spring 1982): 51–56.

7. Tanner, *Politics of God*, 220.

8. Ibid., 222, 223.

9. Kathryn Tanner, *Jesus, Humanity, and the Trinity* (Minneapolis: Fortress Press, 2001), 78.

10. Ibid., 94.

11. Kathryn Tanner, *Theories of Culture: A New Agenda for Theology* (Minneapolis: Fortress Press, 1997), 56.

12. Ibid., 125.

13. Ibid., 155.

14. Stanley Hauerwas, *Sanctify Them in the Truth* (Nashville: Abingdon Press, 1998), 64–65 n. 6, 158–159 n. 5.

15. Tanner, *Theories of Culture*, 97.

16. Ibid., 101–2.

17. Hauerwas, *Sanctify Them in the Truth*, 74.

18. Tanner, *Theories of Culture*, 107–19.

19. Hauerwas, *Sanctify Them in the Truth*, 57.

20. Tanner, *Theories of Culture*, 70.

21. Hauerwas, *Sanctify Them in the Truth*, 11.

22. Ibid., 2.

23. Tanner, *Theories of Culture*, 77.

24. Ibid., 175.

25. Tanner, *Jesus, Humanity, and the Trinity*, 57.

26. Ibid., 61. Tanner's appeal to virtues here and elsewhere in her work nevertheless counsels against drawing sharp boundaries between saints and sinners, as well as against isolating the "Christian virtues" of individuals from their social embodiment in perfecting human relations in church and world. See Kathryn Tanner, "Justification and Justice in a Theology of Grace," *Theology Today* 55, no. 4 (January 1999): 521–23.

27. See H. Richard Niebuhr, *The Meaning of Revelation* (New York: Macmillan, 1941), 21–31, and *The Responsible Self* (New York: Harper & Row, 1963), 150–51.

28. James M. Gustafson, "Just What Is 'Postliberal' Theology?" *Christian Cen-*

tury (March 24–31, 1999): 353–55, and "Liberal Questions: A Response to William Placher," *Christian Century* (April 14, 1999): 422–25.

29. For a start, see William C. Placher, "Being Postliberal: A Response to James Gustafson," *Christian Century* (April 7, 1999): 390–92.

30. Tanner, *Theories of Culture*, 72–79.

31. Ibid., 105ff.

32. Ibid., 107.

33. Ibid., 113.

34. Ibid., 248–49.

35. Ibid., 87–88. Cf. Tanner, *Jesus, Humanity, and the Trinity*, xv, where she argues that the task of systematic theology, gaining some vision of the whole of what Christianity is all about, requires "selection and emphasis."

36. Ibid., 113, 115; italics in original.

37. Ibid., 114, 116, 151.

38. Ibid., 77. For Gustafson's doubts about "coherence," see his "Response to Francis Schussler Fiorenza," in Ronald F. Thiemann, ed., *The Legacy of H. Richard Niebuhr* (Minneapolis: Fortress Press, 1991), 73–82.

39. Kathryn Tanner, "Jesus Christ," in Colin E. Gunton, ed., *The Cambridge Companion to Christian Doctrine* (Cambridge: Cambridge University Press, 1997), 269.

CHAPTER ELEVEN

Eight Theses for Theological Ethics

At the end of chapter 1, I asked eight questions that move from an inquiry about "church and world" to the character of the Christian faith and ethics and then on again to a proper understanding of human beings related to God. My study leads me to these eight responses.

Church and World

First, what is the relation between the church and the world? Life before God in Christ is a permanent revolution of mind and heart that aims to refer all things to the glory of God. That aim does not concretely specify any one normative relation between church and world; but no proposal is acceptable that rests on an unfaithful denial or ignorance of God's work as Creator, Preserver, and Redeemer.

Let me elaborate these three simple claims in reverse order. Paul Ramsey's ethics, I have argued, were intended to be especially attentive to "the whole idea of God." Seeking to avoid both the "Egypt" of the natural law and Christian ethical theory's "Exodus" from it whole and entire, he worked out his characteristic position, "love transforming natural justice." The line of argument seems to follow H. Richard Niebuhr's analysis of problematic sorts of cultural Christianity and sectarianism. What makes these accounts problematic is the way they move past the dynamism of God's redemptive work, on the one hand, and God's creative and sustaining work, on the other.

Niebuhr's understanding of the responsibility of the church for society takes us in a similar direction. The worldly church is irresponsible because it is faithful not to God but to some form of human society itself. The warrants for this worldliness, Stanley Hauerwas may be quick to remind us, are perhaps some appeal to God's ordering of creation realized prominently in a nation or group. Also excluded is the isolated church, in which the Christian community responds only for itself. This cannot be, for the God to whom Christians are responsible creates and sustains and wills the well-being of all human persons in the world.

I proposed that Niebuhr's conversionism or motif of Christ transforming culture can be employed not as normatively overwhelming other motifs but as internally correcting them. Admitting that even on this score there is a point to the charge that he is an imperialist in taking the transformation motif to be perfectly self-correcting, I held out for an interpretation of *Christ and Culture* that cautions against denying the goodness of creation, the fallenness of cultural life, and the redemptive work of God. Attention to God's activity as Creator, moreover, must heed James Gustafson's plea that the activity of the church include attention to the intersections between theology and the insights of the sciences (see question five).

Thus—and here we move to the second simple claim—an infinite dialogue about the church's faithfulness to God and its relation to and responsibility for the world may go forward. Niebuhr fittingly wrote of a rhythm of identification and withdrawal; but one ought not set the meter in advance of response to matters of time and circumstance. The Christian community must withdraw from and oppose whatever opposes the grace of God in Christ, and this includes the idols of nationalism, capitalism (more generally, economism) and liberalism (but see below). Yet a temporally invariant opposition is no more warranted than a similarly static Christian identification with the world (though such an identification may also be correct in its time and place).

Kathryn Tanner posits over against Niebuhr a position that I believe is more to his liking than she thinks: "In the Christian case relations with the wider culture are never simply ones of either accommodation, on the one hand, or opposition and radical critical revision, on the other, but always some mixture."[1] Ramsey takes him to mean that every one of his types belong "in the ongoing historical wrestle of Christ with culture in the conscience of Christians"; but he may go too far in adding that no one "can belong to more than one predominantly." Why not, in the timely rhythm of identification and withdrawal?[2] And "putting it crudely, the Christian response to modern

Western culture's affirmations of women's rights does not have to be the same as its response to that culture's practice of sending Jews to concentration camps."[3]

My third simple claim suggests, in the order of the three, that Niebuhrian conversionism is a basis for denying monolithic relations of opposition, identification, and even a kind of transformation between church and world. Conversion is also a basis for affirming the distinction but not the separation between church and world. "The important difference between the church and the world is that the church knows itself to be 'world' before God while the world does not know this but thinks that it can be like God."[4] Just so, "Insofar as Jesus Christ is seen by us as seated at the right hand of the Father, as very God of very God, the distinction of ourselves from Jesus Christ is primary; we are not Christ. But we identify ourselves with the Christ who has identified himself with man and mankind. We are related to the Christ who is related to the world; and who is not related to the world through us but by his own action."[5]

Oppositionally, to define the world as "nonchurch" may keep us from our necessary identification with it in Christ, and tempts us to ignore how worldly societies stand as covenant communities with their own commissions. But simply to identify church and world misses the challenge of conversion in ourselves and our fellows as well. Finally, to parade a single requirement of transformation specifically applicable in every circumstance narrows options where, in the name of the permanent revolution, something more like identification with the world in its creatureliness or opposition to the world in its sinfulness is more fitting.

Christian Communities and Liberalism

Second, what is the relation between Christian communities and liberalism? Liberalism, democracy, or America, for that matter, assaults the identity of Christian communities if it sets up an idol (e.g., freedom, the American dream), or tempts us to adopt self-deceptive moral ideals of neutrality or individual autonomy. But the church's boundaries must not be drawn so rigidly as to rule out the possibility of faithful, fruitful, limited appropriations and identifications.

As part of his positive project of critically interpreting the virtues and bonds that identify a distinctive people faithful to God in Jesus Christ, Hauerwas has sought to display how American liberalism removes an intelligible context for virtuous practices, dissolves bonds into the terms of contractual and consumerist choice, and accommodates Christian ethics to the social requirements of the United States. A focus on the primacy of individual choice can make Christian faith look like one of many lifestyle options; a focus on the public relevance of Christian moral norms can be co-opted by values that compromise with national violence and the celebration of personal autonomy. Hauerwas effectively questioned Ramsey's ethics for making Christianity appear too much like a worldview and for relying so much on American political and medical institutions to establish his faith's intelligibility.

Christian moral discourse, I said in chapter 7, needs to be rooted in the practices of the church to avoid problems of abstraction and illicit accommodation. These should include activities of Baptism, reconciliation and peacemaking, the Eucharist, and common unforced decision making that serves one another's good. The requirement and its enactment ought not to exclude the possibility of legitimate borrowings of cultural materials from other contexts and arenas. We learned from Tanner that the particular use of borrowed materials is a matter of course in all cultural activities, including Christian ones. Features of liberal belief and practice may not be excluded in principle, but only if they create problems that jeopardize Christian faithfulness to God and neighbor.

Here are two illustrations. The first is familiar. Tanner holds up three kinds of rights possessed by human beings as creatures of God. They are a right to care and concern for one's very existence, a right to self-development in one's activities, and a right "to be oneself, a right to have one's personal integrity respected."[6] She holds that these "are not like rights in liberal theory that define a sphere of independence or noninterference by others on a conflictual model, thereby accentuating the distance of even absence of relation among people." Instead, these rights "establish relations among people," and "establish spheres of obligation . . . in which one has a valid claim on the attentions of others."[7] Recent Roman Catholic social teaching that "human rights" establish basic conditions for life in community makes analogous distinctions. One could claim in response that the language of rights is thoroughly liberal, either because it cannot intelligibly be removed from its conceptual context or because it cannot practically be removed from a prevailing cultural context of individualism.

Neither conceptual worlds nor social worlds, however, are all that tightly bound; moreover, the normative implications of human creatureliness provide good reasons for saying that creatures have rights. My response to the second question also permits saying that there is something important and correct about the liberal idea that human beings, however communal or nonconflictual their life ought to be, are inviolable and owed respect as living, self-determining, unique individuals. Tanner takes that truth and places it theologically in a web of belief that changes the normative goal of respect from isolated, suspicious independence to a community of mutual fulfillment and reciprocal concern.

Second, when Niebuhr presents "Christianity's relation to democracy," he says that faith in God the Father of Jesus Christ can lead to democracy "in a limited and pragmatic sense." It can lead to a commitment to limited political power, free participation in the political life of state and society, equality of respect for citizens, and the expansion of personal liberties. These features are reoriented in the life of faith. Limited government correlates not with protection of a measureless freedom but with free allegiance to a God beyond political loyalty. Participation correlates not with a politics of self-interest but with a politics of social obligation for the common good. Equality and liberty fund not "a pure commercialism that resents restraint" but relations of mutual respect, as Tanner might commend.

It is true, and true perhaps in a way that Niebuhr never acknowledged, that these implications of a democracy to which faith leads require social practices in the church that fill them with content; the implications otherwise become abstract beliefs or ideologies that underwrite the values they are meant to criticize. Still, these features of democracy, or even a certain revisionist liberal democracy, are not transformed beyond recognition. We see what is true about them in the light of faith in divine truth, and in doing this we give honor to God as part of our "permanent revolution."[8]

Nonviolent Discipleship and the Violent Nation-State

Third, what is the relation between the church that aspires to a life of nonviolent discipleship and the violent character of the nation-state? As they challenge one another, just war and pacifist Christians may witness to the state through distinct enactments of a shared practical pacifism. The church ought to criticize all realist justifications of violence, where "realism" means that no moral norms apply, or that they do so only regarding the ends and not the means justifying violence. So our question becomes one of the relation between a people's commitment to nonviolence and the violence of nations (for our purposes, especially, in war) when it is claimed to be just and limited.

I agree with Ramsey that just war and pacifism are equally Christian discipleships. But just as Ramsey asked, "How, in thought and action, can we make just war possible?" I ask, "How can we make just war as a form of Christian discipleship possible?" If it is to be that at all, I believe we should seek some convergence between traditions of nonviolence and just war in forms of practical pacifism.

My criticisms of Ramsey in chapters 4 and 6 were intended to stress the significance of social context and social practice for securing the integrity of just war discourse. Just war rightly practiced would show only that warfare may be a barely human activity. If the doctrine insulates us from the horror of armed conflict, it cannot credibly do good moral work; instead, it tends to become a tool of forces that confuse justice with mere assertions of national interest. Practical pacifism would expose self-congratulatory ideologies of statecraft that tend to render war ordinary, inevitable, and unqualifiedly righteous. Christians who stand up for just war must not aid and comfort the state if it trumpets the ideologies. They will unmask false and inadequate reasons for war along the following lines:

> Being against war . . . means opposing the idea that war is "necessary" or "inevitable," and that peace is not "possible." Finally it means opposing the idea that wars are waged for noble motives: to restore a universal order of justice and peace or simply to make amends for injustices. For at most these noble motives—which some people do not lack—in most cases provide a juridical and moral cover for the true rea-

sons of war: political domination and economic interest. In other words, to oppose the "ideology of war" means to do what is needed to unmask war by showing it as it really is by uncovering its motives and results, by demonstrating that it is always the poor and the weak who pay for war, whether they wear a military uniform or belong to the civilian population.[9]

The last sentence is reminiscent of Niebuhr's own image of war as crucifixion.

I call this practical pacifism because, in the case of Christian proponents of just war, it names the concern to limit the state's use of violence from a standpoint practically rooted in Christian practices of peaceableness and reconciliation. The wager is that Hauerwas is right in his suspicion that "if we could force just war thinkers (and churches) to recognize the kind of communities necessary to sustain the discourses and practices necessary for just war, it would make it increasingly difficult to accuse pacifists of being hopeless 'idealists' and/or 'sectarians.'"[10] Such a community would nurture a sense of war's horror and of the idolatrous claims and tendencies of nation-states in an internal life attuned to embodying and extending mercy in witness to God's own. It need not reject, absolutely and in principle, the possibility of justifiable recourse to arms, though it may at the far limit conclude with Karl Barth that in our time "all affirmative answers to the question are wrong if they do not start with the assumption that the inflexible negative of pacifism has *almost* infinite arguments in its favor and is *almost* overpoweringly strong."[11]

So just war thinkers and churches must use just war criteria to test and question all too easy uses of them by, for example, asking what sort of peace really is envisioned as the end of this war, or whether war in that case really was a reasonable last resort, or whether a conflict that devastates the poor can possibly be proportionate. Ramsey dismissed these questions as dangerous maneuvers meant to discredit all wars one by one; but he saw them as dangerous because he opposed the principled pacifism that he believed lay behind them. I am saying, again, that these strategies need not presuppose absolute pacifism. Alternatively, a principled Christian pacifist witness to the state, based on a view of what God in Christ rejects, affords, and welcomes, may yet practically engage the state by creatively challenging it with its own moral lingo, including just war discourse.

Just war as Christian witness requires a peaceable community in which courage is expressed in restraint, where love casts our fear, and where hope for reconciliation triumphs. It is hard to improve upon Hauerwas's insights in this regard. But just war may also afford Hauerwas an avenue of Christian witness to the state that seeks to make all life, even life in war, less violent, even, perhaps, along a continuum of decreasing intolerability. In short, Christian adherence to just war ought to be a commitment to the serious questioning that practical pacifism affords; and for a Christian to stand up for pacifism should mean, practically, to make an analogous commitment that uses just war to make prophetic criticism pertinent and plain.[12]

Christian Ethics and Public Morality and Politics

Fourth, how does Christian ethics fittingly bear on broader public discussions of moral and political matters? Christian ethics must not give up its distinctive voice by simply conforming it to popular general idioms or sets of normative options. But it ought not simply dismiss these idioms or options in advance. Christian ethics also should not try to prove its usefulness to the issues of the day; but neither should it step away from them because it has no use for the concerns of the world. Christian communities, which are responsible to God, are rather to be responsible for society by calling themselves and their fellows to repent of their false and vicious loyalties; by seeking reconciliation and fellowship between persons within and between various communities; and by being a pioneer and representative, leading in its conversion to God by demonstrating itself as a world society.

Christian ethics, then, being responsible to God and God's creation, will denounce injustice, defend and help create conditions of creaturely covenant, and present to society an internal life that really does attest to God's faithfulness at the heart of things. The pioneering example will help render social critique more intelligible and credible. The analysis that accompanies the critique, itself a gesture toward community or fellow humanity, should be cogent and self-critical. The forms of covenant community commended should be described with wisdom, and the virtues that attend them should be articulated imaginatively.

For example, churches may oppose the direct taking of unborn human life once the process of conception is complete. A number of theological convictions about God's unconditional care for human beings, the special claims of the weak and vulnerable, and the significance of family and especially the mother–child bond underlie this conclusion. But a public ethic emerging from the churches that seeks the protection of unborn life, I am saying, should attempt centrally to help create a social environment in which children are welcomed in the world as gifts; for Christians "see children as a sign of the trustworthiness of God's creation and his unwillingness to abandon the world to powers of darkness."[13]

This ethic can include an effort to change the law, but by itself that effort is not sufficient; moreover, Christian communities themselves must display a commitment to the care of children that extends to addressing the unjust burdens faced by specific parents, especially mothers, in the tasks of caretaking. The intelligibility of caring about the fetus depends, Niebuhr and Hauerwas might say, on this pioneering and representative activity that originates in a common life of a particular people faithful to God in Jesus Christ. And the more general appeal of this moral stance depends on the success with which this activity overlaps and resonates with the moral lives of fellow creatures who, though not explicitly Christian, also care about children and parents.[14] In this way and in keeping with Gustafson's concerns, Christian ethics may and must include their moral sentiments and natural piety.

Christian Ethics and Nature, History, and Culture

Fifth, why and how should Christian ethics deal with—to quote Gustafson again from chapter 1—"the ways in which nature, history and culture are interpreted and understood by investigations proper to them?" The investigations can indicate something about what God is doing in the world. Theologians and ethicists depend on these investigations by "taking up the best thought about the cosmos and its inhabitants and subjecting it to their particular angle of vision, by investigating how all this appears when one understands the world in its relation to the God of all."[15] Theological dependence in this sense allows an independence in which a self-critical language of faith claims certain truths about God's relation to the world that cannot be reduced to the conclusions of the natural and social sciences. Hence, "Human beings are made for a destiny of which the human and natural sciences may know nothing."[16]

Consider Pope John Paul II's 1996 message on evolution to the Pontifical Academy of Sciences. He recognizes that this scientific theory about the origin and development of life "has been progressively accepted by researchers, following a series of discoveries in various fields of knowledge; . . . the convergence . . . of the results of work that was conducted independently is in itself a significant development in favor of this theory." Not being a scientist, the pope does not rule on the truth or falsity of evolution. He notes that there are in fact different evolutionary theories based on different explanations of its operation and on varying "materialist, reductionist, and spiritualist interpretations." He then outlines an argument for a "spiritual soul" as the ground of the transcendent dignity of the person, and concludes that evolutionary approaches taking the human mind to emerge from "the forces of living matter, or as a mere epiphenomenon of this matter, are incompatible with the truth about man."[17]

Let us consider the theological strategy used here. John Paul II's message hails scientific advance and convergence, asserts that "transition to the spiritual cannot be the object of [scientific] observation," and recognizes that scientific observation "nevertheless can discover at the experimental level a series of very valuable signs indicating what is specific to the human being." I think this clears the way for learning a whole lot about humanity, though the spiritual ground and fulfillment of persons in God is held to be independent of scientific inquiry. Perhaps Gustafson might see this route to be defective because it insulates an interpretation of spirit from scientific accounts of mind and will. He might want more crossing from sciences to theology at the intersections where they meet in taking up the same subject matter.

But the proposal defended here allows for two-way traffic. It does not deny that the sciences are a source for what Christians are to say about God's relation to the world. Theological independence from the sciences remains. John Paul II's case for independence includes observations about a theory's dependence on philosophical presuppositions that may or may not comport with theological conceptions of human dignity. In chapter 8, I made a different claim for independence, pointing out Gustafson's uncertain commitment to the cognitive status of Christian tradition and the language of faith.

Theology and other disciplines may intersect in a number of ways, and Gustafson has described them masterfully.[18] So other disciplines can revise traditional theological theses, as Stephen Pope's analysis can revise excessively universalist interpretations of neighbor love.[19] Sociological and political critique of a logic of identity that excludes authentic respect of personal differences can be redescribed from a theological perspective, as Tanner has done. Theological perspectives may also be explicated nontheologically in illuminating ways.[20]

These maneuvers, however, may be an ingredient in a theological style of justification that seeks the most coherent account of a Christian way of life, the way the beliefs, values, and practices of that kind of life hang together in a particular time and place. Gustafson criticizes this method for granting Christian theology an extreme malleability; one can always tinker with a contextual web of belief and practice to evade serious challenges from the sciences about how the universe came to be or what happens when we die.[21] Generally, he sees a temptation for Christians to disengage from critical questions posed by the sciences and other forms of inquiry as the meaning of our social world depends less and less on religious interpretations and explanations. They find themselves too willing to abide by a norm of "faithfulness to what gives distinctive identity to the religious community."[22] A straightforward response is that fidelity to God may constitutively include commitment to a Christian community's distinctive common life and service to God and neighbor in truth and love. The commitment ought never to exclude openness at the intersections to whatever is true and good, just as such openness ought not to exclude the church's distinctive witness to what is true and good.

Tanner strikes a noteworthy balance in her own recent reflections on the meaning of Christian eschatology "without a future"—that is, its meaning in light of the compelling scientific understanding that "death is the end towards which our solar system and the universe as a whole move." With Gustafson, she does not directly contest this understanding; still, she reckons with the possibility that there might yet be a "Christian hope that can cope with, make sense of the end of things that scientists describe." Her theological thought experiment draws from parallel developments in a doctrine of creation, and identifies eternal life or "life *in* God" as a present reality the full consequences of which are not now manifest. She allows that our death may need to be construed as a creature's good and natural end, but holds out for an "overcoming of mortality" in which

> after death (as before death) we are taken up into the life of God as the very mortal creatures we are. . . . Immortality is not, then, granted to the world in the form of some new natural principles that prevent loss or transience; instead, God's own animating eternity shines through or suffuses the very mortal being of those who hold their existence in God. . . . This immortality is properly considered ours . . . insofar as, living in God, we are no longer our own but God's. A new identity is in this way given to the world.[23]

I present the simplest outline of this position to show how responsible attention to the result of scientific inquiries may work in a theological construction that develops traditional Christian discourse in its proper integrity and independence. More work needs to be done in comparing this view with others for overall theological adequacy, and the comparison ought to include Gustafson's approach—with special reference, I think, to his denials regarding anthropocentrism.

Christian Particularity and Universal Intent

Sixth, how does the particularity of the Christian tradition relate to more general or even universal understandings of human value and fulfillment? In their particularity, Christian identity and tradition are not isolated from more general or other particular normative visions within sharply drawn boundaries. Nor does an affirmation of Christian distinctiveness require a Christocentric henotheism that makes Christian community rather than God revealed in Christ a final object of loyalty. Nevertheless, a particular nondefensive, Christian loyalty to God may yet be universal and nonexclusive in affirming Jesus Christ as the unique mediator of salvation. This response continues the discussion of our last theme and ends in a query that is worth studying further.

Tanner has shown us the futility of securing Christian particularity by way of closely guarded boundaries. Christians are always coming to an understanding of who they are at the boundary between inside and outside, internal self-description and external viewpoints. Christian traditions are historically developed arguments about what Christian identity is and what it means to live it out. Gustafson's senses of natural piety reflect sorts of human experiences that a Christian point of view works over and develops within its particular context of commitment, belief, and moral practice. Niebuhr's analysis of the symbolic form of Jesus Christ shows in a striking way how a more general "ethos of citizenship in a universal society" under God is yoked to and modified by the specific and unsubstitutable agent's work of redemption through death and resurrection.

Niebuhr's assaults on turning theology into Christology and his criticism of a Barthian Christocentrism are directed above all against an ethos of a closed society, or an ecclesiasticism that identifies Christians as "members of a special group, with a special god, a special destiny, and a separate existence."[24] Gustafson carries this line forward, and it ought to be heeded, especially as it reflects his positive call for a conversion that enlarges and thus corrects our constricted vision, loves, and moral standards. The criticisms represent one pole of self-defense in which persons evade their responsibilities before God by anxiously clutching at what makes them (supremely or smugly or complacently) different from their fellows.

Another pole of defensiveness (as we saw in the last chapter and at the end of chapter 2) is the attempt to leave the standpoint of the faith one confesses to justify it from a neutral standpoint, to show its usefulness to other societies and their values, or to prove its rational superiority through some systematic apologetic. This form shares with the other a self-justifying desire to prove claims to superior knowledge and virtue, and an accompanying disrespect or dismissal of other points of view. One approach is more imperial; the other is more a matter of self-congratulatory isolation.

Niebuhr states: "As we begin with revelation only because we are forced to do so by our limited standpoint in history and faith so we can proceed only by stating in simple, confessional form what has happened to us in our community, how we came to believe, how we reason about things, and what we see from our point of view."[25] Read this text "in the double Niebuhrian sense of confession—saying what we believe and repenting of our sin and lack of faith in the same breath."[26] Now what if someone said that our confession includes the faith that Jesus Christ uniquely reconciles us to God and in so doing mediates salvation for us in our history and for all the world? Would this affirmation necessarily amount to Christian arrogance and faithlessness?

No one can dispute that the claim can and does amount to this a lot of the time. It can focus attention on Jesus Christ as "our" wonderful possession that you need (but do not have yet, or do not have the way we want you to). It may use Jesus Christ to shield Christian communities from their own sin and misery (because all these others who do not have him have got sin abounding). It can make Jesus Christ merely a predicate of some teaching authority rather than the living Lord and Savior. But must a claim about the nonexclusive particularity of Jesus Christ's salvific mission have these implications?

J. A. DiNoia argues that the meaning of salvation in a Christian context is specific. It has to do with human fulfillment through loving communion with the Triune God in which our own identities are conformed to Christ while deepened and perfected as the very particular creatures we are. This view may bear a likeness to a number of other accounts of human flourishing, as Niebuhr would remind us. But he would also remind us, I think, that it is particular and not identical to the others. Now, to confess Christ as the unique mediator of this specific final end might not offend at all other human persons seeking other final ends. It may even be a condition for respecting one another's particular and different confessions that the possible universality of each be acknowledged rather than rejected.[27]

But does not a commitment to Jesus Christ's universal salvific mission lead necessarily or inevitably to that self-justifying face-off where the Christian says to the non-Christian, "I'm right, and you're wrong"? The question is a little unfair because it gives us no context; but in asking it we mean to worry about lording it over non-Christians in self-justifying defensiveness. It is not clear to me (or to DiNoia) that this is the consequence.

A Christian confession of faith may allow that non-Christians serve God's purposes (and God's desire for salvation of all in Christ) in ways that do not require giving up their (non-Christian) religious loyalties. It can allude to God's working (in Christ) outside the borders of the church, and even especially so. It can identify the truth of God in Christ as not being alien to but in some sense continuous with human persons' natural capacities to know the truth and love the good, and with other religious insights into these. It can acknowledge Christian failure to grasp the true and good in Christ, and to profess a faithful, humble agnosticism about where other people stand before God. Di-Noia wonders what Christians have to offer the world unless it is a message about universal salvation in Christ.[28]

Niebuhr may not have accepted this line. Gustafson's interpretation of him is relevant, as is, perhaps, Robert Bellah's general observation that "Niebuhr was nervous about any mediation of God, even through Christ, certainly through the Bible or the church."[29] A closer look at this question nevertheless makes sense, given the seriousness with which he takes the particularity of Christian belief and the way it could play out along the lines presented above. Stating in confessional form what has happened to us in our community, we include "how we reason about things and what we see from our point of view." We cannot reason about the meaning of human flourishing in any terms but those revealed to us, and what we see when we see some big or little hint of that flourishing is, well, the work of God in Christ.[30]

Of course, this feature of what Christians confess, if it is not to become a piece of idolatry, must be measured by the reality of the sovereign God, whose free Word may reverse expectations and open up theological interpretations of what is going on. Perhaps the universal claim from a Christian standpoint that I am considering practically precludes response to that free Word, given that we are sinful creatures. Perhaps, however, this is a counsel of despair to be avoided just because it gives up on the graciousness of the sovereign God. And in fact, for Christians this graciousness is Jesus Christ. "To whom else shall we go for words of eternal life, to whom else for the franchise in the universal community?"[31]

The Emancipatory Potential of Christian Belief

Seventh, what is the emancipatory potential of Christian belief? Our study suggests a number of sources for a Christian ethic that condemns injustice and pursues human dignity in solidarity. These include the respect owed to human creatures of God, a Christological focus on love as answering to the need of the vulnerable neighbor, a critique of all forms of henotheism that exclude others as beings of worth before God, a rejection of both self-seeking ecclesiasticism and functional or utilitarian Christianity, and a call to repentance and constant vigilance among Christians whose traditions have all too often supported an unjust status quo.

One could say that these themes are unified in a graced capacity for nonidolatrous self-esteem that empowers the oppressed and humbles the mighty in anticipation of conflict and struggle for the sake of life in authentic community. Tanner's answer to what she calls realism corrects fatalistic tendencies in the Niebuhrian tradition. Nevertheless, the tradition as represented by Niebuhr himself will not understand human freedom and responsibility apart from a social, interactive context. I tried to show one way that works without falling to Tanner's criticisms at the end of chapter 9.

Our Dignity before God

Eighth, what is the full meaning of our dignity before God? Our dignity as creatures, and as sisters and brothers for whom Christ died, is realized in our flourishing as the particular beings we are in communities of solidarity. To claim this dignity theologically may presuppose that human beings possess a special distinction in being made in God's image and destined for a unique fellowship; but these presuppositions need not imply a perverse anthropocentrism. Questions remain, however, regarding exactly how respect for creatures in community is to be theologically conceived and practically enacted.

One might say that Niebuhr's legacy also includes this polarity: We are to honor God's human creatures as individual members of a universal society, and hence as nonreducible individuals before God, while recognizing that that respect is historically embodied in a variety of communal bonds and loyalties. Our four authors address the polarity differently. Ramsey depends on a covenantal anthropology derived in part from Barth. Hauerwas suspects individualism but honors all human persons as gifts to be cherished with responsibilities in the forms of common life.

Gustafson also suspects that overemphasis on individual claims or rights gives up on responsibilities in the processes of interdependence which we inhabit. Tanner is far more insistent on the theological importance, if not centrality, of respect for human creatures in their full individual particularity in relation to God; but she commends a communal ideal that highlights communion among gifted creatures sharing their gifts. Further reflection on these and other options is a necessary and recurring requirement for theological ethics. So we come full circle, because my goal throughout has been to work within and not to collapse the polarity in a response of permanent revolution to God's gracious creative, preserving, and redeeming activity.

In chapter 2, I referred to Stephen Crocco's observation: Niebuhr's description of Ernst Troeltsch "as one in whom antithetical interests were combined in the unity of his personality without being fused" makes sense of Niebuhr himself. Bellah sounds the same point when he refers to Niebuhr's penchant for "holding together two almost incompatible things neither of which we can abandon without peril."[32] My responses above should be understood to reflect an appreciation of his sort of dialectical or polar approach to Christian theology and ethics. The church possesses a distinctive identity, but just so seeks to be a universal society in and for the world. Liberalism may be alien to Christian witness but also may capture truths about loyalty to God. Pacifism and just war may converge in a Christian life that maintains a contrastive distance from the violence of the state while witnessing responsibly to it.

Moreover, Christian self-description maintains its independence even as it is deeply dependent on scientific and other sources external to it. A Christian confession may make universal claims but must avoid both imperialistic and priggish defensiveness. A preferential option for the poor is theologically justified, but with reference to our fundamental equality and our ultimate need for correction. Christian ethics should seek to defend and realize bonds of human loyalty that maximally respect human individuality projected toward the closest sort of creaturely communion.

My study moves to a defense of a number of theological commitments that govern the shape and character of a Christian ethic of faithfulness. Lest we think this ethic would be conservative and static, it may be instead be progressive, pioneering, and prophetic. Faithful witness to God's sovereign grace requires as much. Should we think the ethic to be divisive and (henotheistically) judgmental, it may well be loving, merciful, and reconciling even in its call to repentance. Faithful witness to God's activity whole and entire requires as much. Rather than being insulated and self-congratulatory, an ethic of faithfulness to God may be vigilantly self-critical, open to challenge and humble conversion. The church's fidelity to God for the world requires just this. And lest this dynamic go astray through unfitting accommodation to or co-optation by the world, or risk incoherence through an excessive malleability or ceaseless searching for itself, this ethic may be richly nourished by the practices and common life of the church.

My book as a whole, finally and throughout, has taken up Niebuhr's legacy of calling for a Christian life and theology that admits a variety of voices who uplift and correct one another. I have tried to write a critical conversation between Christian thinkers who differ in many things but share a common, very complex legacy. The conversation moves theological ethics forward, as does Niebuhr's recommended communal, situated wrestling with the issue of Christ and culture. There is also his "ecumenical approach to the restatement of Trinitarian doctrine," which calls upon the churches together to overcome the three Unitarian tendencies in the history of Christianity (those of Father, Son, or Spirit):

> The Trinitarianism of the whole Church must undertake to state what is implicit in the faith and knowledge of all its parts though it is not explicit in any one of them. It must attempt to correct the over-emphases and partialities of the members of the whole not by means of a new over-emphasis but by means of a synthesized formula in which all the partial insights and convictions are combined. . . . Truth, after all, is not the possession of any individual or of any party or school, but is represented, insofar as it can be humanly rep-

resented, only by the whole dynamic and complementary work of the company of knowers and believers.[33]

What is unapologetically irenic is also unapologetically critical, and vice versa.

Ramsey's ethic is helped by Hauerwas's attention to social context, and Hauerwas is helped by Ramsey's attention to the whole idea of God. Both ought to be corrected by Gustafson's criticisms of the disciplines; but insofar as they are overcorrections, these should be modified in turn. Tanner alerts us to the dangers of realism and joins Gustafson against defensiveness, but these perspectives stresses would profit from the challenge of Hauerwas's embodied social ethic. And so forth. Yet all of our theologians contribute to the common faith, and their insights remain considerable. To say this is not a matter of cheap tolerance or accommodating pluralism. It is to address, in the matter of Christian ethics, our shared lot and possibility as unprofitable servants seeking to be faithful to the promise of one another's blessings, because we all are blessed by a faithful God.

Notes

1. Kathryn Tanner, *Theories of Culture* (Minneapolis: Fortress Press, 1997), 119.
2. Paul Ramsey, "Tradition and Reflection in Christian Life," *Perkins Journal* 35 (winter–spring 1982): 51.
3. Tanner, *Theories of Culture*, 119.
4. H. Richard Niebuhr, "The Church Defines Itself in the World," *Theology, History, and Culture*, ed. William Stacy Johnson (New Haven, Conn.: Yale University Press, 1996), 72.
5. Ibid., 73.
6. Kathryn Tanner, *The Politics of God* (Minneapolis: Augsburg Fortress Press, 1992), 177. Cf. Kathryn Tanner, *Jesus, Humanity, and the Trinity* (Minneapolis: Fortress, 2001), 89.
7. Ibid., 180–81.
8. H. Richard Niebuhr, "The Relation of Christianity and Democracy," in idem., *Theology, History, and Culture*, 151–58.
9. La Civilta Cattolica, "Modern War and Christian Conscience," in Paul T. Jersild and Dale A. Johnson, eds., *Moral Issues and Christian Response*, 5th ed. (Fort Worth: Harcourt Brace Jovanovich, 1993), 223–24. The quoted pas-

sage lines up with my proposal if we take it to "oppose the *ideology* that wars are waged for noble motives." My concern is that the notion of "noble motives" could foreclose or forestall sure and vigorous critical consideration of engagements and conduct in war.

10. Stanley Hauerwas, "Epilogue," in Paul Ramsey, *Speak Up for Just War or Pacifism* (University Park: Pennsylvania University State Press, 1988), 152.

11. Karl Barth, *Church Dogmatics* (Edinburgh: T. & T. Clark, 1961), vol. 3, part 4, p. 455; my italics.

12. An anonymous reviewer from Georgetown University Press thinks that my standpoint effectively collapses just war into pacifism and writes, "I would think an approach more consistent with the author's basic dialectic would be to call for a very strong presumption against violence but recognize that in certain circumstances that presumption might not hold."

    I believe my view intensifies and contextualizes just this view with regard to just war as a form of discipleship making witness before God to the state. Or at least that is what I am trying to do from the just war side. Make the presumption very strong indeed, and inquire again and again about the "might not hold" in a context in which one is attuned to nationalist presumption and disciples' practices of reconciliation and nonviolent love.

    The polar dialectic I seek may meet with the idea that just war requires an astonishingly challenging combination of principles, commitments, attitudes, and emotions. It requires that wars be fought with resolve but also with horror. It calls for a stance that readies to kill but without hatred. It defends to the death just causes belonging to nations that will, with all creation, one day perish in God's final reckoning in justice and mercy. It insists that the end of war is peace. From the principled pacifism side, I call for a practical commitment to make good use of just war tradition with respect to a continuum of decreasing intolerability. See my brief discussion of Karl Barth on this issue in William Werpehowski, "Hearing the Divine Command: Realism and Discernment in Barth's Ethics," *Zeitschrift fur dialektische Theologie* 15, no. 1 (1999): 72–74.

13. Stanley Hauerwas, *A Community of Character* (Notre Dame, Ind.: University of Notre Dame Press, 1981), 227.

14. William Werpehowski, "The Promise and Pathos of Christian Ethics," *Horizons* (fall 1985): 282–302, and William Werpehowski, "Persons, Practices, and the Argument from Conception," *Journal of Medicine and Philosophy* 22 (1997): 479–94.

15. Kathryn Tanner, "The Difference Theological Anthropology Makes," *Theology Today* 50, no. 4 (January 1994): 568.

16. Ibid., 578.

17. John Paul II, "Message to the Pontifical Academy of Sciences," October 22, 1996, www.cin.org/users/james/files/message.htm.

18. See especially James M. Gustafson, *Intersections: Science, Theology, and Ethics* (Cleveland: Pilgrim Press, 1996), 126–47.

19. See, e.g., Stephen J. Pope, *The Evolution of Altruism and the Ordering of Love* (Washington, D.C.: Georgetown University Press, 1994).

20. In *Intersections*, p. 141, Gustafson cites as a good example James B. Nelson's *Moral Nexus* (Philadelphia: Westminster Press, 1971), a study of Christian moral identity in terms of socialization theory.

21. James M. Gustafson, "Response to Francis Schussler Fiorenza," in Ronald F. Thiemann, ed., *The Legacy of H. Richard Niebuhr* (Minneapolis: Fortress Press, 1991), 79–82.

22. James M. Gustafson, "Liberal Questions: A Response to William Placher," *Christian Century* (April 14, 1999): 425.

23. Kathryn Tanner, *Jesus, Humanity, and the Trinity* (Minneapolis: Fortress Press, 2001), 98, 100, 116, 118.

24. H. Richard Niebuhr, *Radical Monotheism and Western Culture* (New York: Harper & Row, 1960), 60.

25. H. Richard Niebuhr, *The Meaning of Revelation* (New York: Macmillan, 1941), 29.

26. Robert N. Bellah, "Religious Pluralism and Religious Truth," *Reflections* (summer–fall 1995): 13.

27. Here I draw primarily from DiNoia's essay, "Is Jesus Christ the Unique Mediator of Salvation?" in Ronald F. Thiemann and William C. Placher, eds., *Why Are We Here?* (Harrisburg, Pa.: Trinity Press International, 1998), 56–68. For a book-length treatment, see J. A. DiNoia, *The Diversity of Religions: A Christian Perspective* (Washington, D.C.: Catholic University of America Press, 1992).

28. Jerry Walls and J. A. DiNoia, "Must the Truth Offend?" *First Things* 84 (June–July 1998): 34–40.

29. James M. Gustafson, "Making Theology Intelligible," *Reflections* (summer–fall 1995): 2–8; Bellah, "Religious Pluralism and Religious Truth," 15. Also consider Hans Frei's observation that while Niebuhr was very sympathetic with Karl Barth's radical theology of grace, "increasingly what he could not swallow was the startlingly consistent Barthian identity of universal divine action with divine action in Christ alone. There were, for H. Richard Niebuhr, other mysterious forms of the *logos asarkos*, not only in the world's religions but in its philosophies, too." Hans W. Frei, *Theology and Narrative*, ed. George Hunsinger and William C. Placher (New York: Oxford University Press, 1993), 228.

30. Cf. H. Richard Niebuhr, "Reformation: Continuing Imperative," *Christian Century* 77 (March 2, 1960): 249: "I do not have the evidence which allows me to say that the miracle of faith in God is worked only by Jesus Christ and that it is never given to men outside the sphere of his working, though I may say that where I note its presence I posit the presence of something like Jesus Christ."

31. H. Richard Niebuhr, *The Responsible Self* (New York: Harper & Row, 1963), p. 178. Note the full context of these words, 177–78.

32. Bellah, "Religious Pluralism and Religious Truth," 15.

33. H. Richard Niebuhr, "The Doctrine of the Trinity and the Unity of the Church," in *Theology, History, and Culture*, ed. William Stacy Johnson (New Haven, Conn.: Yale University Press, 1996), 62. Cf. Tanner, *Theories of Culture*, 171–75; and see Gustafson's plea for a division of labor in moral communities: James M. Gustafson, *Ethics from a Theocentric Perspective*, vol. 2, *Theology and Ethics* (Chicago: University of Chicago Press, 1984), 216–19.

Index

anthropocentrism: Barth on, 154–55; Gustafson and attack on, 7, 122–27, 135, 136, 138, 150–51, 161; and science, 7, 135, 150–51

apologetic theology: and defensiveness, 196; and divine sovereignty, 19; Gustafson on, 197; and Niebuhr's confessional theology, 19; Tanner on, 159, 197

Audi, Robert, 136

Augustine, Saint, 56, 100–101, 113, 114

Barth, Karl: on anthropocentrism and human afflictions, 154–55; Christocentrism of, 147, 215; and covenant and creation, 38, 41, 47, 62; and Frei's typology, 144; and Hauerwas, 90, 106, 114; Niebuhr on, 147, 157, 215, 223n29; on pacifism, 209; and radical theology of grace, 223n29; and Ramsey, 38, 41, 44, 47, 62; and social gospel, 30n6; theological overcorrections of, 157

Basic Christian Ethics (Ramsey), 36, 37–38, 40–41

Bellah, Robert, 217, 219

Character and the Christian Life (Hauerwas), 75–76

Christ and Culture (Niebuhr): and conversionism, 108, 110–12, 204; and dialogue, 110–11; Hauerwas's criticism of, 74, 95, 107–13; and Jesus' identity, 146–47; and monolithic treatment of culture, 108–9, 112–13; and Ramsey, 38, 112; and theological language, 20; and typological solidity, 107–8, 109–10; and view of culture, 109, 113, 204; Yoder's criticism of, 107–13

Christian belief, emancipatory potential of, 12, 218

"The Christian Church in the World's Crisis" (Niebuhr), 68

Christian Ethics and the Sit-In (Ramsey), 41–42, 51, 62–63, 187

Christian particularity and universal intent, 12, 214–17; criticisms of defensiveness and Christocentrism, 196–200, 215–16, 221; and Niebuhr, 215–17, 223n29, 224n30; and salvation, 216–17; Tanner on, 196–200, 215, 221

Christocentrism: of Barth, 147, 215; Gustafson and, 138, 158, 197, 215; Niebuhr's resistance to, 12, 138, 158

"The Church against the World" (Niebuhr), 89

church and world, 26–27; and apostolic church, 120–21; and Christian inactivity, 88–89; and the church's isolationism, 120; and the church's responsibility to God and society, 27, 101–2, 120–21, 138–39, 140n2, 179–80, 203–4; and conversionism, 204–5; and Gustafson, 121, 139, 204, 212; and Hauerwas, 80–85, 203; and "love transforming natural justice," 203;

church and world (*continued*)
   and Niebuhr, 26–27, 28, 203–5; and
   polarities, 28; and Ramsey, 68–69,
   121, 203, 204–5; and Ramsey on
   Niebuhr, 204–5; and Ramsey's just
   war theory, 68–69; and Tanner, 10–11,
   199–200, 204–5; and theology of permanent revolution, 69; as thesis for
   theological ethics, 11–12, 203–5
confessional theology, 19–20, 28, 157
conversionist ethics: Barth on, 38, 41,
   44, 47, 62; basic difficulties of, 41;
   and church and world, 204–5; critique of ambiguities of, 111–12; and
   divine sovereignty, 22, 28; faithfulness
   and exceptionless moral norms,
   45–46; of Gustafson, 24, 121, 137,
   139; and Hauerwas, 24, 108, 110–12,
   113, 139; and Maurice, 111; and
   Niebuhr, 22–24, 25, 28, 38–44, 108,
   110–12, 113, 137, 139, 204–5; and
   pluralism, 108; and Ramsey, 24,
   38–44, 62–63, 139; and Ramsey's
   Christian Ethics and the Sit-In, 41–42,
   62–63; and symbol of responsibility,
   25; and Tanner's Christological ethic,
   24; as theological perspective, 22–24,
   38–39; and transformation in history,
   23–24
Crocco, Stephen, 29, 219
"Culture Protestantism," 26

defensiveness: and Christian particularity, 196–200, 215–16, 221; Gustafson's critique of, 138, 196–200, 215,
   221; Niebuhr's critique of, 29, 138,
   196–97; Tanner's critique of, 196–
   200, 221
Diefenthaler, Jon, 30n1
DiNoia, J. A., 216, 217

Earl Lectures, Niebuhr's, 147
Ellul, Jacques, 187

Ethics from a Theocentric Perspective
   (Gustafson), 137

Farley, Edward, 150, 151
Finnis, John, 70n21
Frei, Hans: on Niebuhr, 27, 32n47,
   146–48, 223n29; and Ramsey's use of
   Scripture, 49n5
Frei, Hans, and typology of modern
   Christian theology, 143–46, 159; type
   one, 144, 145, 146; type two, 144,
   145, 146, 151; type three, 144, 145,
   146, 159; type four, 144–45, 146,
   159; type five, 145, 146

Gifford Lectures, Hauerwas's, 90,
   118n60
"The Grace of Doing Nothing"
   (Niebuhr), 74
Gustafson, James, and theocentric ethics,
   6–9, 11, 121–39; ambiguity of, 148–
   52; ambiguity of, examples, 152–59;
   and anthropocentrism, 7, 122–27,
   135, 136, 138, 150–51, 161; and
   apologetic theology, 197; and Christian traditions, 131–32, 148–51, 158,
   213; Christianity and history, 124–25,
   134; and Christocentric theologies,
   138, 158, 197, 215; Christology of,
   152–53; church and the world, 121,
   139, 204, 212; and "composite rationale," 135; and conversionism, 24,
   121, 137, 139; corrections and overcorrections, 157–59, 160; and defensiveness, 138, 196–200, 215, 221; divine intentions and human activity,
   128; and divine sovereignty, 18, 150,
   161–62; ethic of responsibility and social change, 173–76; four risky readings of theocentric ethics of, 134–36;
   general ideas of, 6–9, 11; and God
   as personal agent, 129–30, 135–36;
   and Hauerwas, 7, 8, 121, 138, 139,

158–59, 162; and human dignity, 219; human experience and religion, 123–24, 148; "human fault" and corrections of, 131–32; and human loyalties, 127–28; and human moral agency, 8, 132–34; and independent isolated theology, 159–61; and "in-group" confessionalism, 157; interdependence and nature, 8, 130–31, 135; language of faith and narratives of tradition, 131–32, 148–51, 213; and nature of God, 128, 129–30, 135–36, 148–49; and Niebuhr, differences from, 12–13, 143–62; and Niebuhrian legacy, 12–13, 18, 22, 24, 121, 137–38, 141n49, 158, 161, 196–97; and piety, 7–8, 126–27, 128, 129, 134, 135, 137, 148, 149, 150, 215; and postliberalism, 197–98; practical force of his ethics, 154–55; and radical monotheism, 12, 22, 24, 121, 137; and Ramsey, 8, 33, 158, 162; Ramsey in contrast to, 8, 121, 136, 139, 142n56; and Reformed tradition, 125, 150; and religious symbols, 126, 127–29, 149; resurrection and experience, 155–57; science and anthropocentrism, 7, 135, 150–51; science and constraints on theology, 150–51, 158; science and the church, 204, 212; science and theological construal, 129–30, 135, 138, 148–49, 150–51; and sociality of experience, 123–24; and Tanner, 173–76, 196–200, 221; theocentric anthropology of, 130–33; and theocentric ethics, summary and method, 6–9, 122–25, 140n6; and unsure commitments, 151, 213; and utilitarian ethics, 136

Hauerwas, Stanley: and Baptism, 86; and Barth's theology, 90, 106, 114; on character, virtue, and vision, 75–77, 90; Christ and culture, 103–13; and Christian grammar, 72–73, 90; on Christian identity, 192–93; and Christian works, 194–95; church and world, 80–85, 203; and communal provenance of moral agency, 76; and community and character, 4–6, 75–76; community and liberalism, 80–85; and conversionism, 24, 108, 110–12, 113, 139; and creation/creatureliness, 104–7, 113–14, 119; critics on sectarianism of, 72, 91, 158–59; discipleship and, 85, 86–88, 105, 106; and Eucharist, 86; general ideas of, 4–6, 11; and Gustafson, 7, 8, 121, 138, 139, 158–59, 162; and historical relationism, 18; and human dignity, 219; and internal and external history, 74, 79–80; and Kingdom of God, 85–86; on moral ideal of personal autonomy, 73; on narrative and truthfulness, 74, 76–81; and Niebuhr, 12, 18, 22, 24, 73–74, 88–90, 107–13; on Niebuhr's Christ and Culture, 74, 95, 107–13; and O'Donovan, 104–5, 114–15; and pacifism, 4–5, 6, 95, 97–98, 103, 116n14, 209, 210; peaceableness and discipleship, 85, 105, 106; principalities, powers, and peaceable kingdom, 85–89; and radical monotheism, 22; and Ramsey, 73, 74, 88, 96, 114, 206, 221; social context of Christian existence, 73; and Tanner, 10, 189–96; on violence and nationalism, 73. See also Hauerwas, Stanley, and critique of liberalism; Hauerwas, Stanley, and just war

Hauerwas, Stanley, and critique of liberalism, 5, 103–13; Christ and culture, 103–13; community and practices, 80–85, 206; and conversionism, 108, 110–12; and creation/creatureliness, 104–7; criticisms of other Christian

Hauerwas, Stanley (*continued*)
ethicists, 103–5, 107–13; and deform-
ing of human bonds, 66; discipleship
and, 85, 87–88, 89, 105, 106; and
justice, 103; and medical ethics, 6,
106; and monolithic treatment of culture, 108–9, 112–13; and Niebuhr,
107–13; and O'Donovan, 104–5; and
peaceableness, 105–6; and pluralism,
103, 107, 108; political liberalism,
73, 81–82, 83, 84, 87–88, 90–91; and
Protestantism's Constantinian accommodations, 73, 87–88, 95, 96, 109,
120; and Ramsey, 103–4; and respect
for individualism, 103; and Roman
Catholics, 104–5; and social responsibility of church, 121; and suspicion of
theologies of creation and preservation, 103–5, 106–7, 113–14; and typological solidity, 107–8, 109–10;
view of culture as autonomous of
Jesus, 109, 113; Yoder and, 96, 105
Hauerwas, Stanley, and just war,
95–103, 119; and coercive control of
democratic state, 97–98; as Constantinian accommodation to secular
power, 96; criticisms of, 116n14; and
dual character of Christ's redemptive
work, 96–97; and duality of Christian
witness, 97–98; endorsing just war
theory, 96; just war and domestic police function, 98; and Niebuhr, 74;
opposing just war theory, 95–96; and
pacifism, 97–98, 103, 116n14, 209,
210; and Persian Gulf War, 98–99;
and Ramsey, 88, 96, 99–103, 206; requirements for just war, 99; social and
moral credibility of just war, 99;
Yoder and, 96, 97, 98–99, 100
henotheism: Niebuhr's theology of radical monotheism, 21; and theocentric
theologies of Niebuhr and Gustafson,
138, 158, 196–97

Hollenbach, David, 104, 105
human dignity before God, 12, 218–21
Hunsinger, George, 154

Jenson, Robert, 194
John Paul II, Pope, 212–13
just war. *See* Hauerwas, Stanley, and just
war; Ramsey, Paul, and just war

The Kingdom of God in America
(Niebuhr), 19

liberalism and Christian communities,
205–7; and creaturely rights, 190–91,
206–7; Hauerwas's critique of, 206;
Niebuhr and, 205–7; Ramsey and,
5–6, 206; Tanner and, 190–91,
206–7. *See also* Hauerwas, Stanley,
and critique of liberalism

Maurice, F. D., 111
McCann, Dennis, 104, 105
Mead, George Herbert, 24
The Meaning of Revelation (Niebuhr),
19, 20
medical ethics: and Barth on creation
and covenant, 62; and canons of loyalty, 62–67; and care for the dying,
64, 66; and children, 63–64, 66; and
external conditions of covenants,
62–64, 65–66; and fellow humanity,
62–66; Hauerwas and critique of liberalism, 6, 106; and informed consent, 8–9, 63–65; and "love transforming natural justice," 66; and
marriage bond, 186–87; and *Planned
Parenthood v. Danforth*, 64–65; problems in discourse, 66–67; Ramsey
and, 3, 8–9, 62–67, 69, 119, 186–87
Miller, Francis, 89
Miller, Richard, 68
monotheism, radical: and Gustafson, 12,

22, 24, 121, 137; and Hauerwas, 22;
Niebuhr's theme of, 12, 20–22, 24,
25, 28, 121, 122, 137, 138, 176; and
Ramsey, 22; and symbol of responsibility, 25; and Tanner, 22, 176

Niebuhr, H. Richard, 15–30; as antiac-
commodationist, 12, 113; and Barth,
147, 157, 215, 223n29; and Christian
particularity and universal intent,
215–17, 223n29, 224n30; and Christocentric theologies, 12, 138, 158;
Christology and, 147, 153, 215; and
church and world, 26–27, 28, 203–5;
and church's responsibility to God,
120; confessional theology, 19–20,
28; and contrast between internal and
external history, 74, 79–80; conversionist theme of, 22–24, 25, 28,
38–44, 108, 110–12, 113, 121, 137,
139, 204–5; correlations of faith and
experience, 146–48; critique of defensiveness, 29, 138, 196–97; and divine
agency and human agency, 173–79;
and divine sovereignty, 13, 16–22, 24,
26, 27, 28, 110, 161–62, 173–75; and
divine transcendence, 12, 13; and
emancipatory potential of belief, 218;
in Frei's theological typology, 146–48;
Hauerwas and, 12, 18, 22, 24, 73–74,
79–80, 88–90, 107–13; Hauerwas's
criticism of approach to Christ and
culture, 107–13; and human dignity
before God, 10, 12, 218–21; and
human moral agency, 164, 174–75;
legacy and Gustafson, 12–13, 18, 22,
24, 121, 137–38, 141n49, 158, 161,
196–97; legacy of, 12–13, 74, 90,
218–21; and pacifism, 74; and polarities in church, 15, 27–30, 218–19;
and radical monotheism, 12, 20–22,
24, 25, 28, 121, 122, 137, 138, 176;
and Ramsey, 12, 22, 24, 38–39, 45,

53–54, 61–62, 67–69; and realism,
175–76, 178, 180, 184–89; reality of
God and human point of view, 16–18;
and Reinhold Niebuhr, 74; relationism and relativism, 17–18, 24, 27, 45,
67, 110; and responsibility, 24–26,
27, 28, 120–21, 173–78, 179–80;
and social responsibility of church,
120–21; Tanner and Niebuhrian resonances, 12, 13, 18, 22, 164, 173–80,
184–89, 204–5; theocentric relativism,
18; theologies of grace, 179–80; theology and ethics of, 15–30; and theses
for theological ethics, 203–21; and
Trinitarian doctrine, 220–21
Niebuhr, Reinhold: and Christian realism, 53–54; as critic of Social Gospel,
88; and H. Richard Niebuhr, 74; as
influential theologian, 15; and just
war theory, 116n14; and nonviolent
resistance, 53; and Ramsey, 4, 53–54
Nine Modern Moralists (Ramsey),
38–42, 45, 184
nonviolence. *See* pacifism

O'Donovan, Oliver, 104–5, 114–15
Outka, Gene, 135

pacifism: Barth on, 209; Hauerwas and,
4–5, 6, 95, 97–98, 103, 116n14, 209,
210; just war and practical pacifism,
208–10, 221n9, 222n12; and Niebuhr,
74; Ramsey and, 53, 58, 60, 61, 103,
208–10; and Reinhold Niebuhr, 53.
See also Hauerwas, Stanley, and just
war; Ramsey, Paul, and just war
Pauck, Wilhelm, 89
Placher, William, 153, 164–65
Planned Parenthood v. Danforth, 64–65
The Politics of God (Tanner), 191
Pope, Stephen, 160, 213
postliberalism, 197–98
Princeton University, 33

Ramsey, Paul: agape and natural law, 3, 37–38; agape as free and binding, 2–4, 35–38; and Barth on covenant and creation, 38, 41, 44, 47, 62; canons of loyalty, 45–47, 48, 58, 62–67; Christian moral discourse, 33–34; and Christian vocation, 36–37; and church and world, 68–69, 203, 204–5; and conversionist ethics, 24, 38–44, 62–63, 139; covenant and creation, 38, 41–44, 47, 51; on "Egypt" and "Exodus," 39–40, 203; and ethics of redemption, 34, 39; and faithfulness, 38, 45–46, 48; and fellow humanity, 2–4, 5, 35–37, 42–44, 46–47, 51–53, 55–57, 58, 60, 61, 62–66, 68, 188–89; general ideas, 2–4, 11, 34; and Gustafson, 8, 33, 158, 162; Gustafson in contrast to, 8, 121, 136, 139, 142n56; and Hauerwas, 73, 74, 88, 96, 114, 206, 221; and human dignity, 219; and language, 33, 34; and liberalism, 5–6, 103–4, 206; and "love transforming natural justice," 4, 34, 37–47, 51, 52–53, 57–58, 66, 203; and medical ethics, 3, 8–9, 62–67, 69, 119, 186–87; and moral rules, exceptionless, 45–47; and natural law, 38–40, 203; and Niebuhr, connections to, 12, 22, 24, 38–39, 45, 61–62, 67–69; and Niebuhr's Christian realism, 53–54; and Niebuhr's conversionist theme, 12, 24, 38–39, 41, 42, 61–62, 67–68; and Niebuhr's relativism, 45, 67; and nonresisting love, 52–53, 68; and political realism, 53–54, 184–89; at Princeton, 33; and public forums, 48–49, 50n36; and redemption, 39, 47; and responsibility, 36–37, 101–2, 121, 187; and Tanner, 184–89; use of Scriptures, 35, 49n5. See also Ramsey, Paul, and just war

Ramsey, Paul, and just war, 3, 4, 51–62, 100–102, 103, 119, 208–10; adequacy of discourse, 59; and agape, 55, 57–58, 60; and Augustine's two cities, 100–102, 103; and canons of loyalty, 58; and Christian political responsibility, 101–2; and church and world, 68–69; in contrast to Hauerwas and Yoder, 100–102; and conversionist theme, 61–62; and covenant and creation, 51; and enemy combatants, 56–57; and fellow humanity, 51–53, 55–57, 58, 60, 61; and government power, 58–59, 100; Hauerwas's criticism of, 88, 96, 99–103, 206; and immunity of noncombatants, 55, 56, 58, 60; on just war as "barely human activity," 56; and keeping faith in political ethics, 57–62; and "love transforming natural justice," 51, 52–53, 57–58; and Niebuhr, 53–54, 61–62, 68–69; and nonresisting love, 52–53, 68; and pacifism, 53, 58, 60, 61, 103, 208–10; pacifism and "bellicism," 58, 60, 103; and political accommodation, 88, 96, 99–103; problems of discourse, 59–62; Ramsey's deference to authorities, 61; and Ramsey's public speaking, 50n36; and Reinhold Niebuhr, 57–58; and relative standards of justice, 55–56; and social responsibility of church, 121; steps in execution of just war, 60–62; and Vietnam war, 50n36

Rauschenbusch, Walter, 16, 88

relativism and relationism: divine sovereignty and, 18, 110; and human moral agency, 24; and Niebuhr, 17–18, 24, 27, 45, 67, 110; Ramsey's criticism of, 45, 67; and theocentric relativism, 17–18

Resident Aliens (Hauerwas and Willimon), 107

responsibility: and church and world, 27, 101–2, 120–21, 139, 140n2, 179–80, 203–4; and divine sovereignty, 24, 28; Gustafson's ethics of, 173–76; and Hauerwas's just war theory, 121; and human relationships, 24–25; Niebuhr's theology of, 24–26, 27, 28, 120–21, 173–78, 179–80; and radical monotheism, 25–26, 176; Ramsey and, 36–37, 101–2, 121, 187; and relativism, 24; Tanner and ethic of, 164, 173–76

resurrection and experience, 155–56, 157

Roman Catholicism: and Hauerwas's critique of liberalism, 104–5; on human rights and community, 206–7; natural law tradition and war, 70n21

Sartre, Jean-Paul, 41

Schleiermacher, Friedrich, 144

science: and anthropocentrism, 7, 135, 150–51; constraints on theology, 150–51, 158; Gustafson and, 7, 127–34, 135, 138, 148–49, 150–51, 158, 204, 212; Tanner on Christian eschatology and, 213–14

Social Gospel theology, 16–17, 19, 30n6, 88

sovereignty, divine: and apologetic theology, 19; and confessional theology, 19–20; and conversionism, 22, 28; Gustafson and, 18, 150, 161–62; and human moral agency and responsibility, 24, 28; Niebuhr's theology of, 13, 16–22, 24, 26, 27, 28, 110, 161–62, 173–75; and radical monotheism, 20–22; and relationism and relativism, 18, 110; Tanner and, 13, 164–67, 168–69, 170, 171–72, 173–75, 178–79

Suffering Presence (Hauerwas), 106

Tanner, Kathryn, 9–11, 164–80; on apologetic theology, 159, 197; Chris-tian eschatology and science, 213–14; and Christian particularity, 215; and Christian virtues, 195, 201n26; and church and world, 10–11, 184–85, 199–200, 204–5; communities and liberalism, 190–91, 206–7; and con-versionist theme, 24; and defensive-ness/defensive particularism, 196–200, 221; divine sovereignty and agency, 13, 164–67, 168–69, 170, 171–72, 173–75, 178–79; and divine transcen-dence and human agency, 9–10, 12, 13, 171–72; and ethic of faithfulness, 179, 196; and ethics of responsibility, 164, 173–76; and Gustafson, 173–76, 196–200, 221; and Hauerwas, 10, 189–96; and human freedom and em-powerment, 166–67; and human hier-archical relations, 10, 170–71; and human individual differences, 10, 188–89, 219; human interpretation of God, 169–70; and human rights, 190–91, 206–7; and irreducible status of Christian theology, 199–200; and Niebuhr on human moral agency and responsibility, 164, 174–75; Niebuhrian resonances, 12, 13, 18, 22, 164, 173–80, 184–89, 204–5; and Niebuhr's approach to agency, 173–78; on postliberalism, 197–99, 202n35; radical monotheism, 22, 176; and Ramsey, 184–89; and real-ism, 175–76, 178, 180, 184–89; and social change, 9–11, 167–71, 174–75, 178; themes, 164; and theocentric rel-ativism, 18; and theology of creation, 167–70; theology of grace, 171–73, 179–80, 182n48. *See also* Tanner, Kathryn, and Christian identity

Tanner, Kathryn, and Christian identity, 10, 189–96, 215; anthropology and patterns of culture, 189–90; Christian culture and way of life, 10, 189–92;

Tanner, Kathryn (*continued*)
  discipleship and ethics, 191; and
  Hauerwas, 191–95; and human individual differences, 10, 188–89, 219;
  and human rights, 190–91; identity
  and community, 191–96; practices
  and struggle against sin, 194–95
theological ethics: and apostolic church,
  120–21; and Christian particularity
  and universal intent, 12, 196–200,
  214–17; and church and world in tension, 11–12, 203–5; and church's responsibility to God and society, 120,
  138–39, 140n2; and communities and
  liberalism, 205–7; and community
  and moral discourse, 119–20; and
  emancipatory potential of belief, 12,
  218; and faithfulness, 13, 120, 220;
  and human dignity before God, 12,
  218–21; and independence of church,
  183; and isolationism of church, 120;
  and nature, history, and culture, 12,
  211–14; and nonviolent discipleship

and violent nation-state, 208–10; and
  public morality and politics, 12,
  210–11; and reflection and witness,
  119–20; theses of, 12, 203–21
*Theories of Culture: A New Agenda for
  Theology* (Tanner), 189
Thiemann, Ronald F., 155–56
Tillich, Paul, 135
"Toward the Independence of the
  Church" (Niebuhr), 74
transformationism. *See* conversionist
  ethics
Troeltsch, Ernst, 29, 219

Willimon, William H., 107, 109

Yale Divinity School, 15
Yoder, John Howard, 93n29; and
  Hauerwas's critique of liberalism, 96,
  105; and Hauerwas's just war theory,
  96, 97, 98–99, 100; and Niebuhr's
  Christ and Culture, 107–13